POSTCARD HISTORY SERIES

The Salton Sea

On the Front Cover: This is Helen's Place, located 234 feet below sea level at the Salton Sea in California. (Author's collection.)

On the Back Cover: Boating on Salton Sea. (Author's collection.)

POSTCARD HISTORY SERIES

The Salton Sea

Karl Anderson

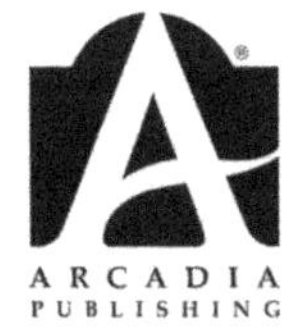

ISBN 978-0-7385-7455-4

Published by Arcadia Publishing
Charleston, South Carolina

Library of Congress Control Number: 2010937904

For all general information contact Arcadia Publishing at:
Telephone 843-853-2070
Fax 843-853-0044
E-mail sales@arcadiapublishing.com
For customer service and orders:
Toll-Free 1-888-313-2665

Visit us on the Internet at www.arcadiapublishing.com

This book is dedicated to the individuals who are committed to preserving and restoring the Salton Sea as a wildlife refuge and sanctuary for future generations.

Contents

Acknowledgments		6
Introduction		7
1.	Early Years of the Salton Sea and Imperial Valley	9
2.	Farming and Crops of the Imperial Valley	21
3.	Life in the Imperial Valley	35
4.	Resorts and Attractions of the Salton Sea	59
5.	Glory Years of the Salton Sea	95
Resources		127

Acknowledgments

Friends and family have endured my longwinded soliloquies and discourse about the Salton Sea for more than two decades. They have been encouraged to thrill over my amateur photographs of birds, waterfowl, abandoned hotels, half-submerged towns, and popular cult destinations.

During recent years, eBay has enticed me to purchase vintage postcards of the Salton Sea and, of late, the Imperial Valley. These photograph cards show the evolution of the Imperial Valley and Salton Sea from a barren desert wasteland to an agricultural giant and popular tourist destination. They present a somewhat romantic and innocent view of a bygone era. More than a throwaway greeting for friends at home, the cards help us to understand the history, creation, and development of the sea.

All of the postcards in this book are from the author's personal collection. The description, name and address of the publisher, and identification number are listed for each postcard.

A special thanks to Debbie Seracini of Arcadia Publishing and to my daughters Kristina and Karla, who helped me complete this project without a single casualty or nervous breakdown.

Introduction

My first visit to the Salton Sea was during the 1960s when I was taken on a weekend trip with my uncle and aunt. We stayed at the Fountain of Youth Spa near Niland. It was a sweaty and uncomfortable experience. How could anyone enjoy the hot desert days, even if it was a dry heat?

In 1979, I started a CPA practice. One of my first audit engagements was the Salton Community Services District in Salton City. My father-in-law, Bob Swenson, was a retired CPA who agreed to assist with the project. Swenson had been fascinated with the Salton Sea since the early 1950s. One of his early clients was a Dutch immigrant named Harry Pond. The client was a land developer who acquired thousands of acres of land from the Southern Pacific Railroad for 50¢ per acre and ultimately became a millionaire.

Since my Palm Springs office was 40 miles north of Salton City, I booked Swenson at the only motel in town. It was a dilapidated, two-story structure on the west side of Highway 86. His "suite" consisted of a small kitchen and bedroom on the second floor. There was a hole in the floor, and you could look down to the first level with little difficulty. In later years, Bob fondly talked about his stay in Salton City for those two weeks during the sweltering heat of mid-August.

When our children were fairly young, the family started taking annual daytrips to the Salton Sea. The excursions were originally taken to accommodate my wife's love of bird watching.

There were only a few grocery markets or places to eat from North Shore to Niland. Restaurants seldom stayed in business for more than a year. Cleanliness could be an issue, but sometimes overlooked because of hunger and limited options. We often brought a cooler and enjoyed a picnic along the way.

We soon learned that there is a strange curiosity about towns that are half submerged and half abandoned. The North Shore Beach and Yacht Club was a $2 million resort, and Bombay Beach was a respectable seaside community. Both dreams vanished with the pollution, fish die-offs, and the rising elevation of the sea. However, the Imperial Valley continues to be among the most productive and profitable agricultural areas in the world.

It was several years before we discovered the fascination of mud volcanoes, Sonny Bono National Wildlife Refuge, Slab City, and Salvation Mountain. These destinations are a must for any novice to the area.

As an avid collector, my motto has always been, "Too much is just a good beginning." Therefore, it was no wonder that my collections include postcards, magazine articles, and memorabilia from this strange but beautiful place. My hope is that readers will enjoy this book and develop a new appreciation of the Salton Sea and Imperial Valley.

—Karl Anderson

One

Early Years of the Salton Sea and Imperial Valley

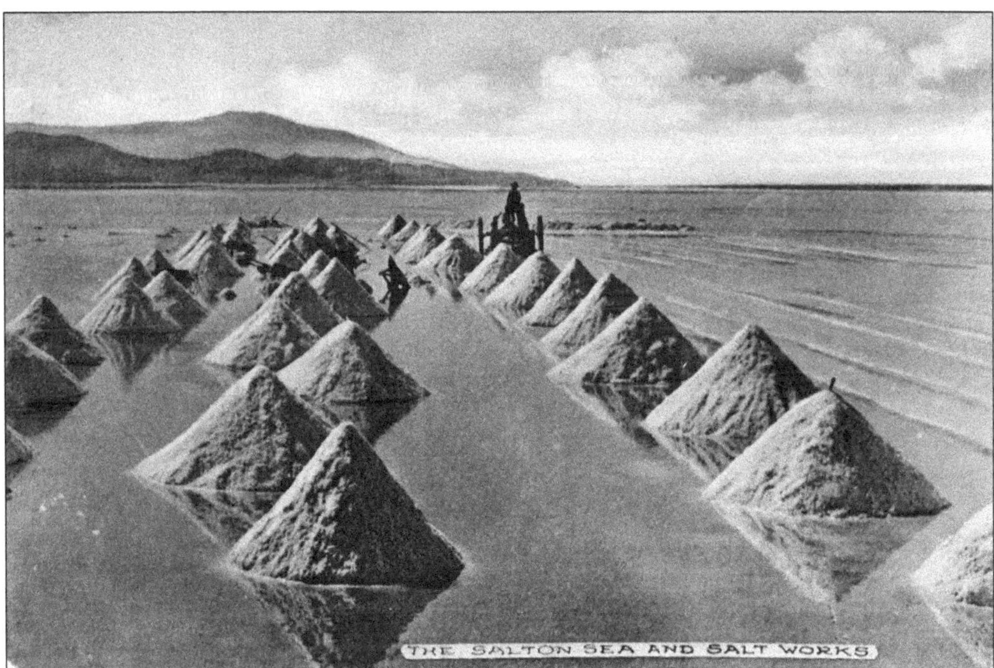

The Salton Sea and Salt Works. Mailed August 20, 1909 from El Paso, Texas, to San Francisco, Cal. In 1885, George Dubrow formed the New Liverpool Salt Company. He operated the Salton Sink's first commercial mine until 1906. The Standard Salt Company began operations in 1901. The Mullet Island Salt Works operated from 1940 to 1942. In 1935, Seth and Chester Hartley opened the Imperial Salt Company and was the biggest of the salt operations. The company was purchased by the Western Salt Company in 1942 and was closed in 1947.

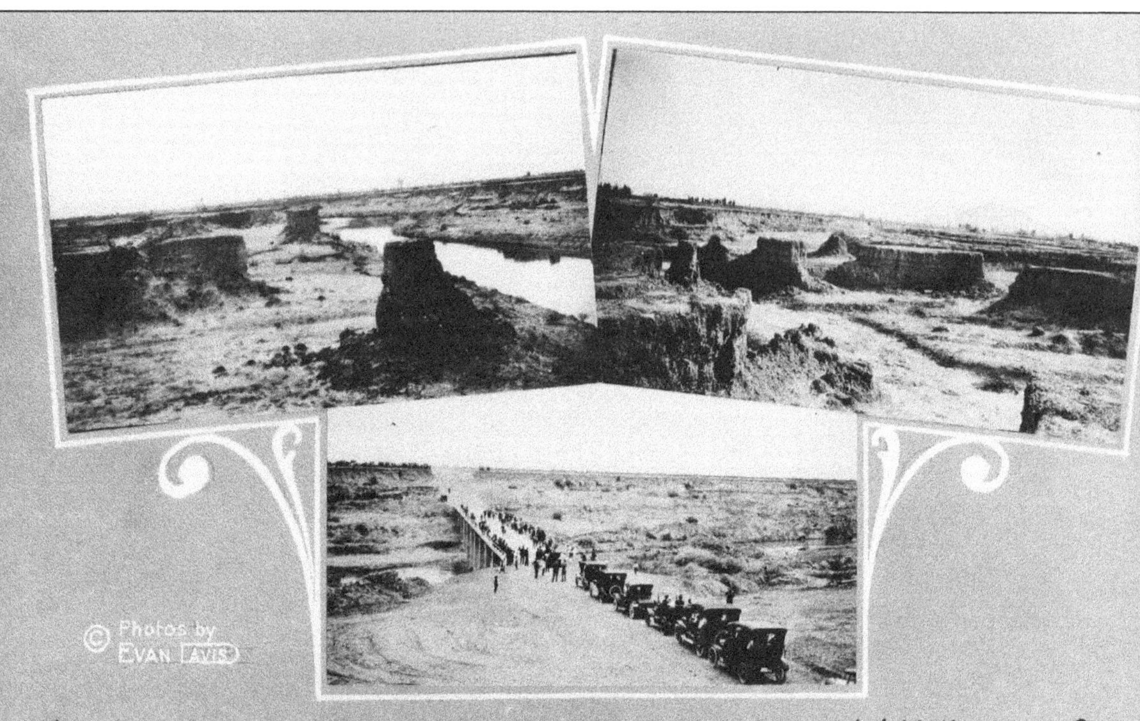

"New River" Results of Flood of Colorado River in 1906. Imperial Valley, Calif. The creation of the Salton Sea began during the winter of 1905, when heavy rainfall and snowmelt caused the Colorado River to swell. A flood of water poured down the canal and breached an Imperial Valley dike. The Southern Pacific Railroad spent $3 million and dumped boxcars of boulders in an attempt to stop the overflow. However, their efforts were unsuccessful. From 1905 to 1907, the Colorado River emptied into the Salton Sink and created the Salton Sea. Unused. (© Photos by Evan Davis.)

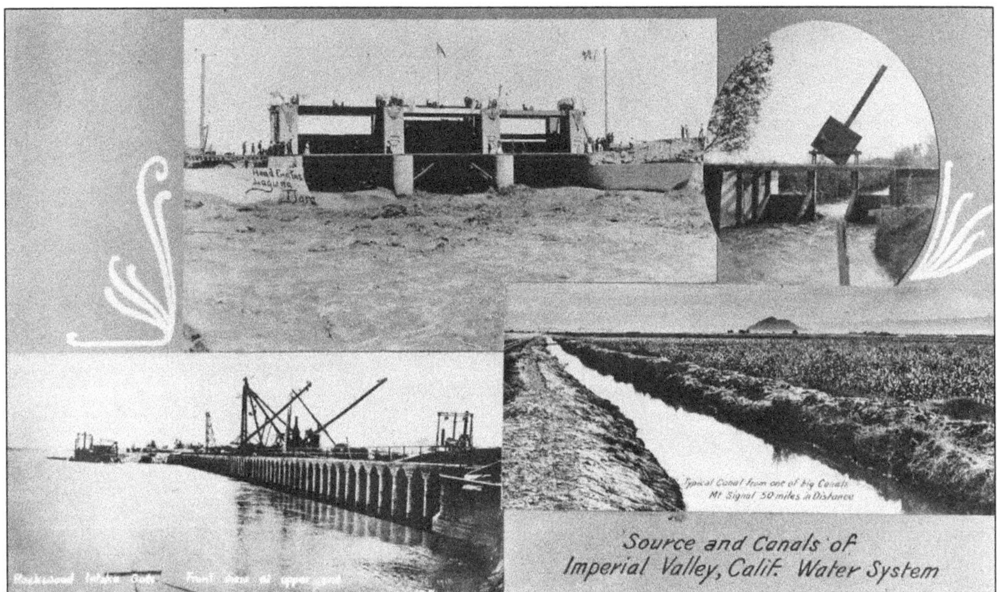

SOURCE AND CANALS OF IMPERIAL VALLEY, CALIF. WATER SYSTEM. Dredging of the canal system began in 1900. According to the City of El Centro's Chamber of Commerce website, "In 1901, few white men inhabited the Imperial Valley other than the surveyors working on the canals. In four years, by 1905, the residents numbered 12,000. Irrigated acreage had increased from 1,500 acres to 67,000 acres." Unused. (© Photos by Evan Davis.)

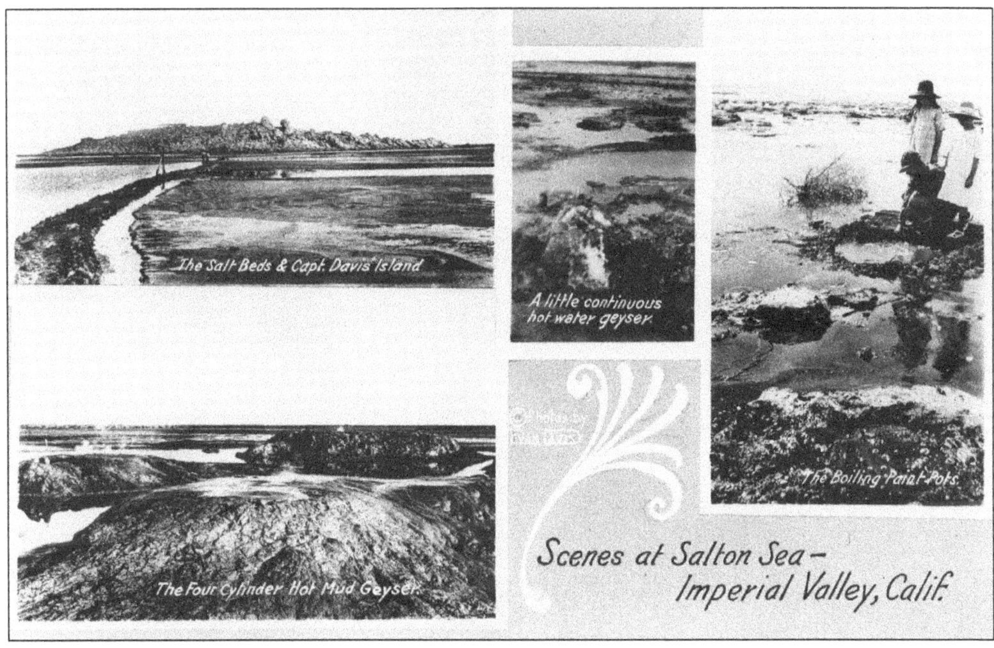

SCENES AT SALTON SEA, IMPERIAL VALLEY, CALIF. Evan Davis published a series of early Imperial Valley and Salton Sea postcards. His name seems to have vanished from local history books and publications. Unused. (© Photos by Evan Davis.)

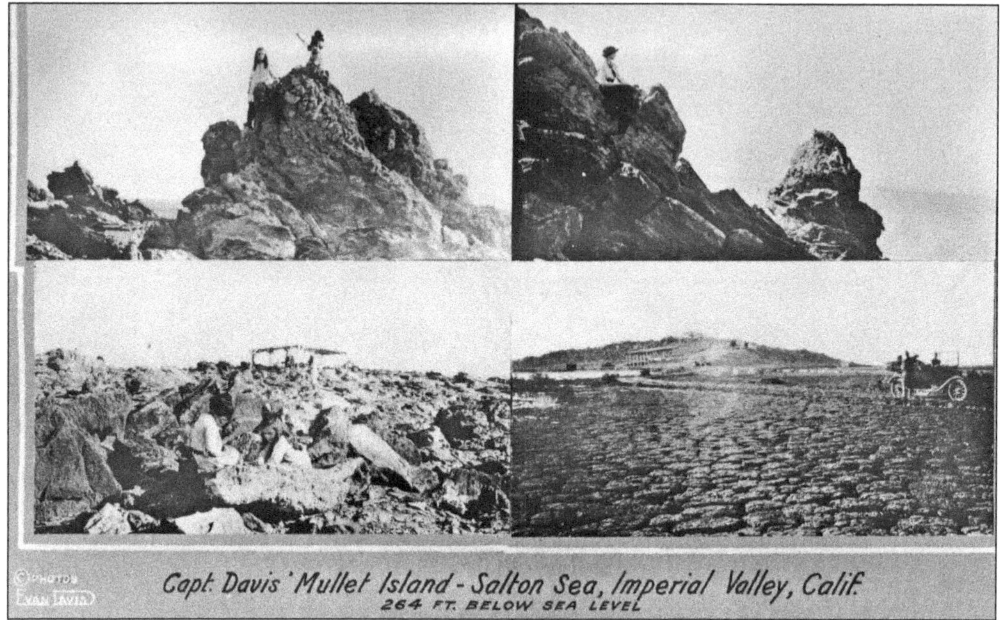

Capt. Davis' Mullet Island – Salton Sea, Imperial Valley, Calif. 264 Ft. below Sea Level. Today, Mullet Island is the only island in the Salton Sea. It is a bird-dropping encrusted hill. The foundation of a building is still visible, as is the old roadway from when this island was a peninsula. Unused. (© Photos by Evan Davis.)

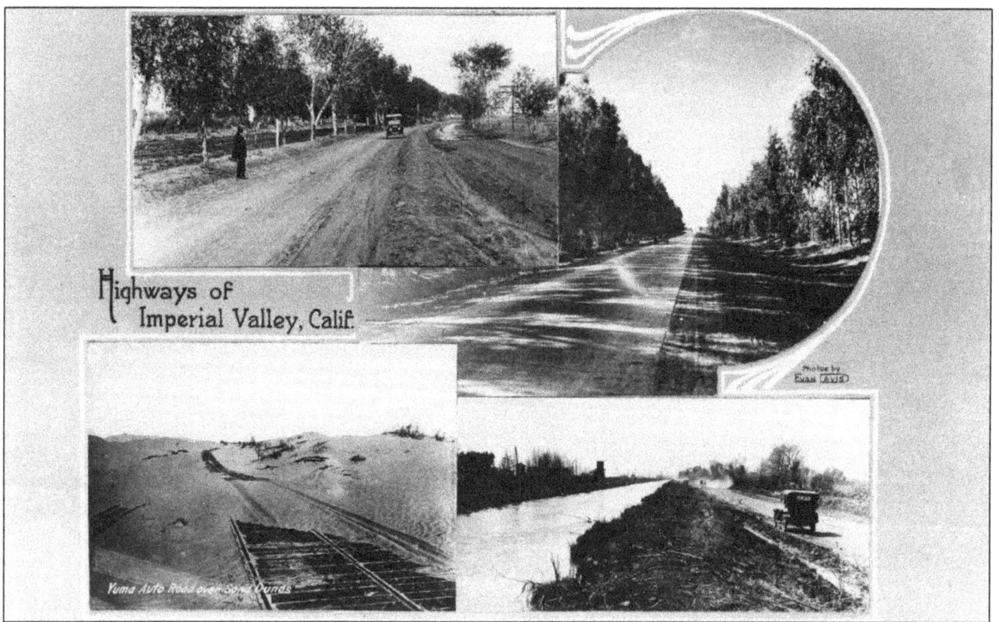

Highways of Imperial Valley, Calif. The Salton Sea is bordered by Highway 111 on the east and Highway 86 on the west. However, the real treasures seem to be located on dirt roads and the side streets of the small towns that surround the lake. Unused. (© Photos by Evan Davis.)

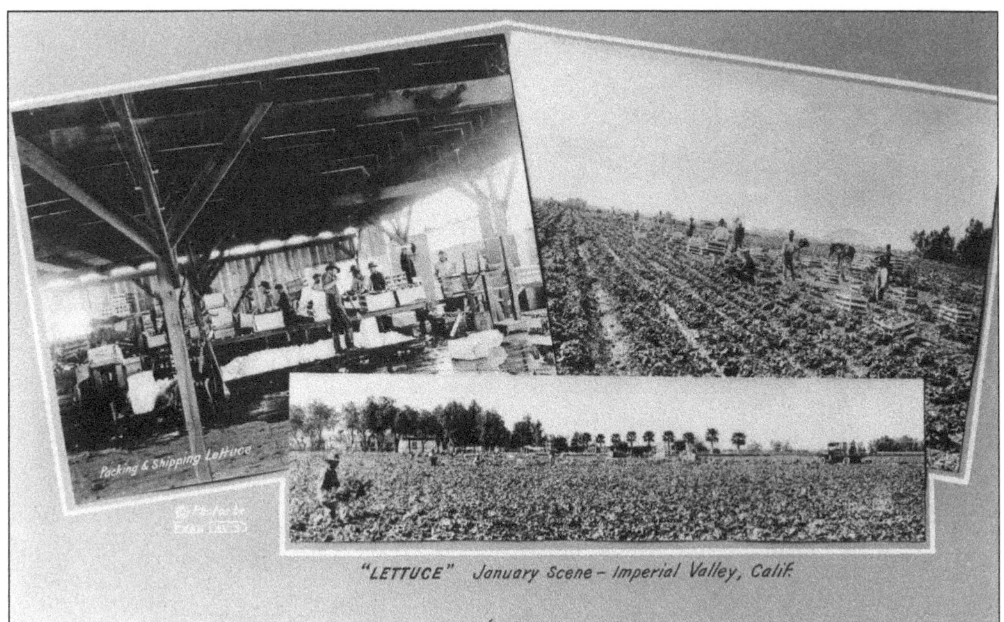

"LETTUCE" JANUARY SCENE—IMPERIAL VALLEY, CALIF. In 2009, the Imperial Valley produced enough lettuce to serve four-ounce dinner salads to 5,175,673,432 people. Unused. (© Photos by Evan Davis.)

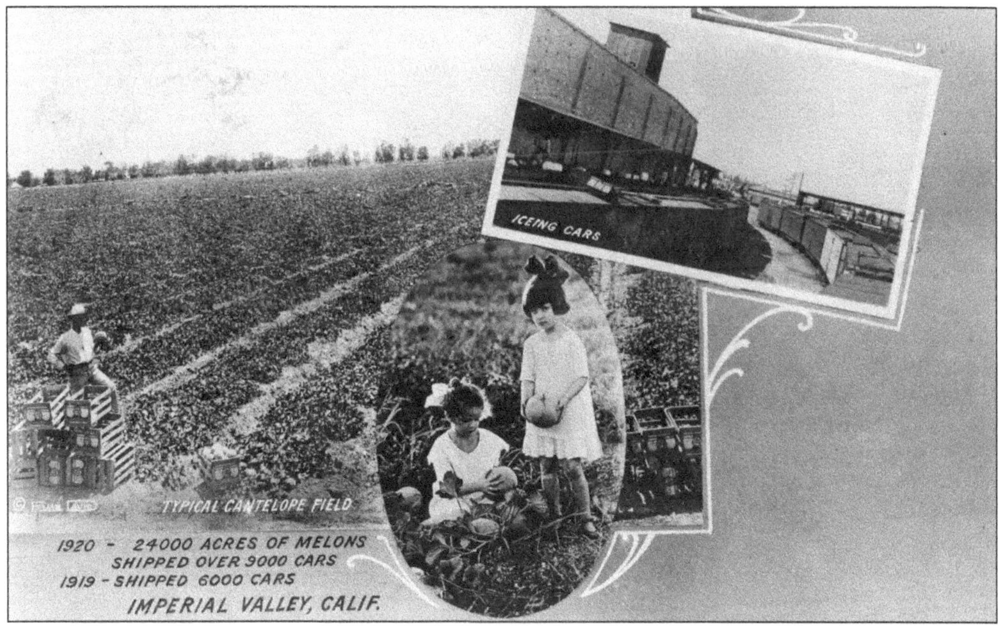

TYPICAL CANTELOPE [*SIC*] FIELD: 1920 – 24000 ACRES OF MELONS SHIPPED OVER 9000 CARS, 1919 – SHIPPED 6000 CARS, IMPERIAL VALLEY, CALIF. According to a 1922 article in the *Imperial Valley Press*, "Southern Pacific service in moving the unprecedented cantaloupe crop of the Imperial Valley, and the foresight of the company in having sufficient equipment on sidings at all times to rush the perishables to markets as rapidly as they were loaded, brought forth commendation of the Imperial Valley Press of recent date." Unused. (© Photos by Evan Davis.)

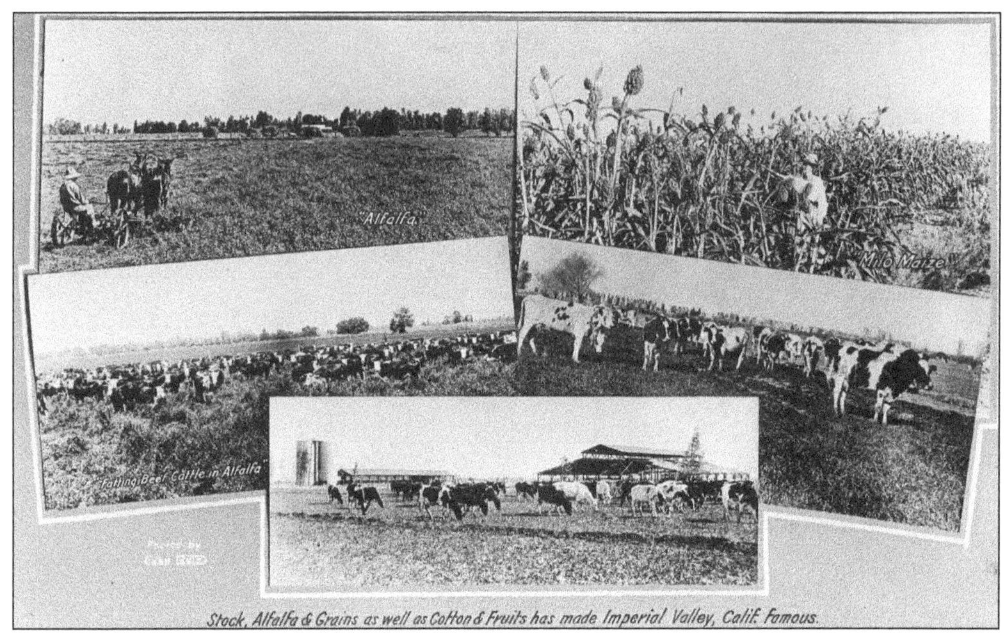

Stock, Alfalfa & Grains as Well as Cotton & Fruits Has Made Imperial Valley, Calif. Famous. In 2008, Imperial County farmers produced 1.622 million tons of hay, including alfalfa, Bermuda grass, Sudan grass, and kleingrass hays, making the region a vital producer of food for the state's vast dairy industry. Unused. (© Photos by Evan Davis.)

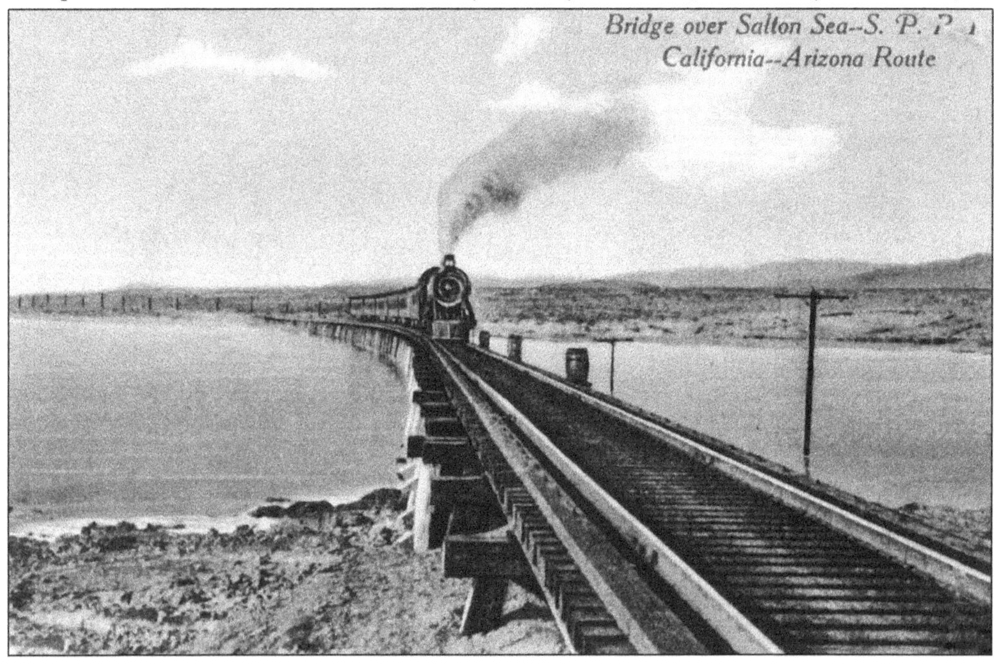

Bridge over Salton Sea - S.P.R.R. California–Arizona Route. The concept of a transcontinental railroad was conceived by James Gadsden, president of the South Carolina Railroad Company. In 1852, Congress paid Mexico $10 million for the Gadsden Purchase, a strip of land south of the Gila River, for the proposed railroad route. Unused. (Published by Newman Post Card Co., Los Angeles and San Francisco.)

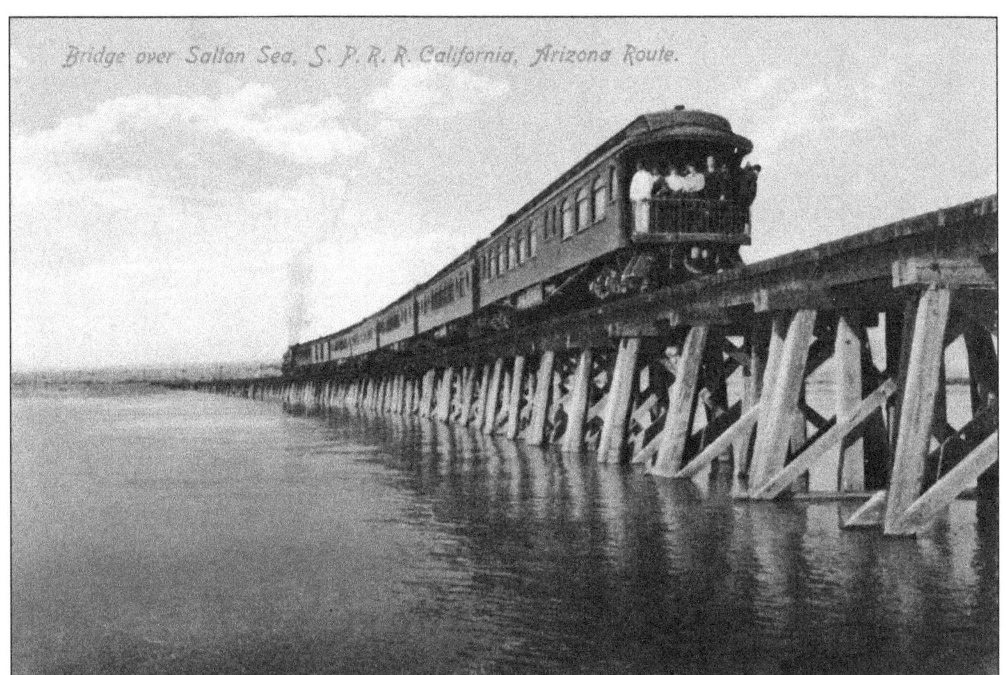

BRIDGE OVER SALTON SEA, S.P.R.R. CALIFORNIA, ARIZONA ROUTE. In 1877, the Southern Pacific Railroad (SPRR) began building east from Los Angeles. The rails reached Tucson, Arizona, in March 1880. Mailed October 21, 1909, to Coldwell, Kansas. (Published by Newman Post Card Company, Los Angeles.)

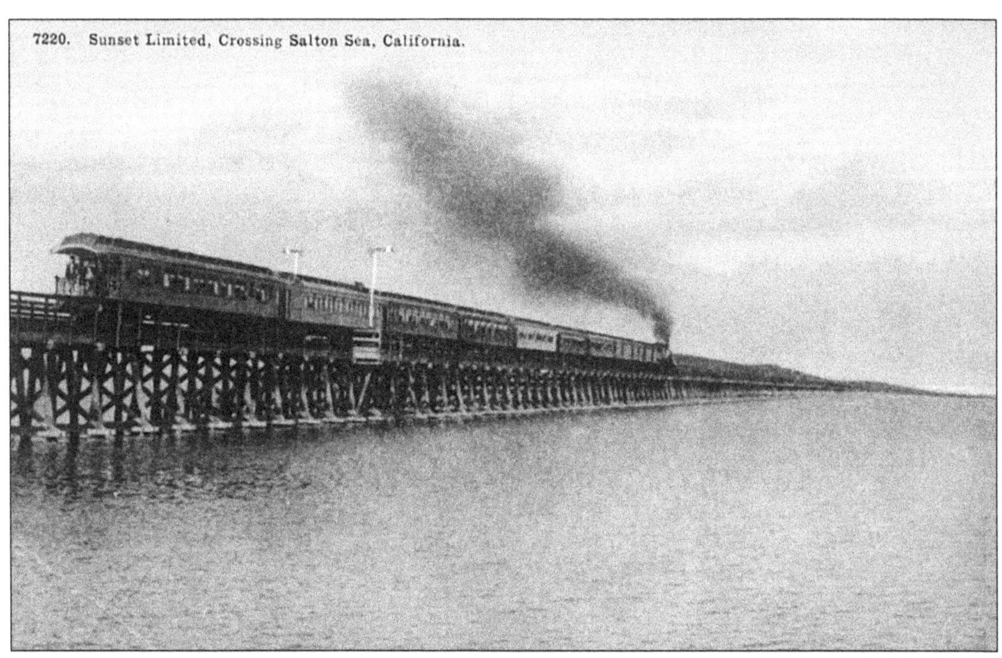

7220 *SUNSET LIMITED*, CROSSING SALTON SEA, CALIFORNIA. The SPRR's premier passenger train on the route was named the *Sunset Limited*. By 1894, winter resorts in Tucson, Phoenix, and Pasadena soon filled the passenger trains with affluent vacationers. Unused.

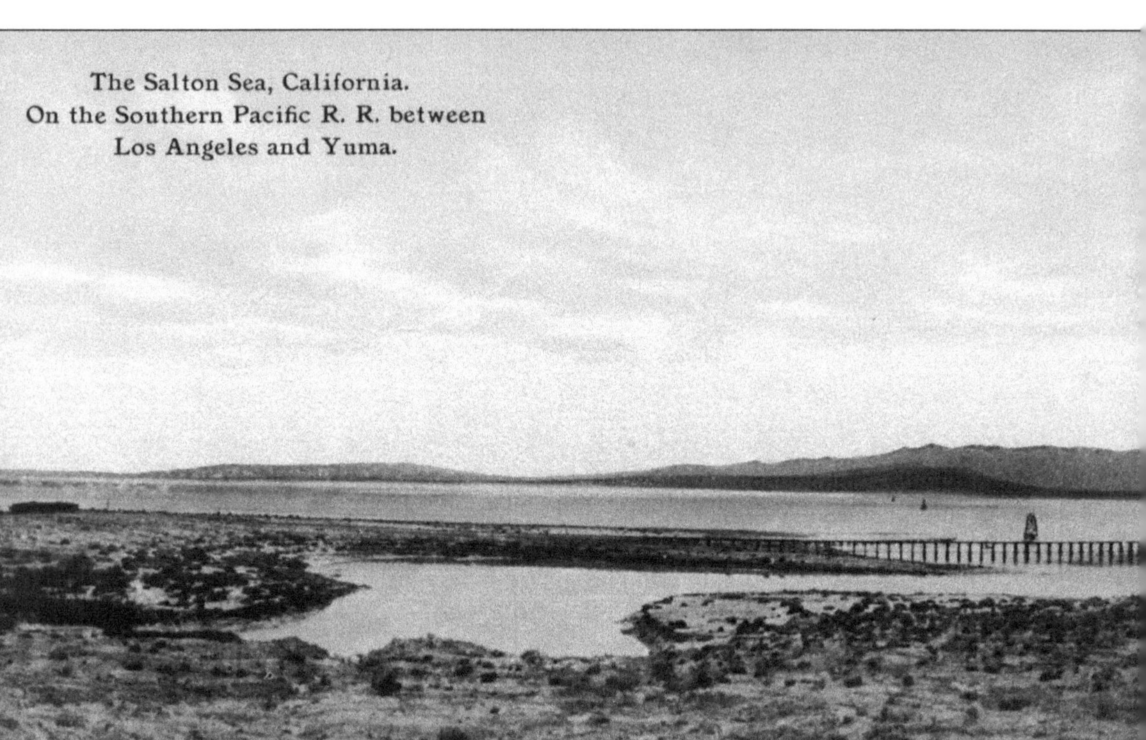

The Salton Sea, California. On the Southern Pacific R. R. between Los Angeles and Yuma. During 1903 and 1904, the SPRR completed its line from the main Sunset Route at Niland (formerly known as Old Reach) to the Mexican border at Calexico. The Imperial Valley rail system (Inter-California Railway Company) through Mexico was connected to the Southern Pacific's main line near Yuma on July 24, 1911. Unused. (Published by the Benham Co., Los Angeles, Cal. Made in U.S.A.)

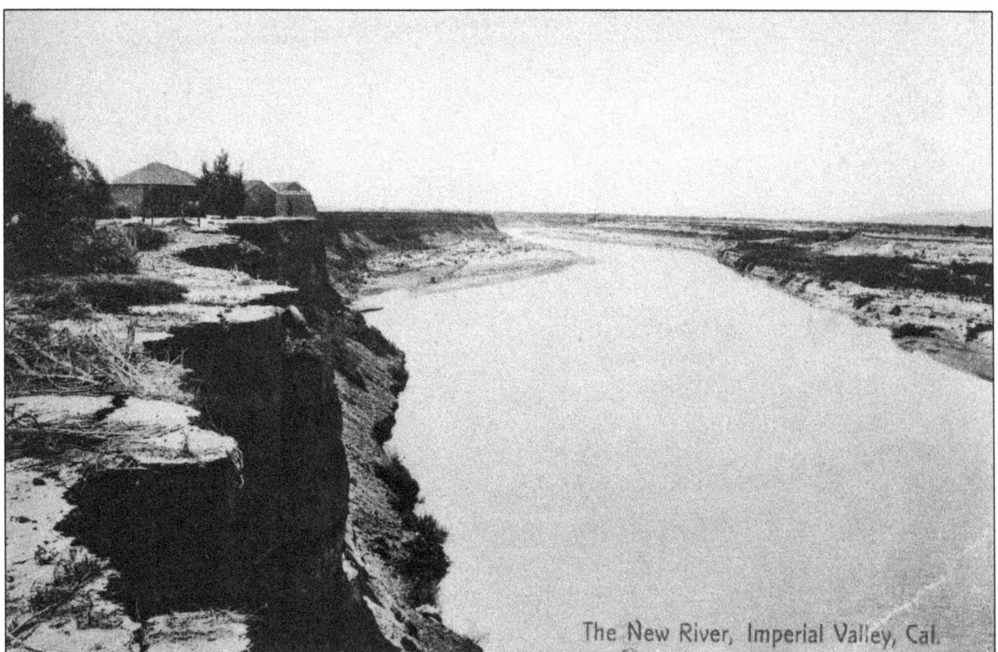

The New River, Imperial Valley, Cal. The New River (*Río Nuevo* in Spanish) flows north from near Cerro Prieto, through the city of Mexicali in Baja California, Mexico, and into the United States through the city of Calexico, California, and finally toward the Salton Sea. Mailed June 20, 1908, to Los Angeles, California. (M. Rieder, Publ., Los Angeles, Cal. 21037; Made in Germany; handcolored work.)

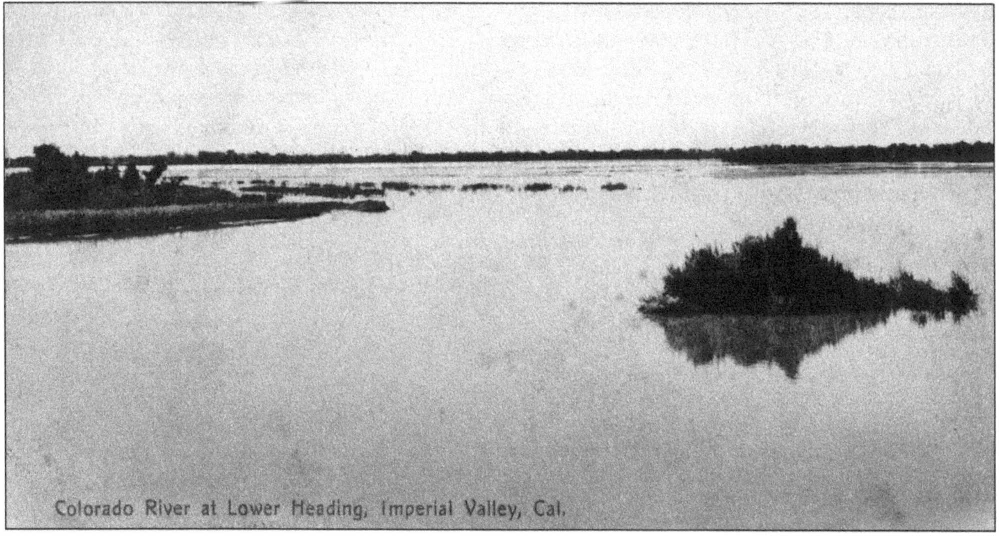

Colorado River at Lower Heading, Imperial Valley, Cal. The volume of discharge from the Colorado River has been greatly reduced by large dams and diversions for irrigation along its lower course through the Imperial Valley. The average flow at the mouth of the Colorado River has been reduced from 22,000 cubic feet per second between 1903 and 1934 to less than 5,000 cubic feet per second from 1951 to 1980. Mailed December 1908 to Milwaukee, Wisconsin. (M. Rieder, Publ., Los Angeles, Cal. 21038; Made in Germany; handcolored work.)

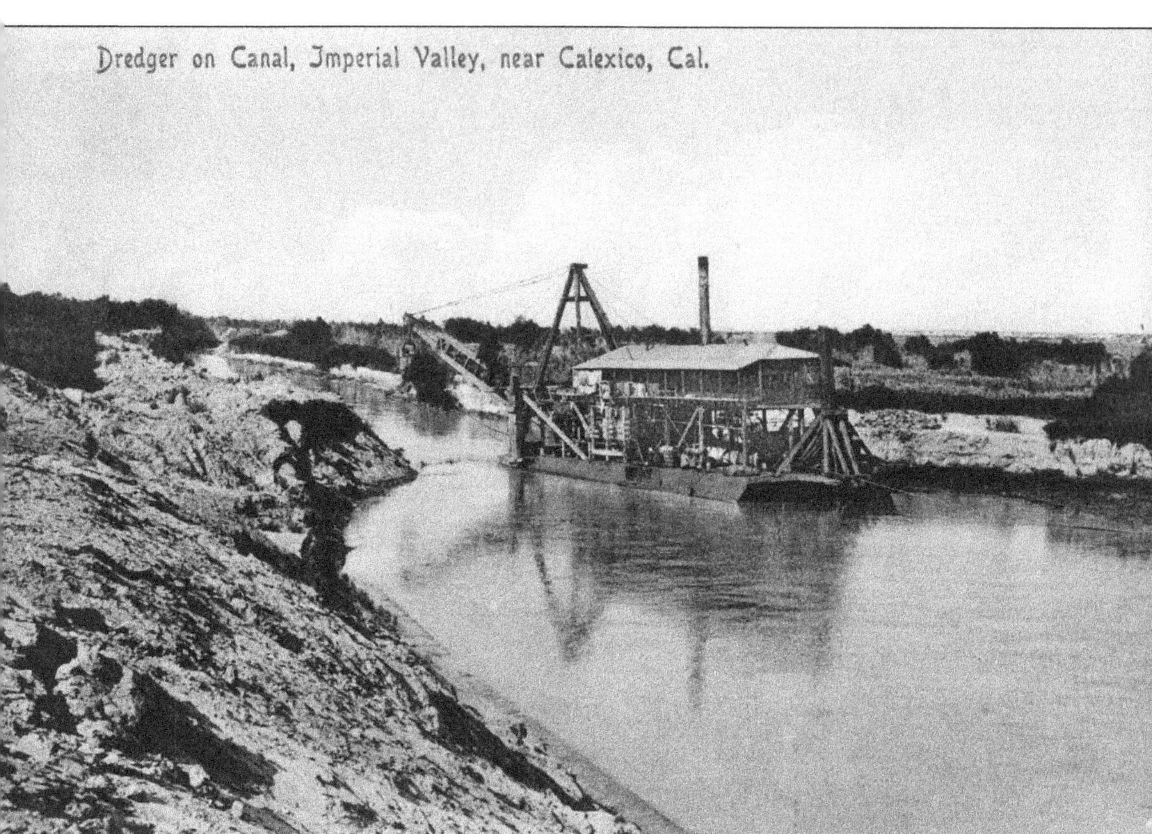

DREDGER ON CANAL, IMPERIAL VALLEY, NEAR CALEXICO, CAL. / ON THE LINE OF THE SOUTHERN PACIFIC RAILWAY. Prior to the construction of Hoover Dam, a single day's supply of water for the Imperial Valley contained enough silt to make a levee 20 feet high by 20 feet wide and one mile long. As a result, sediment and silt deposits of the Colorado River demanded almost continuous dredging of the canal system. Mailed to Valley Center, Kansas. (M. Rieder, Publ., Los Angeles, Cal. 7977; Made in Germany.)

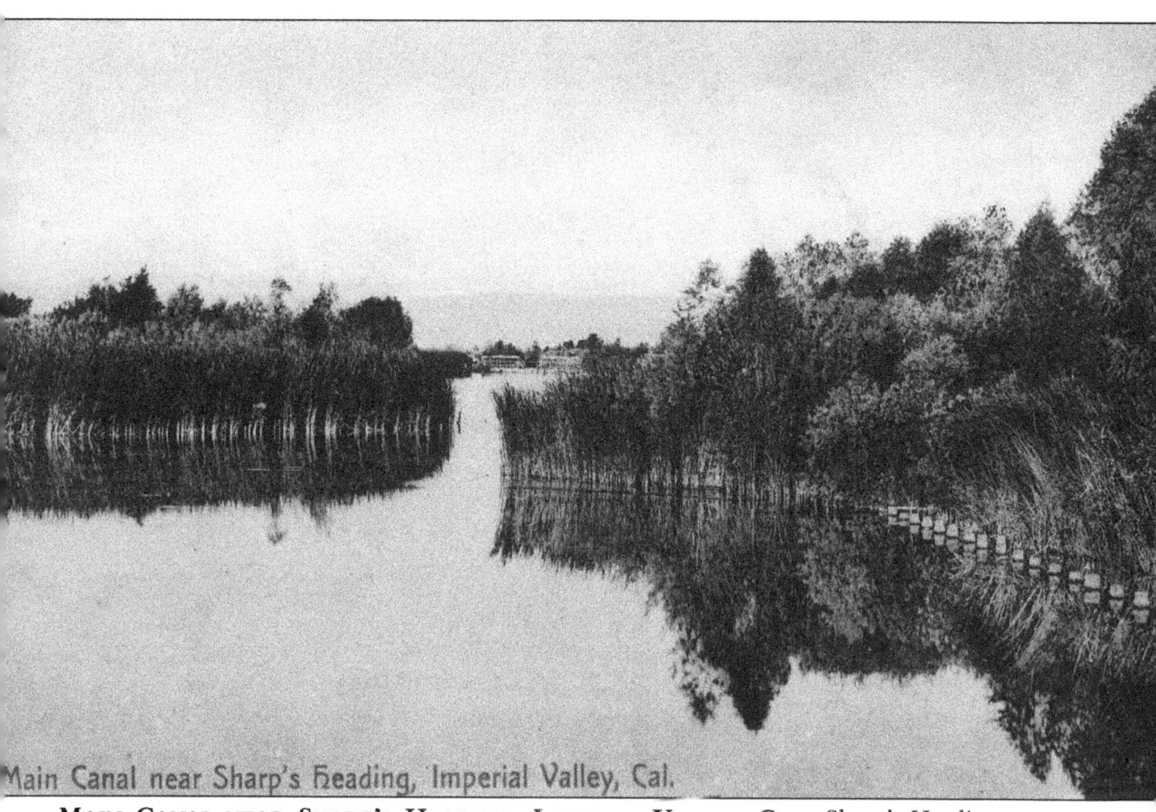

MAIN CANAL NEAR SHARP'S HEADING, IMPERIAL VALLEY, CAL. Sharp's Heading was designed and installed by engineer Charles N. Perry. This timber structure was completed on September 1, 1906. It served as the headgate for the Central Main Canal during the months when the entire flow of the Colorado River was entering the Imperial Valley. Sharp's headgate was located seven miles east of Mexicali, Mexico. Mailed April 20, 1909, to Mendocino, California. (M. Rieder, Publ., Los Angeles, Cal. 21320; Made in Germany; handcolored work.)

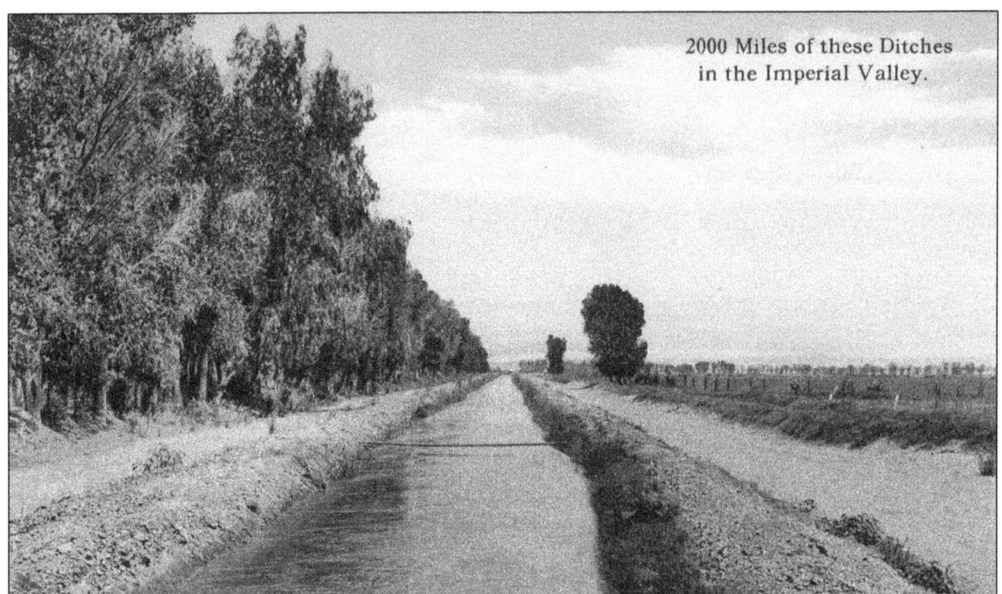

2000 MILES OF THESE DITCHES IN THE IMPERIAL VALLEY. This is an advertising card with the name Juan Felix Brandes of Santa Barbara, California, printed on the backside along with a short text titled "History of the Imperial Valley." This brief history states that 14 years prior to the date of the postcard, there were no residents, sagebrush was everywhere, and there was no irrigation. By 1914, there were 10,000 residents, 10 thriving cities, property valued at $65 million, an annual crop of $25 million, 350,000 acres under irrigation, and an annual cotton production of 80,000 bales.

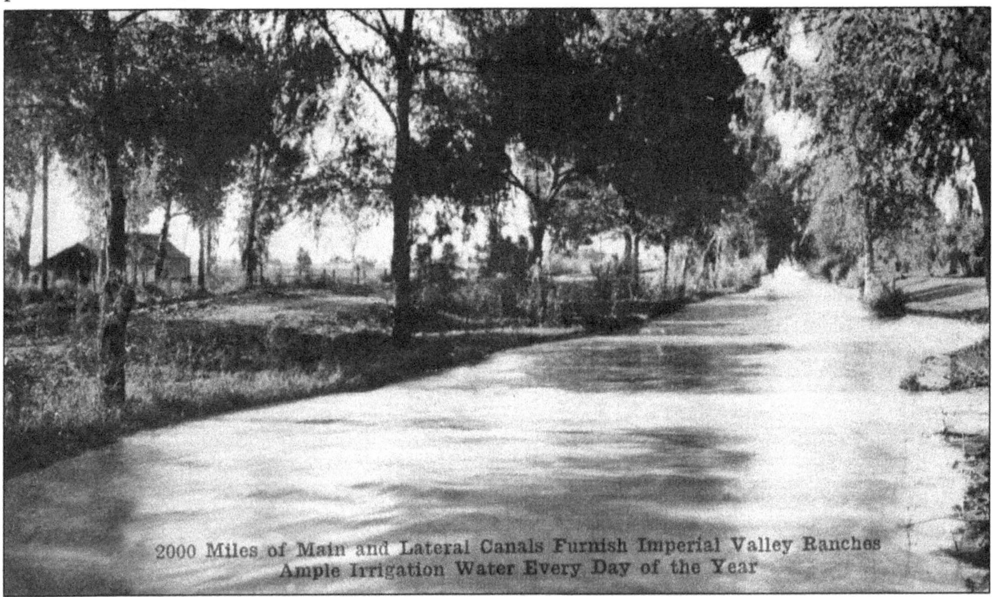

2000 MILES OF MAIL AND LATERAL CANALS FURNISH IMPERIAL VALLEY RANCHOS AMPLE IRRIGATION WATER EVERY DAY OF THE YEAR. "For descriptive literature of the famous Imperial Valley, California, write the Chamber of Commerce at Brawley, Calexico, Calipatria, Dixieland, El Centro, Heber, Holtville, Imperial, Niland, Seeley." (Published by Van Ornum Colorprint Co., Los Angeles.)

Two

Farming and Crops of the Imperial Valley

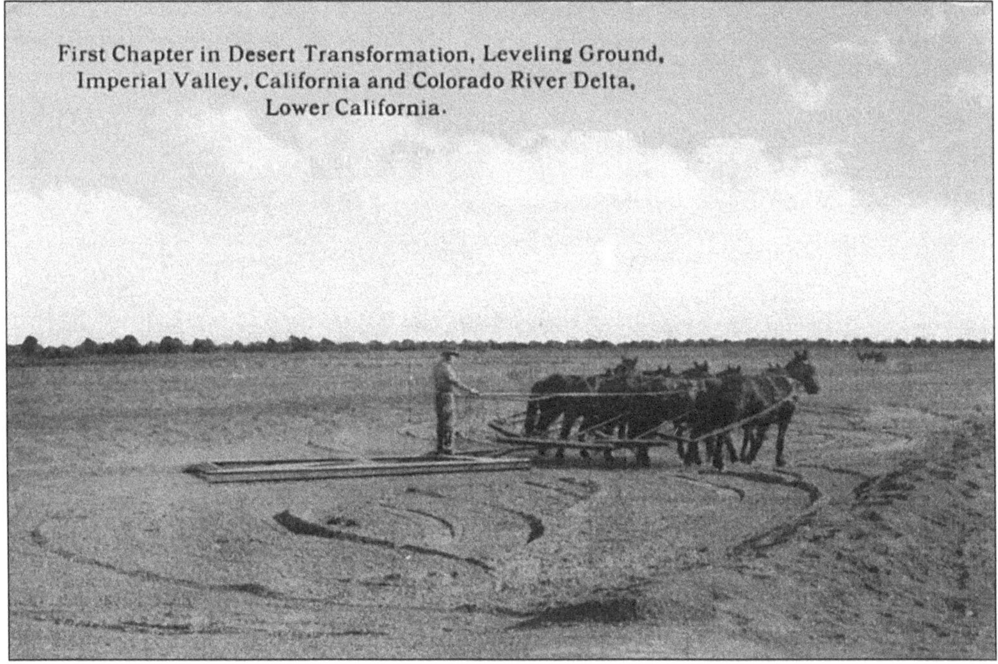

First Chapter in Desert Transformation. Leveling Ground, Imperial Valley, California and Colorado River Delta, Lower California. "Before crops are planted, lands are cleared of brush and leveled, then irrigation ditches are built, connection the lands with the mail Imperial Canal. Within twelve months for the time of starting operations a 2500 acre tract can be transformed into blooming cotton fields." Near the end of the 1800s, the Imperial Valley was virtually uninhabited. In 1901, the Alamo Canal was opened to the Imperial Valley. By 1915, there were 300,000 under cultivation of crops and livestock production. Today, there are nearly 500,000 acres of farmland in the Imperial Valley. Unused.

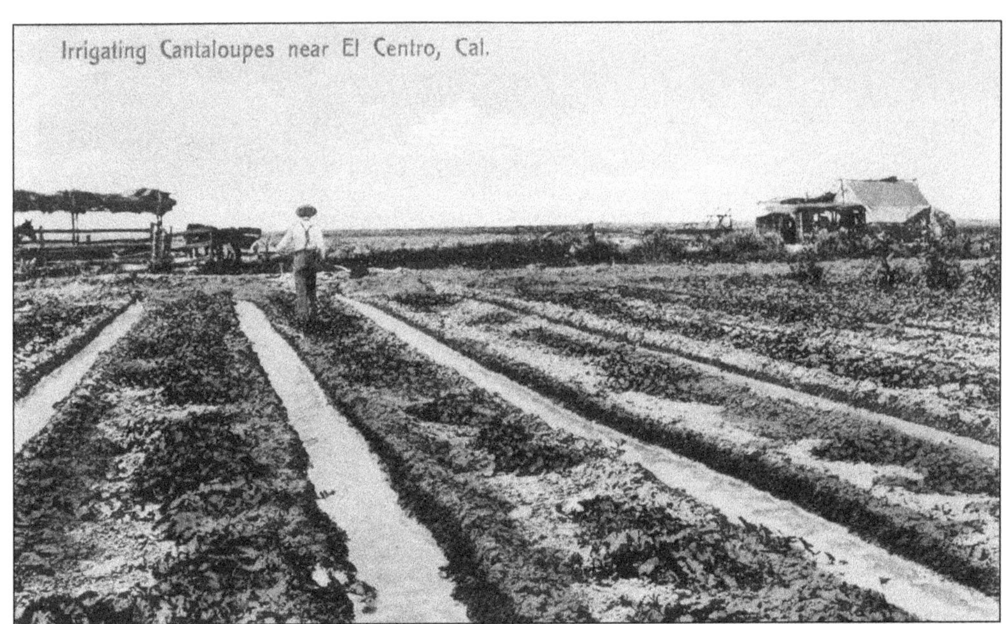

Irrigation Cantaloupes Near El Centro, Cal. Some food historians believe that cultivation of cantaloupes date back to the biblical period in Egypt and Greece. The fruit was depicted in Egyptian paintings and identified as a melon. In ancient times, the Romans obtained their supply of melons from Armenia. Unused. (M. Rieder, Publ., Los Angeles, Cal. 21476; Made in Germany; handcolored work.)

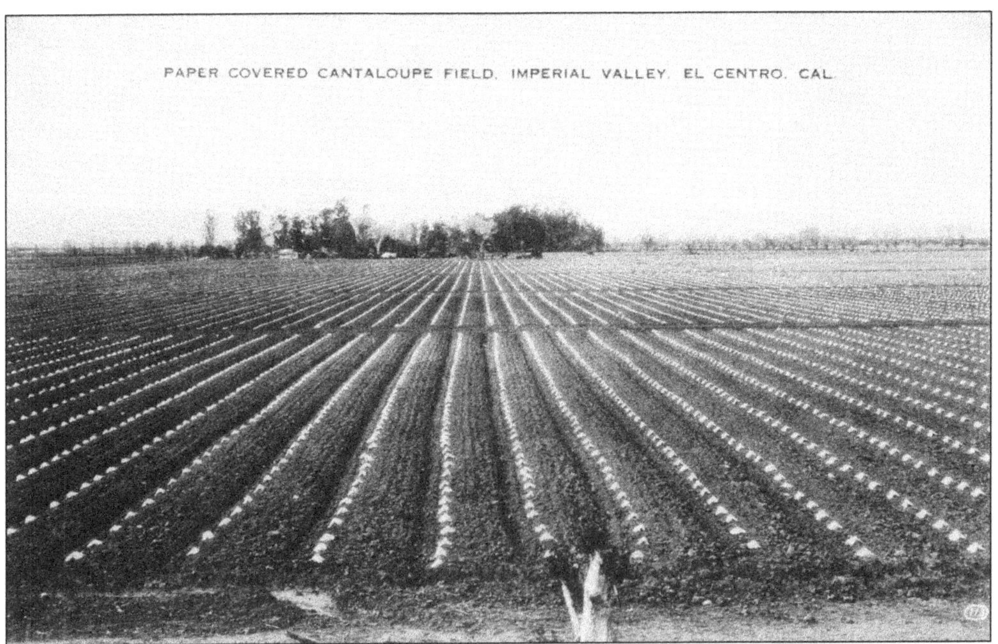

Paper Covered Cantaloupe Field, Imperial Valley, El Centro, Cal. Today, cantaloupes are largely grown in the San Joaquin and Imperial Valleys of California. Unused. (Published by Artvue Post Card Co. – 225 5th Av. N.Y.C.)

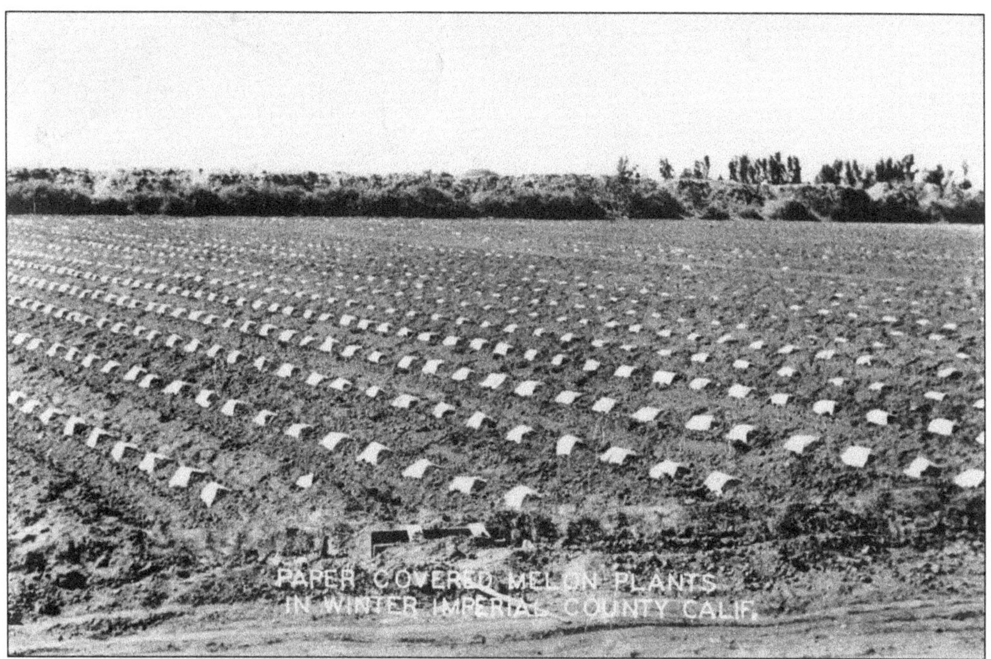

Paper Covered Melon Plants in Winter Imperial Valley Calif. Spring production of warm-season vegetables starts in late April with harvests that include cantaloupes and watermelons as well as sweet onions, bell and chili peppers, and sweet corn. Unused.

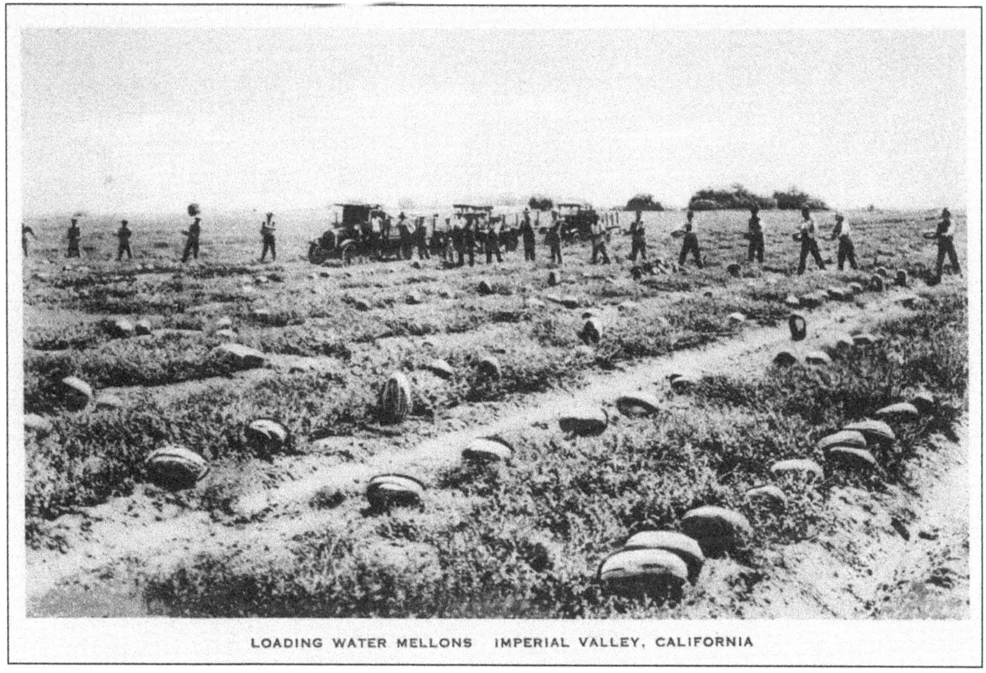

Loading Water Melons Imperial Valley, California. The Imperial Valley remains a large producer of watermelons. However, they are commercially grown in 44 states. Unused. (Published by Western Publishing & Novelty Co., Los Angeles.)

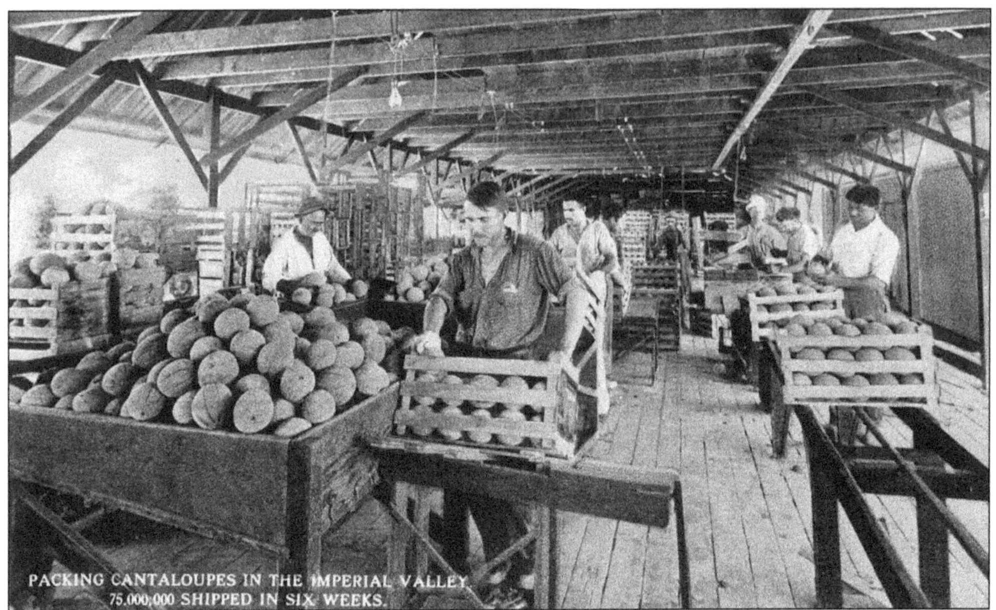

PACKING CANTALOUPES IN THE IMPERIAL VALLEY. 75,000,000 SHIPPED IN SIX WEEKS. Many of the Imperial Valley postcards featured in this book were produced by Leo Hetzel (1877–1949). Mr. Hetzel moved to El Centro in 1910 and began his career as a photographer in 1913. He was not considered to be an "artistic" photographer. Hetzel was a straightforward documentarian and photographed exactly as it appeared to him. He was also a farmer and took great pride in the crops and filed workers of the Imperial Valley. Unused. (Published by Leo Hetzel, El Centro, CA.)

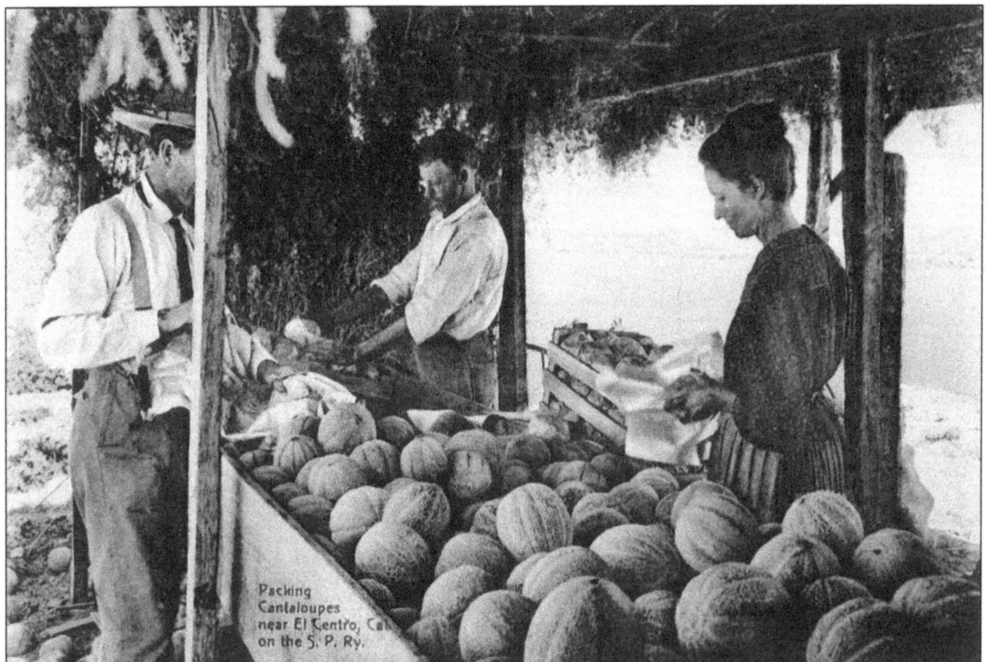

PACKING CANTALOUPES NEAR EL CENTRO, CAL. ON THE S.P. RY. Unused. (M. Rieder, Publ., Los Angeles, Cal. 21525; Made in Germany.)

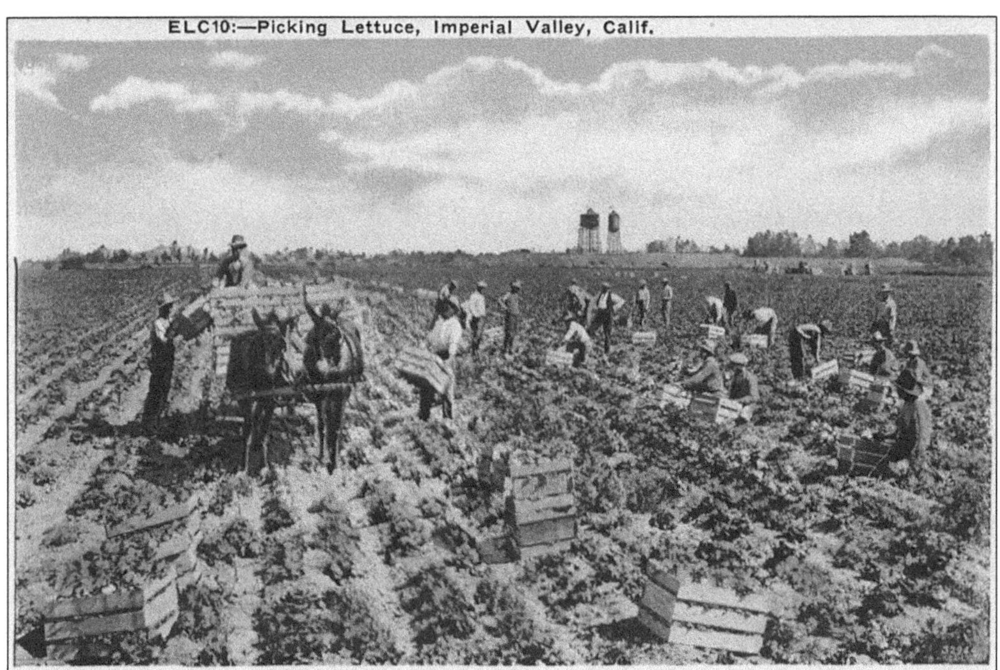

ELC10—Picking Lettuce, Imperial Valley, Calif. Unused. (Published by M. Kahhower Co., Los Angeles, California.)

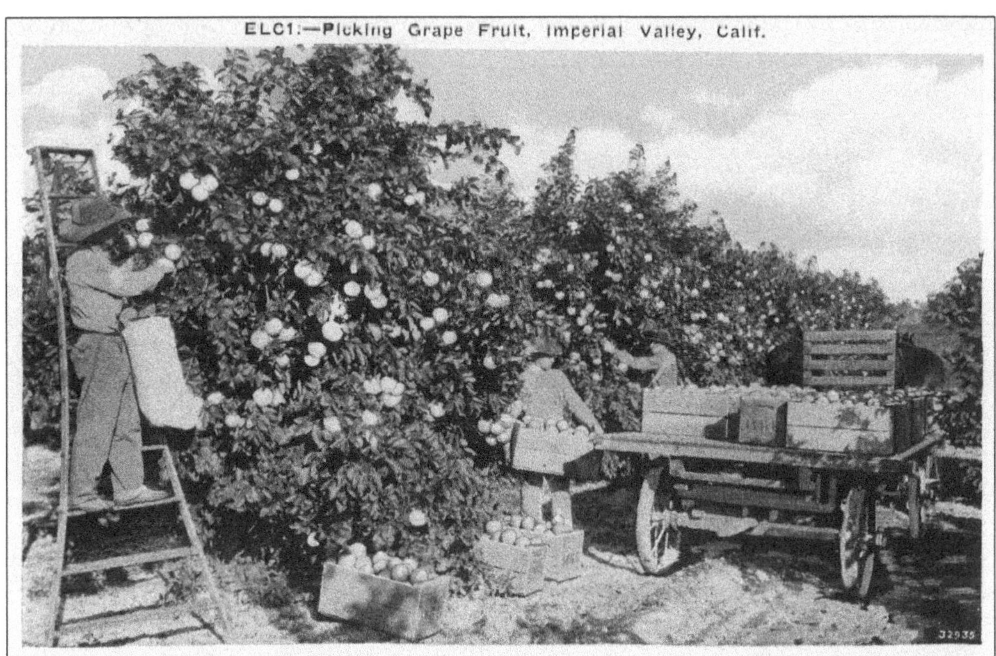

ELC1—Picking Grapefruit, Imperial Valley, Calif. The United States produces 41 percent of the world's grapefruit crop. Florida grows about 75 percent of the country's grapefruit, while California is a distant second. Who was the first US president to eat grapefruit? William Howard Taft. Mailed October 6, 1987, to Wichita, Kansas. (Published by M. Kashower Co., Los Angeles, California.)

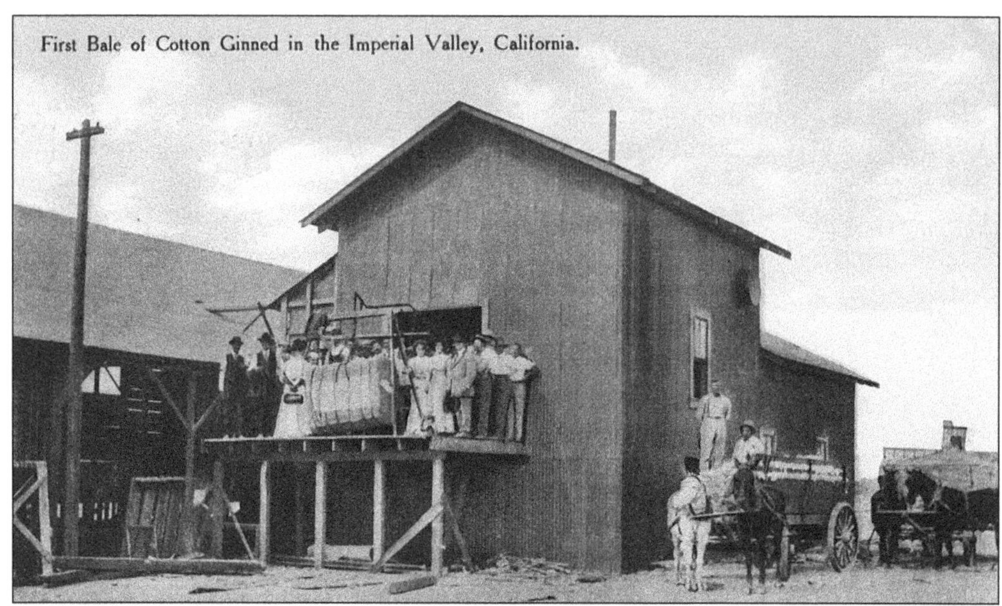

First Bale of Cotton Ginned in the Imperial Valley, California. In 1908, one year before the first commercial crop was produced in Imperial Valley, Texan transplant Ira Aten argued that "the picking of cotton is held to be a drawback to the valley, but that is not true. We mean to get Mexicans for the work and get all we need. Mexicans are the best pickers we know of. They come from Mexico City to do the work and make good pay at it in Texas." Mailed March 24, 1911, to San Bernardino, California. (Published by The Benham Co., Los Angles, California.)

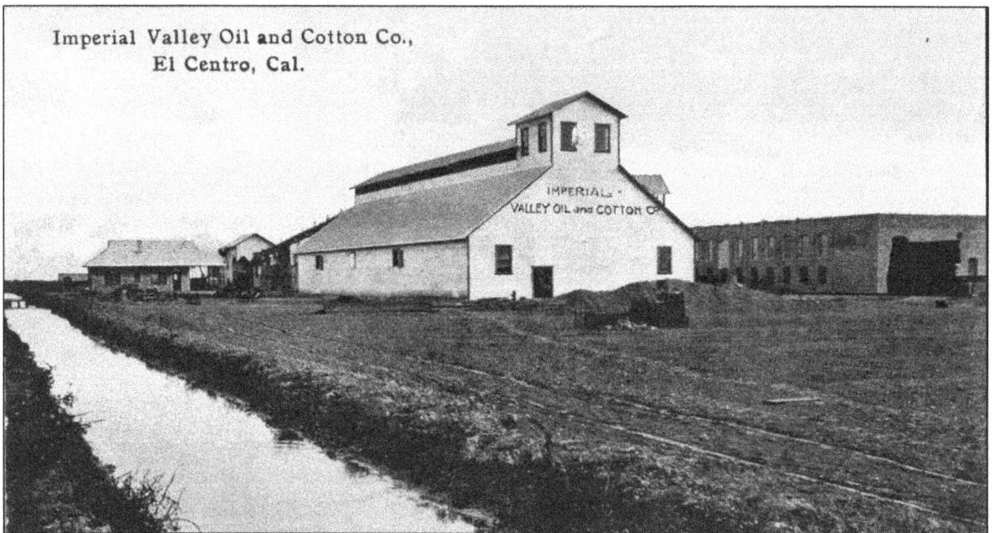

Imperial Valley Oil and Cotton Co., El Centro, Cal.; Panama-California Exposition, San Diego. Cottonseed oil is cooking oil extracted from the seed of a cotton plant. The oil is used as an ingredient in mayonnaise and salad dressing because of its flavor stability. It is also used in fatty foods such as potato chips and is a principal ingredient in Crisco shortening. Many nutritionists claim that cottonseed oil is too high in saturated fats. Research shows that a diet containing cottonseed oil causes infertility in rats. Unused. (Published by The Benham Co., Los Angeles, California.)

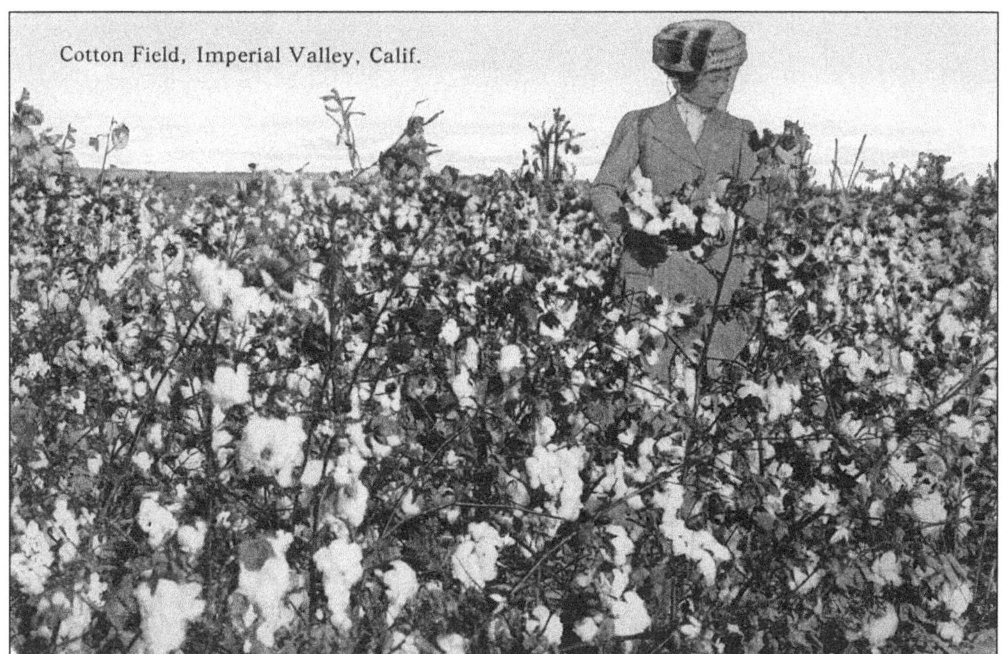

COTTON FIELD, IMPERIAL VALLEY, CALIF. "Imperial Valley is acknowledged the best in the United States. Two bales of long staple to the acre is attainable." Mailed November 23, 1920, to Cranesville, Pennsylvania.

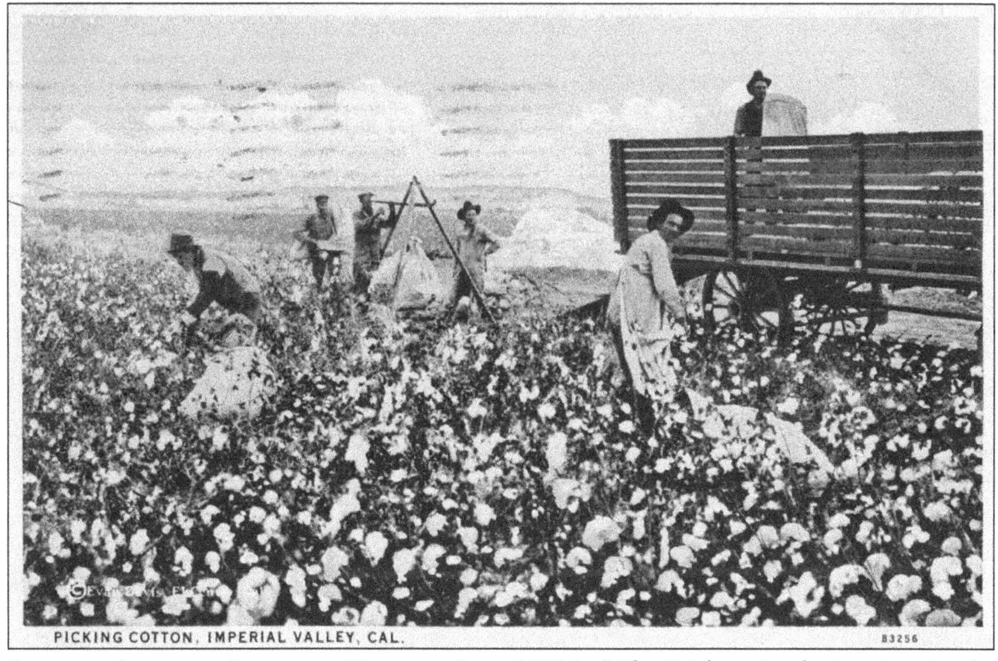

PICKING COTTON, IMPERIAL VALLEY, CAL. 83256. "The Richest Producing Area in the World. Over 60,000 acres in this valley are devoted to growing, with a great many ranches producing better than a bale to the acre. Just across the border, in Mexico, 135,000 acres are also in cotton, which is really part of the Imperial Valley." Mailed January 26, 1929, to Quincy, Illinois. (C.T. American Art, colored.)

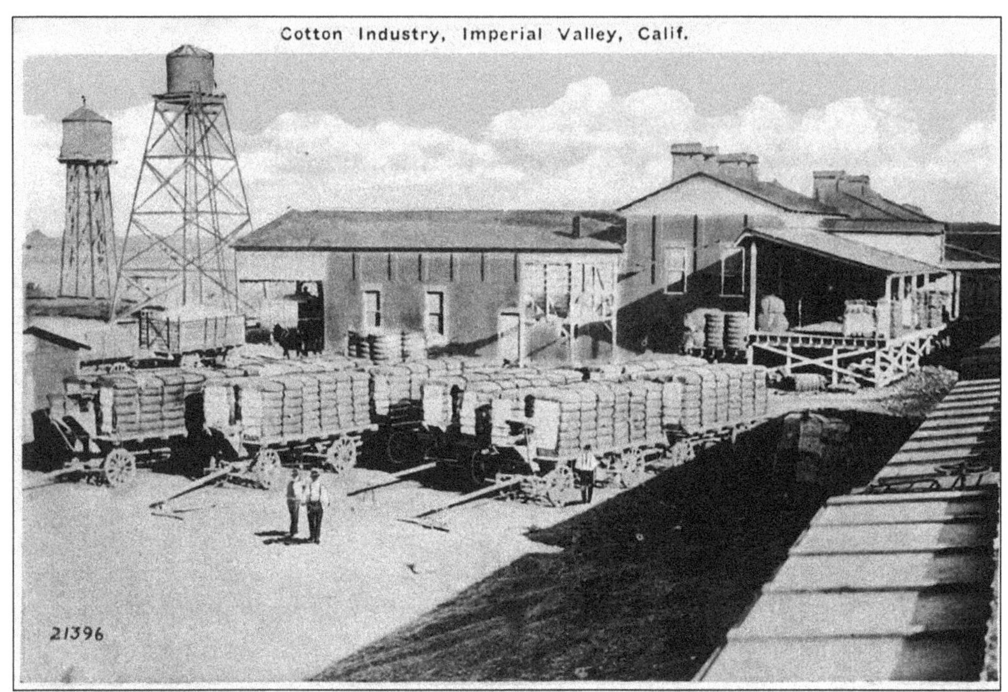

COTTON INDUSTRY, IMPERIAL VALLEY, CALIF. At one time, there were five cotton gins located in the Imperial Valley. However, they have all closed. Unused. (Published by the M. Kashower Co., Los Angeles, California.)

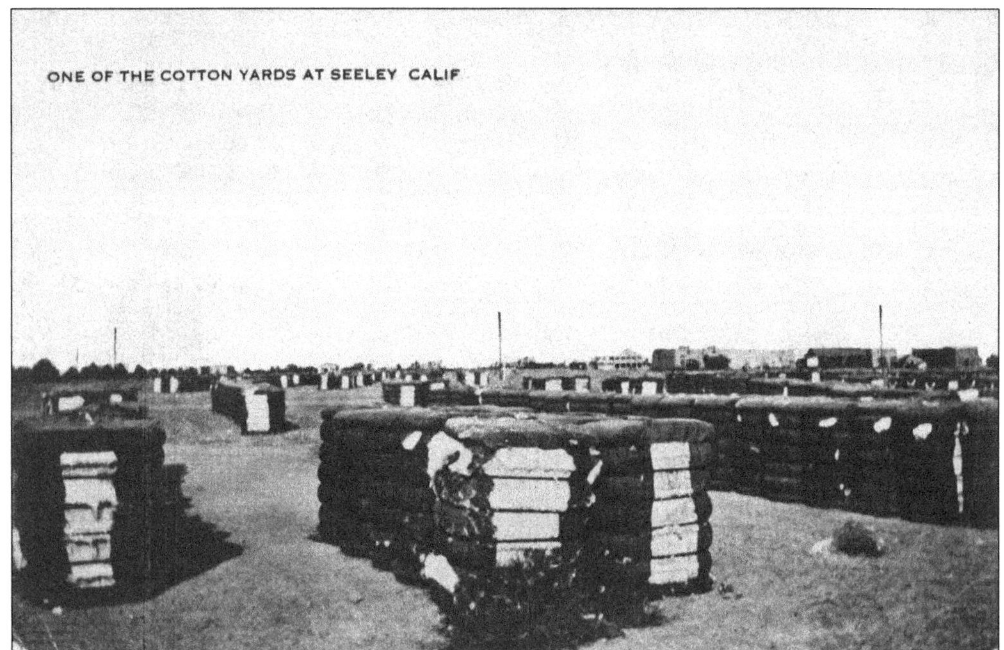

ONE OF THE COTTON YARDS AT SEELEY, CALF. In 1918, the Imperial Valley had 22 cotton gins, three oil mills and two compressors, which represented an investment of over $1 million. Unused photo card.

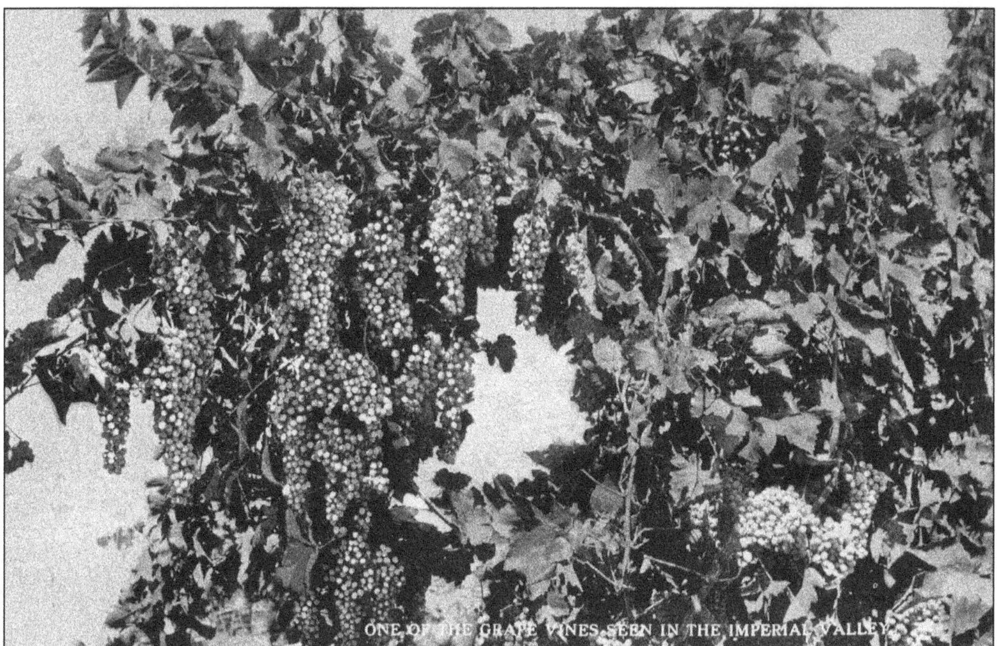

One of the Grape Vines Seen in the Imperial Valley. Today, grape production in the Imperial Valley is not significant. However, 5.8 percent of California's table grape production is in the nearby Coachella Valley. Unused. (Published by Leo Hetzel, El Centro, California.)

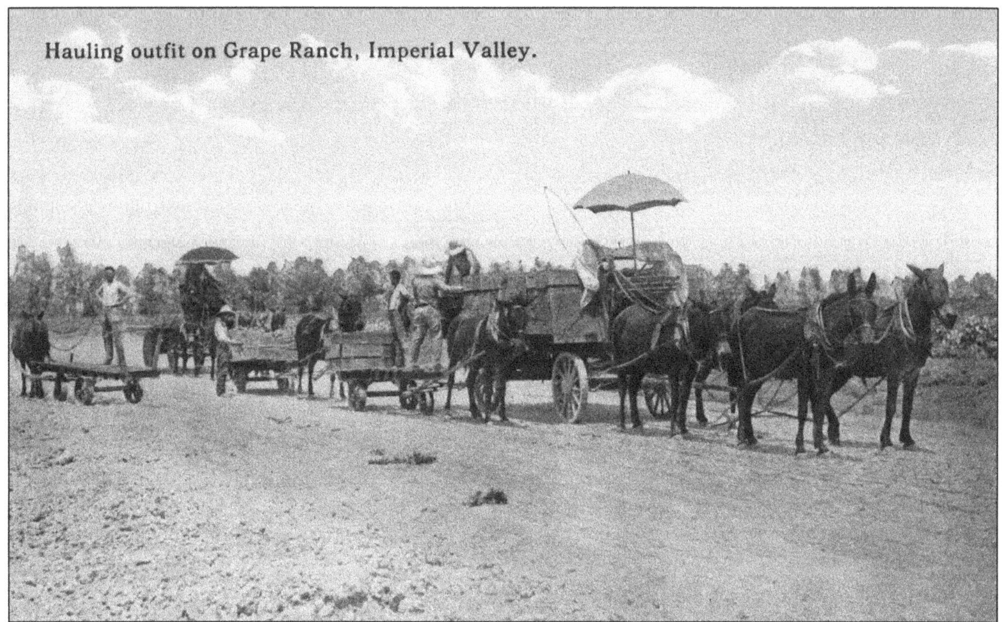

Hauling outfit on Grape Ranch, Imperial Valley. Today, there are nearly 14,000 acres of table grapes grown in the southern end of the Coachella Valley, near the Salton Sea. Approximately two-dozen growers produce $150 million in early-season table grapes. This accounts for 14 percent of the nation's total table grape production. Although the Coachella Valley includes areas of Riverside and Imperial Counties, table grapes are produced exclusively in Riverside County. Unused. (Published by Leo Hetzel, El Centro, California.)

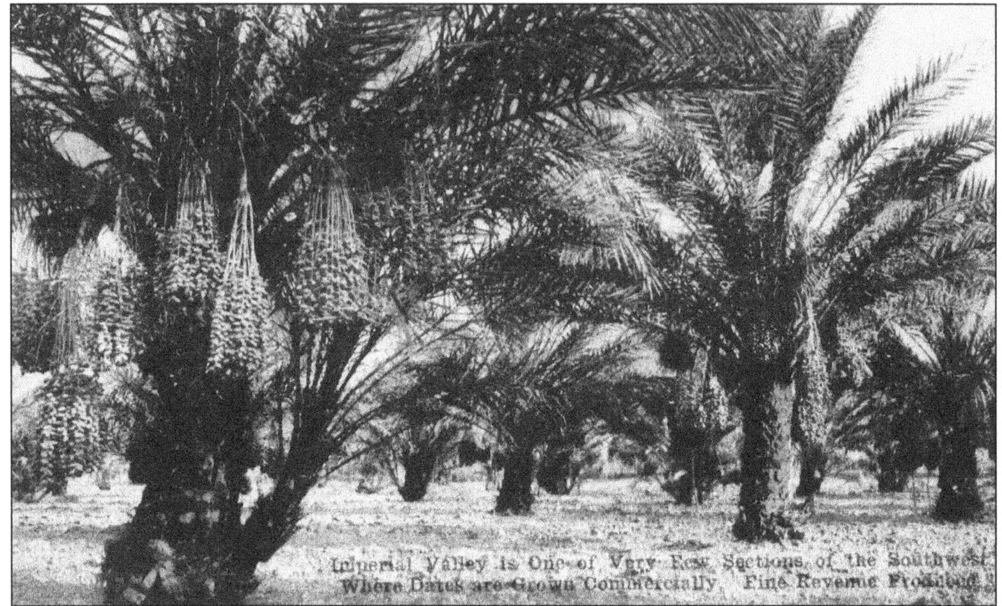

IMPERIAL VALLEY IS ONE OF VERY FEW SECTIONS OF THE SOUTHWEST WHERE DATES ARE GROWN COMMERCIALLY. FINE REVENUE PRODUCED. Unused. (Published by Van Ornum Colorprint Co., Los Angeles, California.)

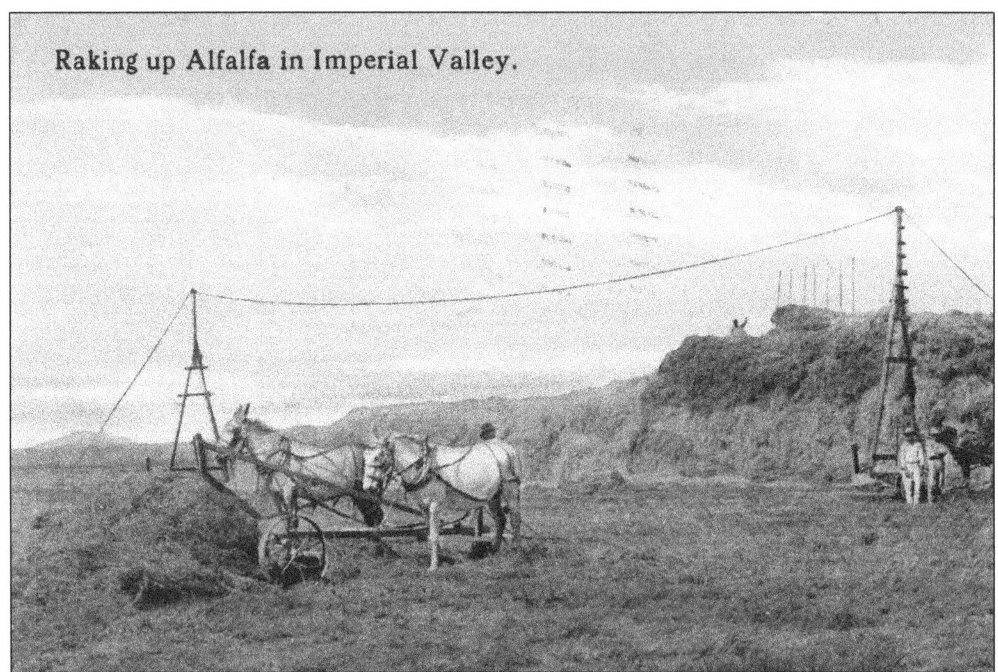

RAKING UP ALFALFA IN IMPERIAL VALLEY. Today, alfalfa is the number one agricultural crop in the Imperial Valley, with over 173,000 acres in production. Mailed April 1, 1918, to Rye, New York. (Published by Leo Hetzel, El Centro, California.)

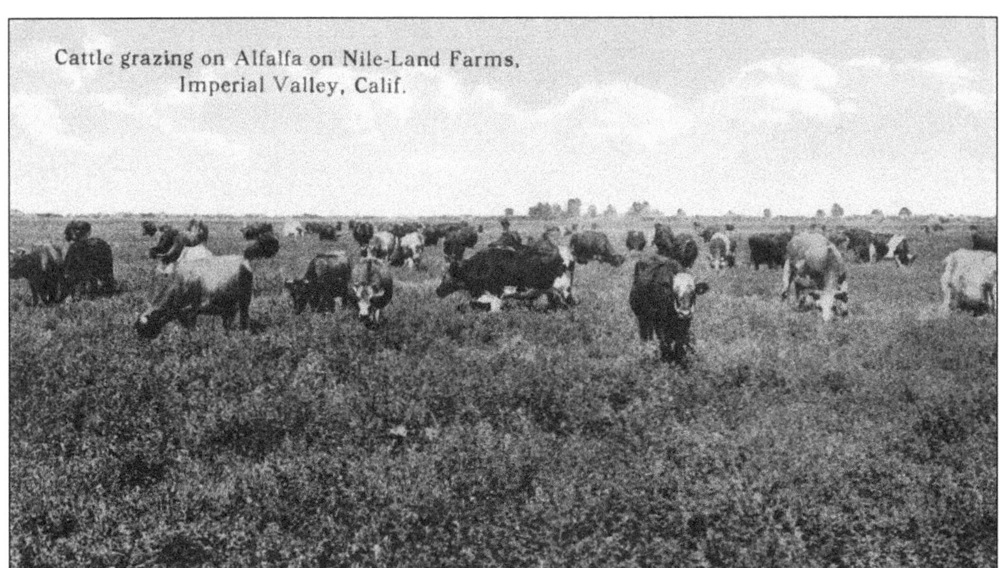

CATTLE GRAZING ON ALFALFA ON NILE-LAND FARMS, IMPERIAL VALLEY, CALIF. "Imperial Valley supports immense herds of livestock on its alfalfa and barley. Nine-Land Farms—47,000 acres at the north end of the Valley—considered ideal alfalfa lands have been opened by coming of irrigation water." California Land & Water Company 609–611 South Springs Street, Los Angeles, Cal. (Made by Curt Teich & Co., Chicago, U.S.A.)

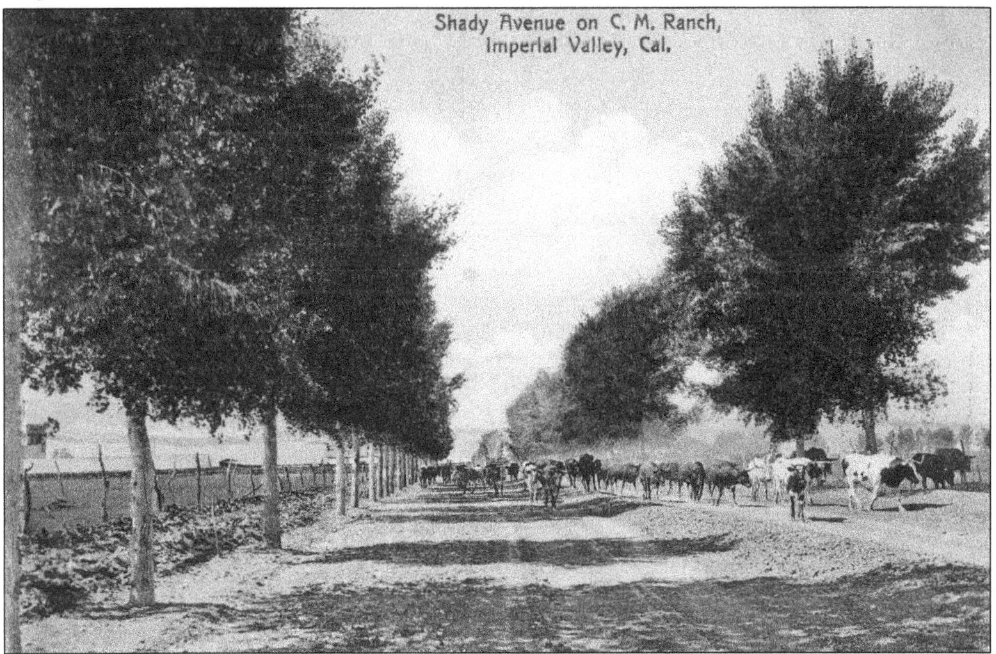

SHADY AVENUE ON C.M. RANCH, IMPERIAL VALLEY, CAL. The C.M. Ranch was also known as the California Land & Cattle Company. The ranch was a stock company owned by Los Angeles businessmen. It was comprised of 1,100 acres of highly developed ranchland in California and 876,000 acres across the border in Mexico. The ranch raised more stock than any other of its kind in Southern California. Mailed on June 29, 1909, to Whittington, Ontario, Canada. (M. Rieder, Publ., Los Angeles, Cal., 21527; made in Germany; handcolored work.)

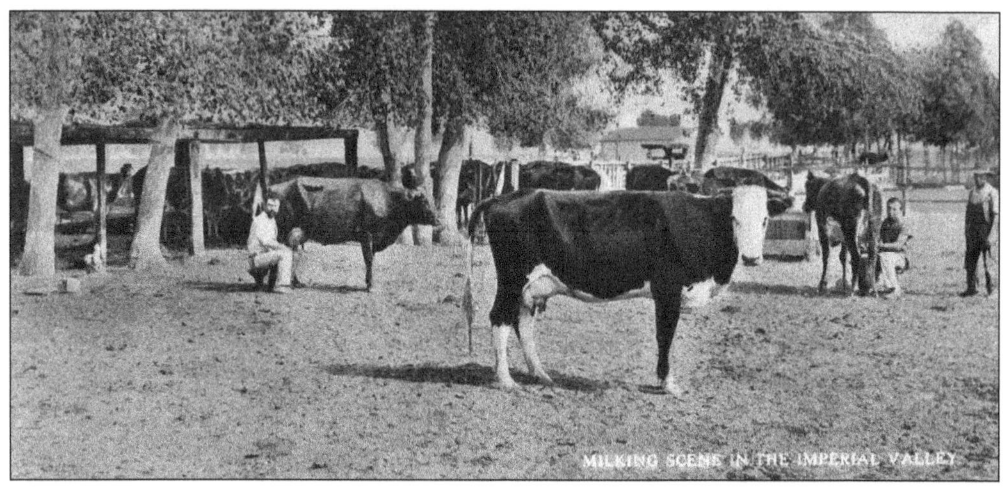

Milking Scene in the Imperial Valley. There is a marker located at 1550 East Worthington Road, Holtville, California, that commemorates persons of Swiss descent who first arrived in the Imperial Valley in 1901. Many of the Swiss began milking cows in the existing dairies. The Imperial Valley was once the favored dairy-producing location in Southern California, with more than 24,000 dairy cows producing six million pounds of butter annually. Today, only one dairy remains, and many of the Swiss descendents have turned to farming. Mailed to Gardena, North Dakota. (Published by Leo Hetzel, El Centro, California.)

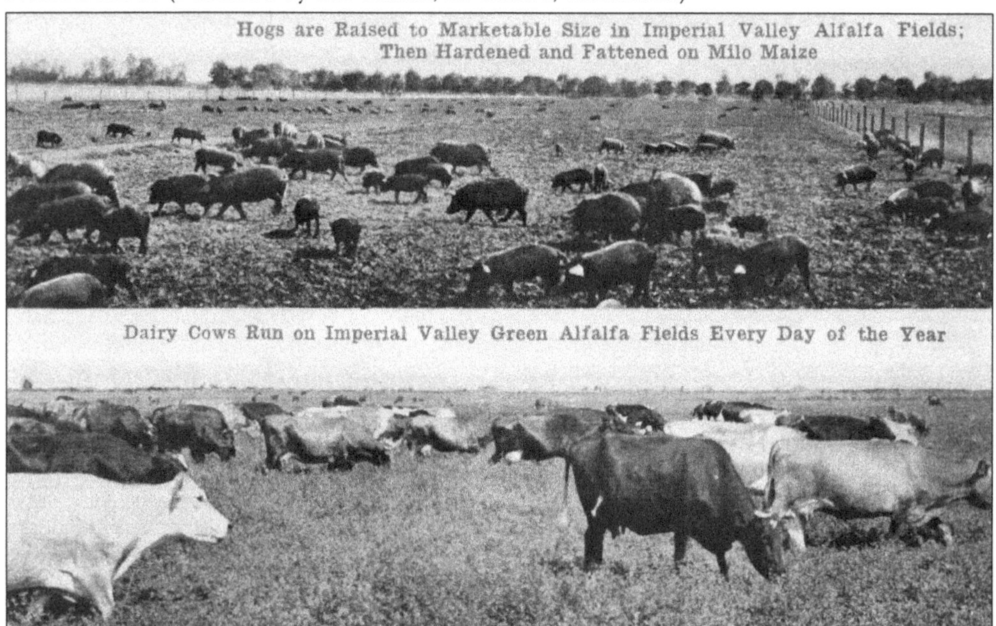

Hogs Are Raised to Marketable Size in Imperial Valley Alfalfa Fields; Then Hardened and Fattened on Milo Maize; Dairy Cows Run on Imperial Valley Green Alfalfa Fields Every Day of the Year. Hog and dairy are no longer major agricultural products in the Imperial Valley. However, local farmers produced 1,622,000 tons of hay and alfalfa in 2008, making the Imperial Valley a vital producer of food for California's dairy industry. Dairy is California's number one agricultural commodity and supplies 20 percent of the nation's production. Unused. (Published by Van Ornum Colorprint Co., Los Angeles, California.)

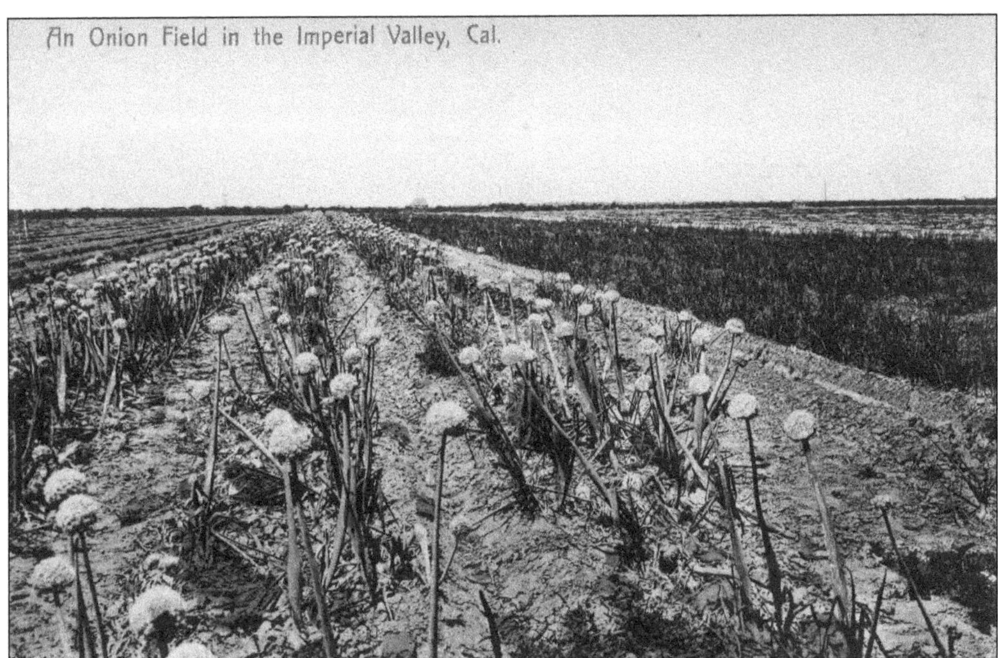

An Onion Field in the Imperial Valley, California. The Imperial Valley is known for the Sweet Imperial onion. In the 1930s, Dr. Henry Jones hybridized a cross between the flat Bermuda and the Grano onion into what eventually developed as the Granex, a yellow, globe-shaped sweet onion with a minimum diameter of 2.5 inches. The valley is the nation's number one producer of sweet onions. Unused. (M. Rieder, Publ., Los Angeles, California; 21043; Made in Germany; handcolored work.)

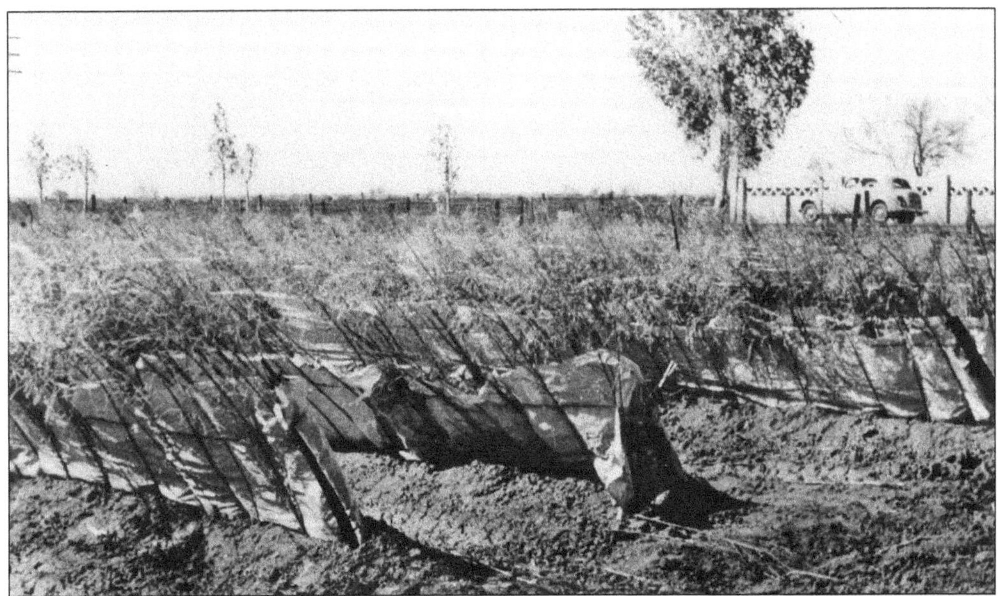

Brush Covered Tomato Plants in Winter Imperial Valley Calif. The Imperial Valley grows about 1 percent of the state's fresh-market tomatoes. Unused photo card.

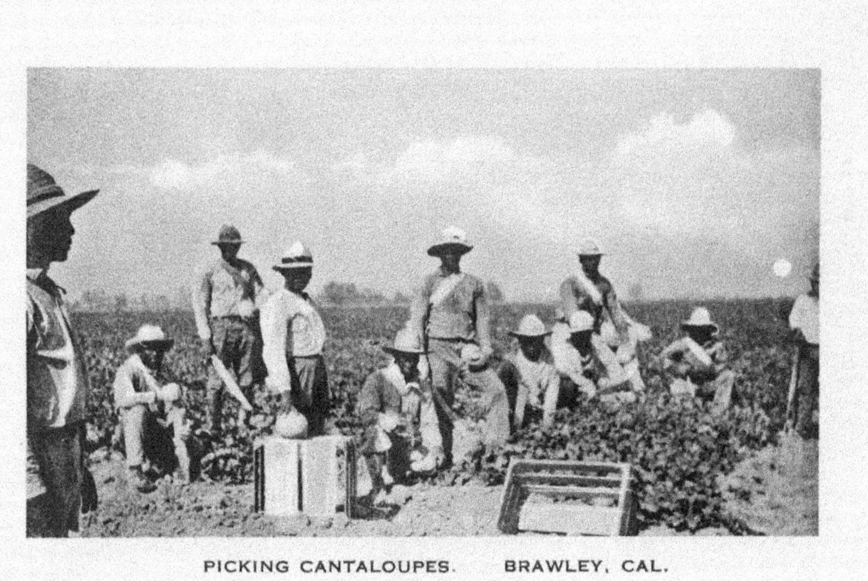

Picking Cantaloupes, Brawley, Cal. Historically, the southern desert valleys in Imperial and Riverside Counties have been one of California's two primary growing areas for cantaloupe and other melons. Harvesting in Imperial and Riverside counties takes place from May through early July. During the early 1990s, a new virus disease in melons caused Imperial Valley melon production to drop from approximately 12,000 acres annually to under 2,000 acres. Unused. (Published by White Cross Pharmacy, Post Cards of Quality, The Albertype Co., Brooklyn, New York.)

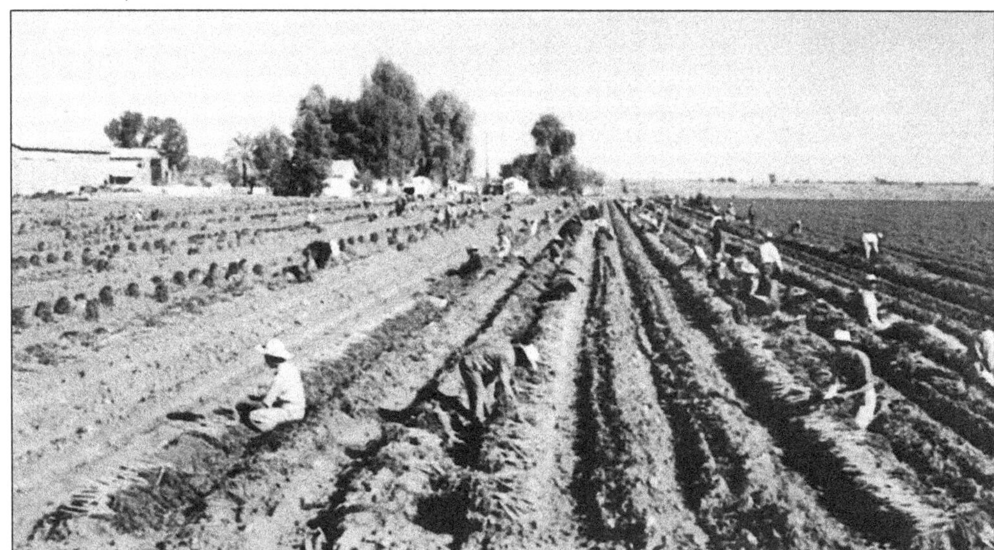

Carrot Harvest in Rich Imperial Valley, near El Centro, Calif. "Winter vegetables from this lush area are shipped to markets in all parts of the United States." In 2008, enough carrots were grown in Imperial Valley to serve a 2.5 pound helping to 75 percent of the world's nearly 5 billion people. Unused photo card. (Pub. & Dist. by Larry Holland, El Centro, California; Plastichrome by Colourpicture, Boston 15, Mass. U.S.A.)

Three

Life in the Imperial Valley

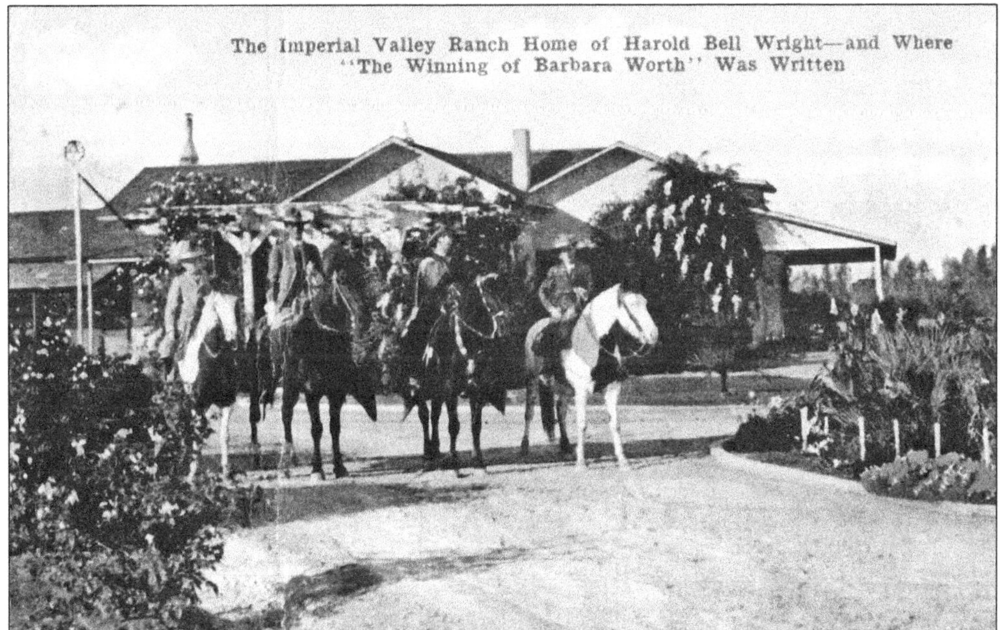

The Imperial Valley Ranch Home of Harold Bell Wright—and Where the "Winning of Barbara Worth" Was Written. Although he is not generally well recognized today, Harold Bell Wright was one of the most popular authors of the early 20th century. He wrote and released 19 books during his career. From his roots as a preacher, his books contained a message of morality. Ronald Reagan once reflected about the impact of reading Wright's book, *That Printer of Udell's*. President Reagan wrote, "That book . . . had an impact I shall always remember. After reading it and thinking about it for a few days, I went to my mother and told her I wanted to declare my faith and be baptized. We attended the Christian Church in Dixon, and I was baptized several days after finishing the book."

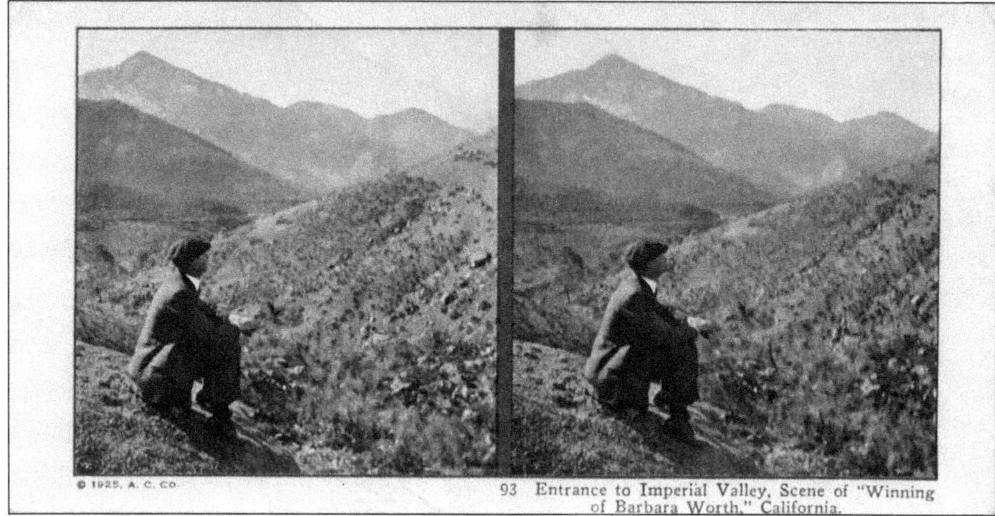

93 Entrance to Imperial Valley, Scene of "Winning of Barbara Worth," California.; Stereoscope Card. The Imperial Valley was the setting for the book and was Wright's home from 1907 to 1914. He lived just to the east of El Centro in a little area he named Meloland. (© 1925, A.C. Co.)

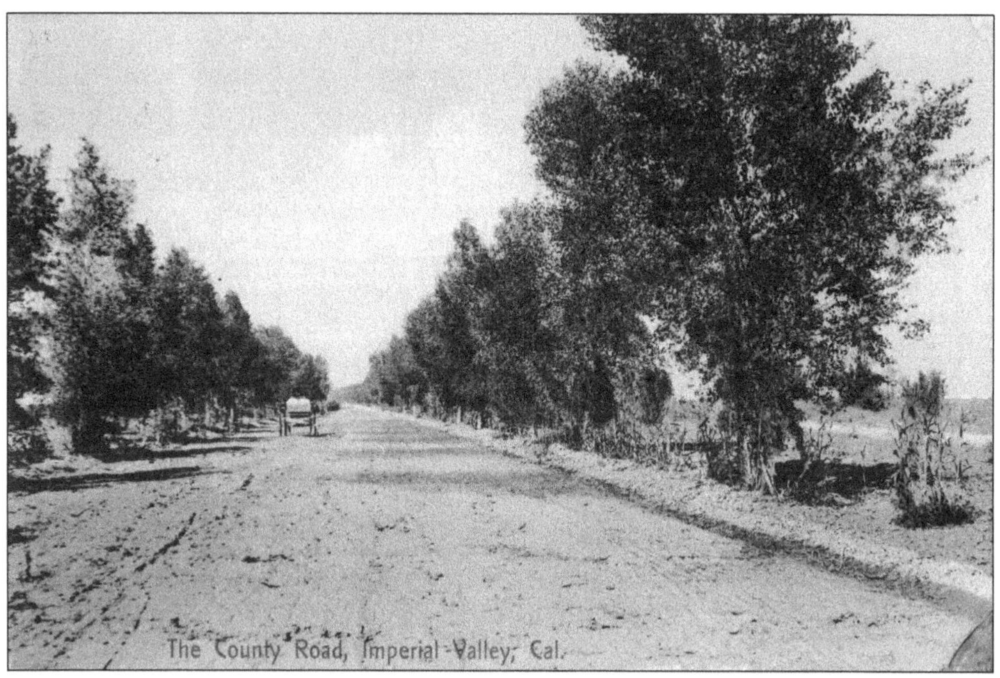

The County Road, Imperial Valley, Cal. Driving along the highways of the Imperial Valley is always an adventure for the urban dweller. Beautiful farmland, huge cattle feedlots, desert landscape, fish farms, geothermal plants, and migratory birds are examples of the rural lifestyle of Imperial County. Mailed to Redlands, California. (M. Rieder, Publ., Los Angeles, California; 21040; Made in Germany; handcolored work.)

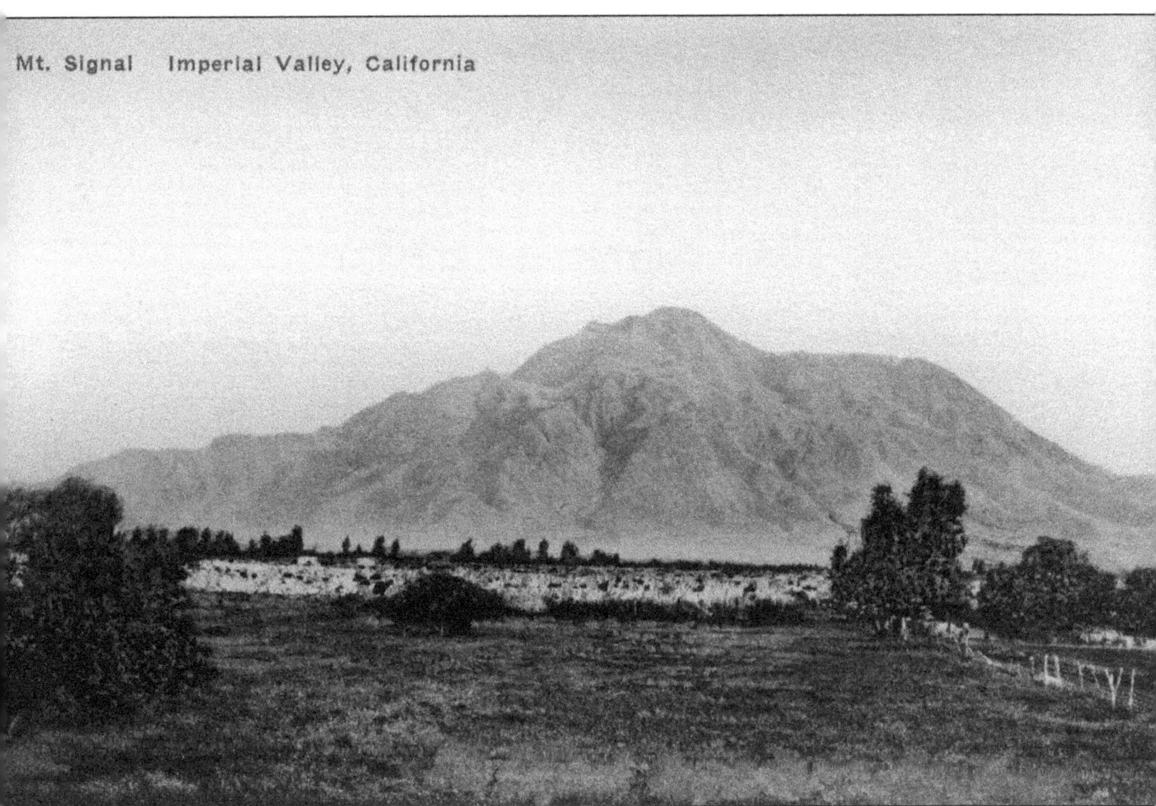

MT. SIGNAL IMPERIAL VALLEY, CALIFORNIA. Mount Signal is an unincorporated town along State Route 98 west of Calexico and about 1.7 miles north of the Mexican border. The actual mountain is 2,300 feet high and located on the Mexican side of the border. Mount Signal was used by Native Americans and early pioneers as a landmark to help guide them through the desert. Unused. (Published by Barbara Worth Hotel, El Cento, California, Post Cards of Quality, The Albertype Co., Brooklyn, New York.)

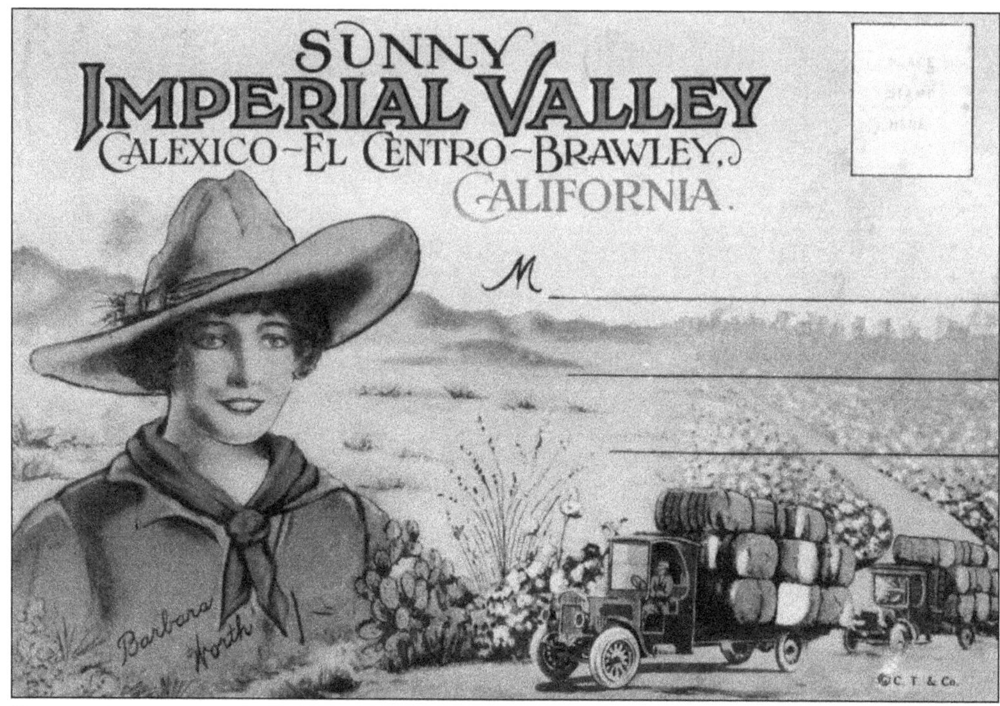

SUNNY IMPERIAL VALLEY / CALEXICO-EL CENTRO-BRAWLEY, CALIFORNIA; A BOOK OF SIXTEEN POSTCARDS WITH A PICTURE PORTRAYAL OF BARBARA WORTH ON THE FRONT COVER. This book of postcards was initially puzzling. Who was young lady prominently featured on the cover? Why did someone sign the name Barbara Worth below the portrait? Was the signature that of the person who owned the book or simply a facsimile signature of the beautiful girl in cowgirl attire? Some research revealed that *The Winning of Barbara Worth* was a bestselling novel by Harold Bell Wright and a defining saga of settler colonization in the Imperial Valley during the first quarter of the 20th century. (Made by Curt Teich & Co., Chicago, U.S.A.)

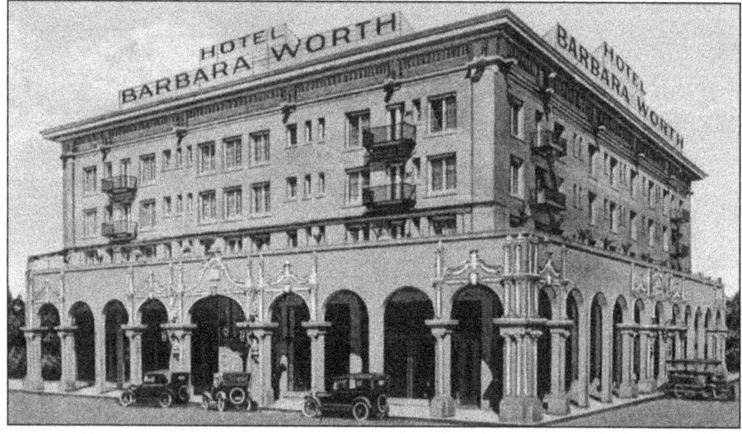

HOTEL BARBARA WORTH, EL CENTRO. This world-class resort was located on the corner of Seventh and Main Streets in El Centro, California. Harold Bell Wright and his family posed for the murals painted on the lobby walls. The name was taken from Wright's best-selling novel *The Winning of Barbara Worth*. Construction began in 1914, and the hotel opened May 8, 1915. It burned to the ground January 21, 1962. All that remains is a vacant lot in the middle of town.

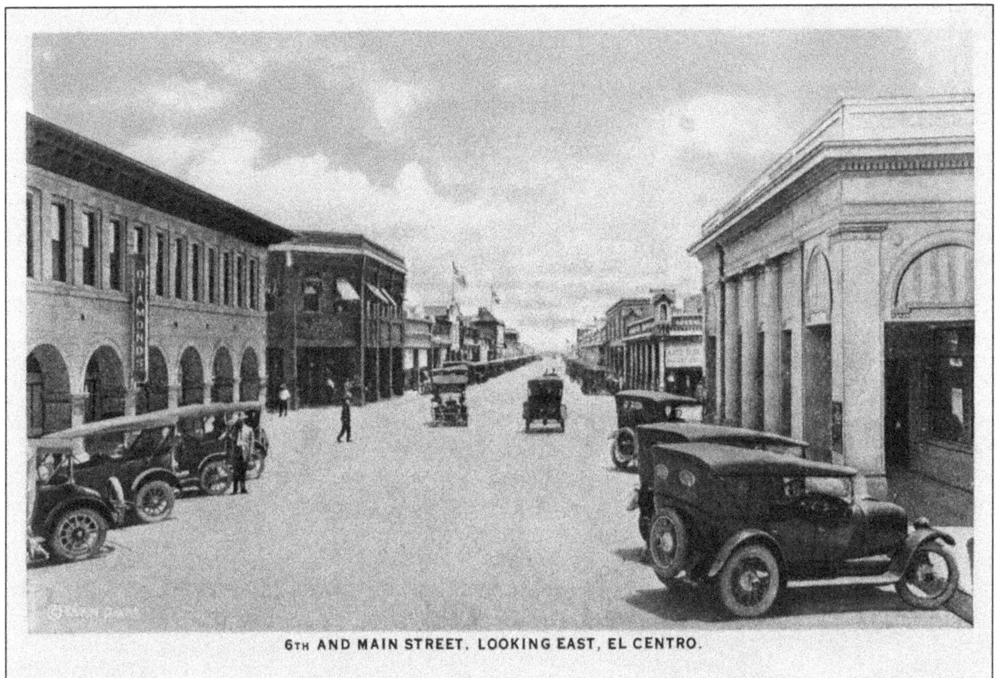

6TH AND MAIN STREET, LOOKING EAST, EL CENTRO. The city was founded in 1906 by W.F. Holt and C.A. Barker. They purchased the land on which El Centro was eventually built for about $40 an acre and invested $100,000 in improvements. As one historian of local life put it, "in only five months, El Centro went from a barley field to a city."

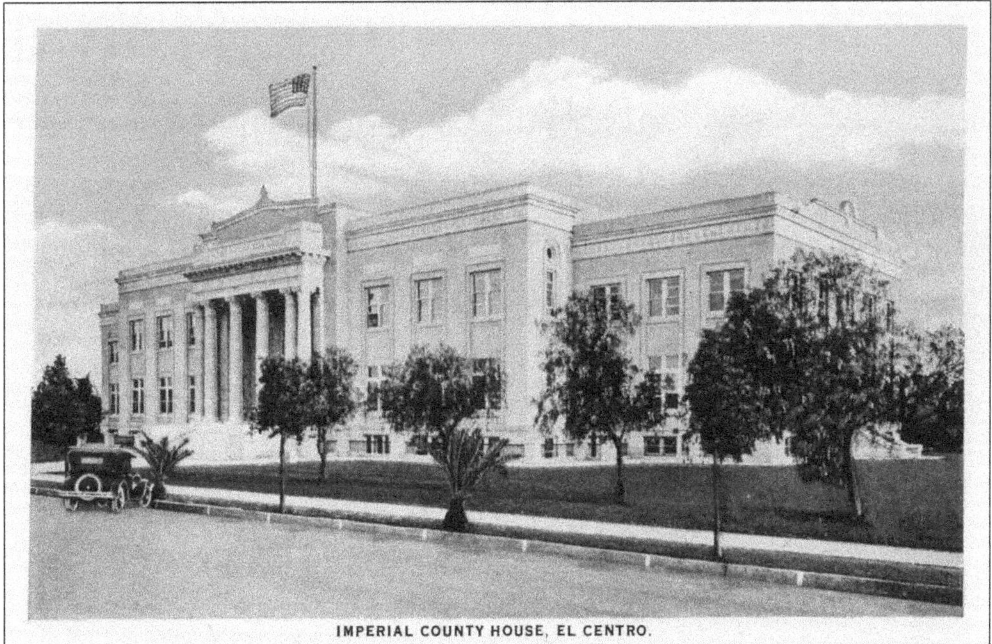

IMPERIAL COUNTY [COURT] HOUSE, EL CENTRO. The Imperial Valley courts occupied offices on the second floor of a bank building until 1924, when the county built the new courthouse on donated land in El Centro.

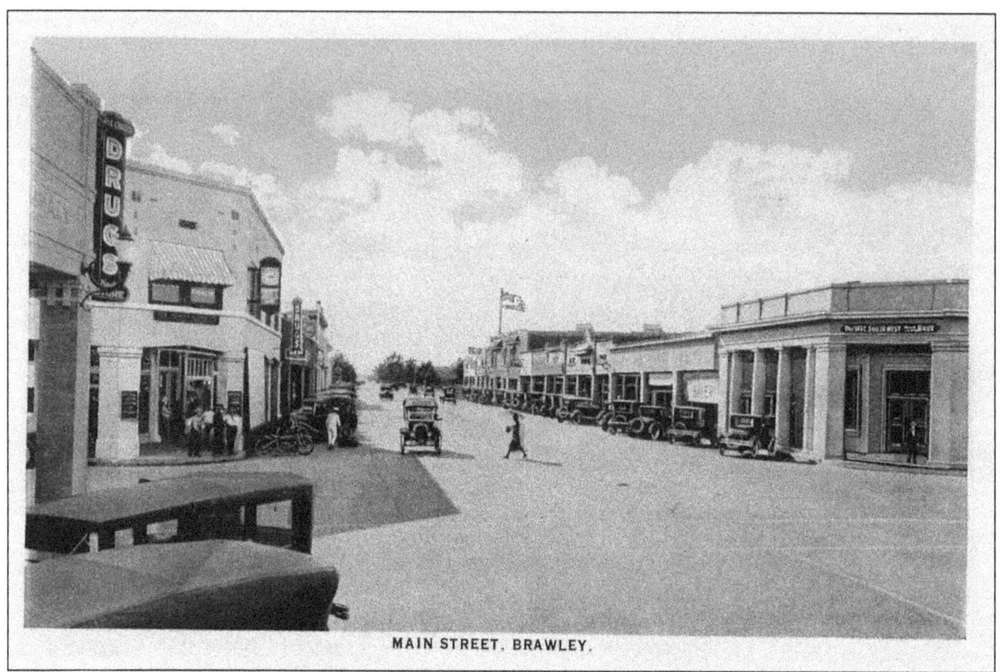

MAIN STREET, BRAWLEY.

MAIN STREET, BRAWLEY. The Imperial Land Company laid out the town in 1902 and named it Braly in honor of J.H. Braly, who owned the land. After Braly refused to permit this, the town name was changed to Brawley.

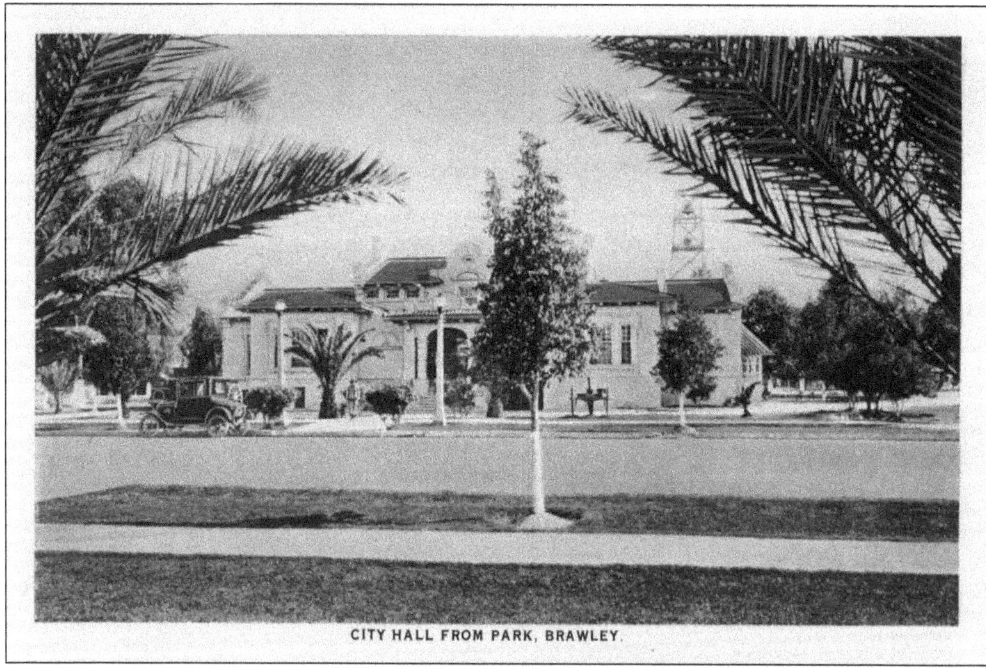

CITY HALL FROM PARK, BRAWLEY.

CITY HALL FROM PARK, BRAWLEY. At the time of the 2000 census, Brawley had a population of 22,052. The town has a significant cattle and feed industry and hosts the annual Cattle Call Rodeo.

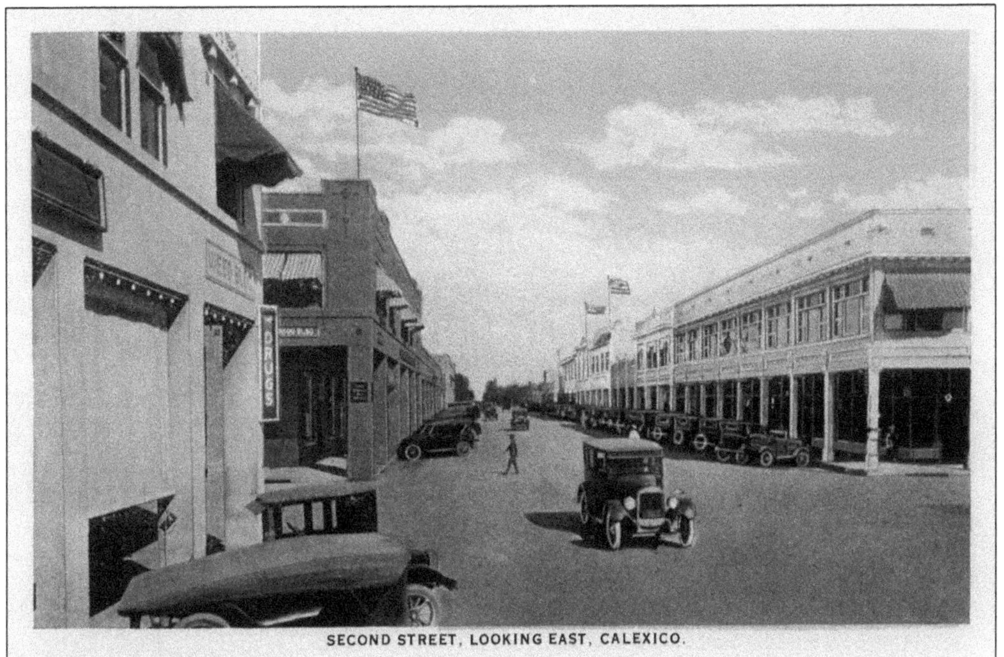

SECOND STREET, LOOKING EAST, CALEXICO.

SECOND STREET, LOOKING EAST, CALEXICO. The name Calexico is a portmanteau, or combination, of California ("Cal") and Mexico ("exico.")

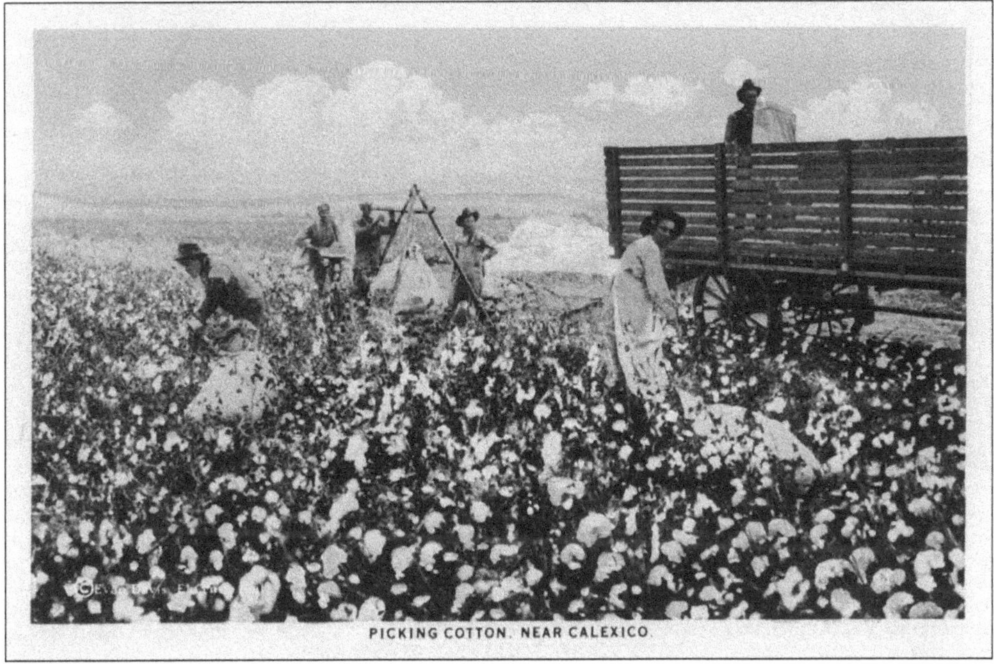
PICKING COTTON, NEAR CALEXICO.

PICKING COTTON, NEAR CALEXICO. A similar postcard reads that the Imperial Valley is "The Richest Producing Area in the World. Over 60,000 acres in this Valley are devoted to growing, with a great many ranches producing better than a bale to the acre. Just across the border, in Mexico, 135,000 acres are also in cotton, which is really part of the Imperial Valley."

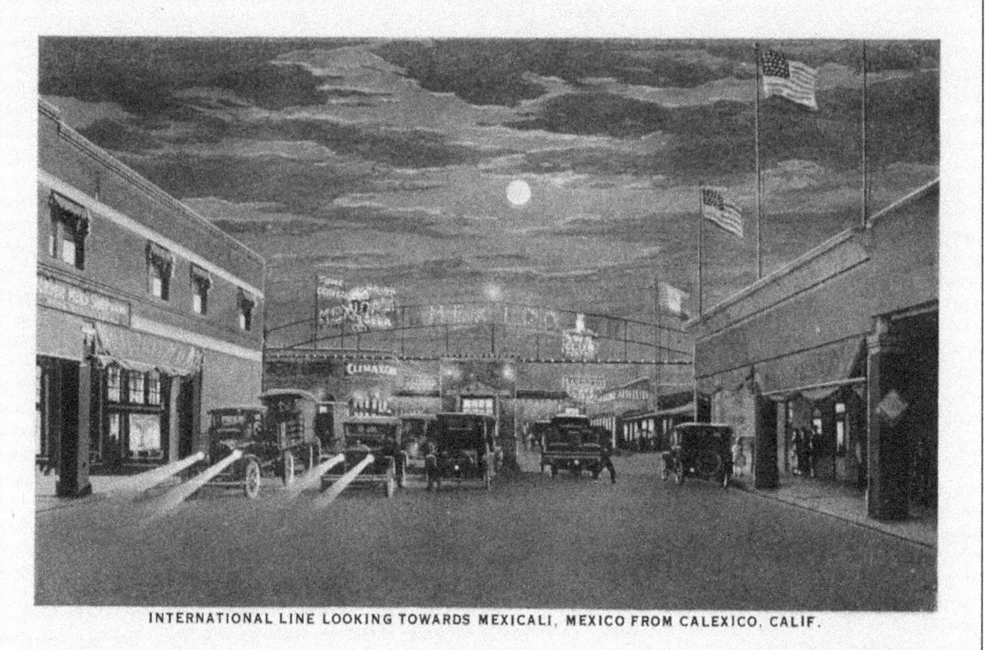
INTERNATIONAL LINE LOOKING TOWARDS MEXICALI, MEXICO FROM CALEXICO, CALIF.

INTERNATIONAL LINE LOOKING TOWARDS MEXICALI, MEXICO FROM CALEXICO, CALIF. According to the 2000 census, Calexico had a population of 27,109, while the city of Mexicali had a population of 764,602.

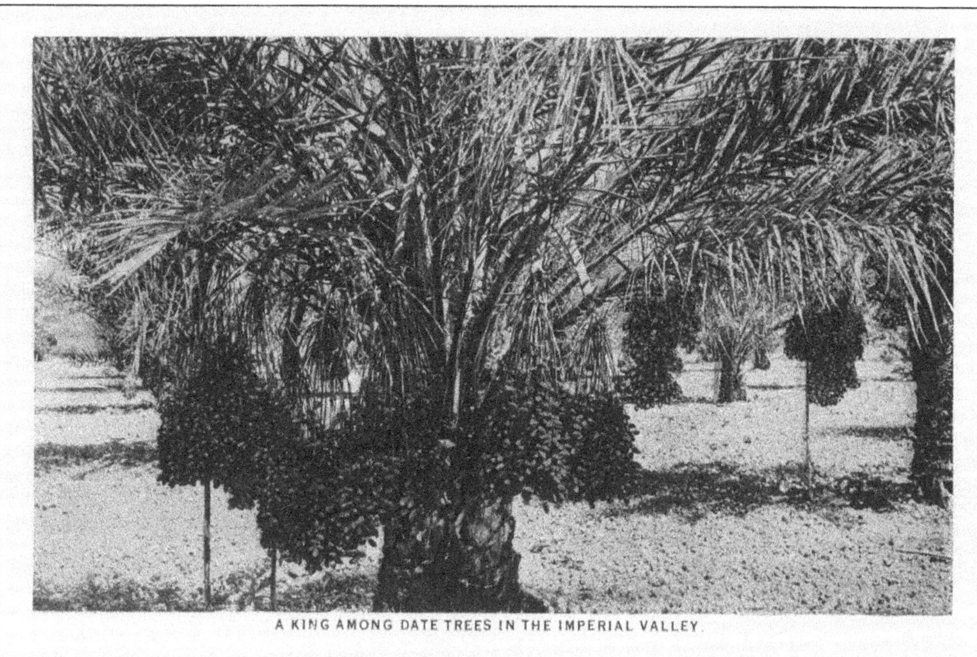
A KING AMONG DATE TREES IN THE IMPERIAL VALLEY.

A KING AMONG DATE TREES IN THE IMPERIAL VALLEY. California ranks first in the nation in date production. The Coachella Valley is the date-growing region in California, with Riverside and Imperial Counties leading in production.

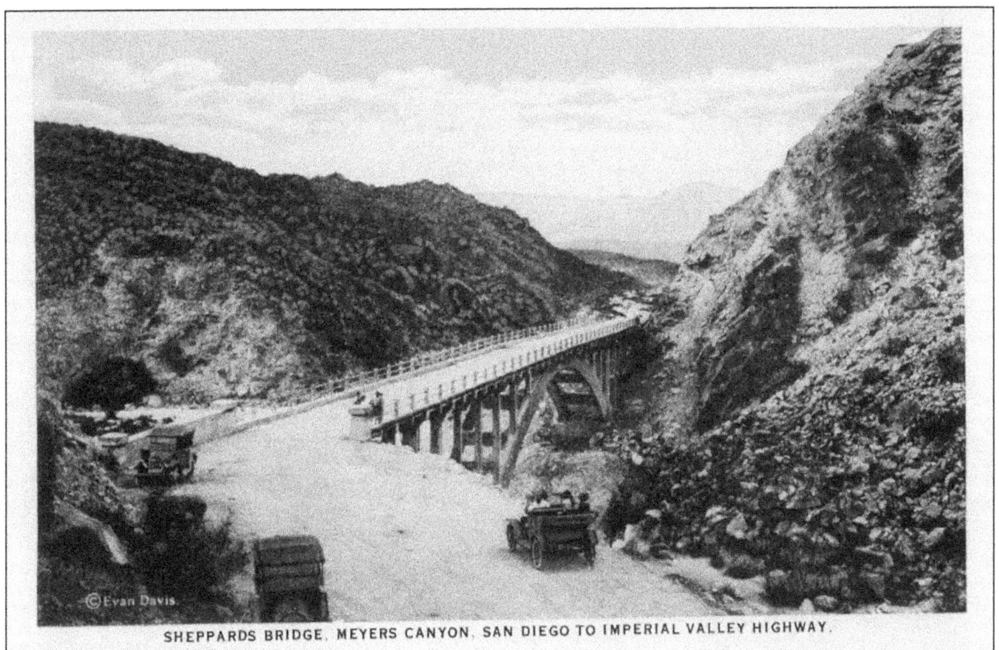

SHEPPARD[']S BRIDGE, MEYERS CANYON, SAN DIEGO TO IMPERIAL VALLEY HIGHWAY. In 1913, a group of San Diego delegates to the Ocean Highway Association raised $60,000 for completing a stretch of roadway that dropped nearly 1,000 feet within three miles. They blasted a 12-foot-wide route down Imperial County's Meyers Canyon at a cost of $37,000 and returned the surplus funds to subscribers.

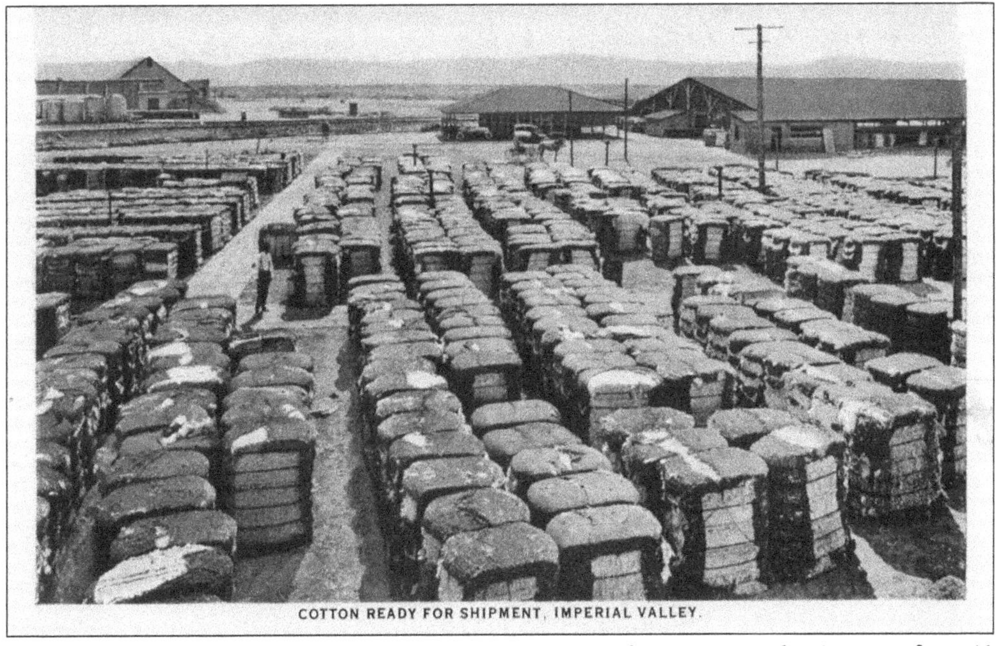

COTTON READY FOR SHIPMENT, IMPERIAL VALLEY. The cotton production rose from 10 bales in 1907 to 80,000 bales in 1914.

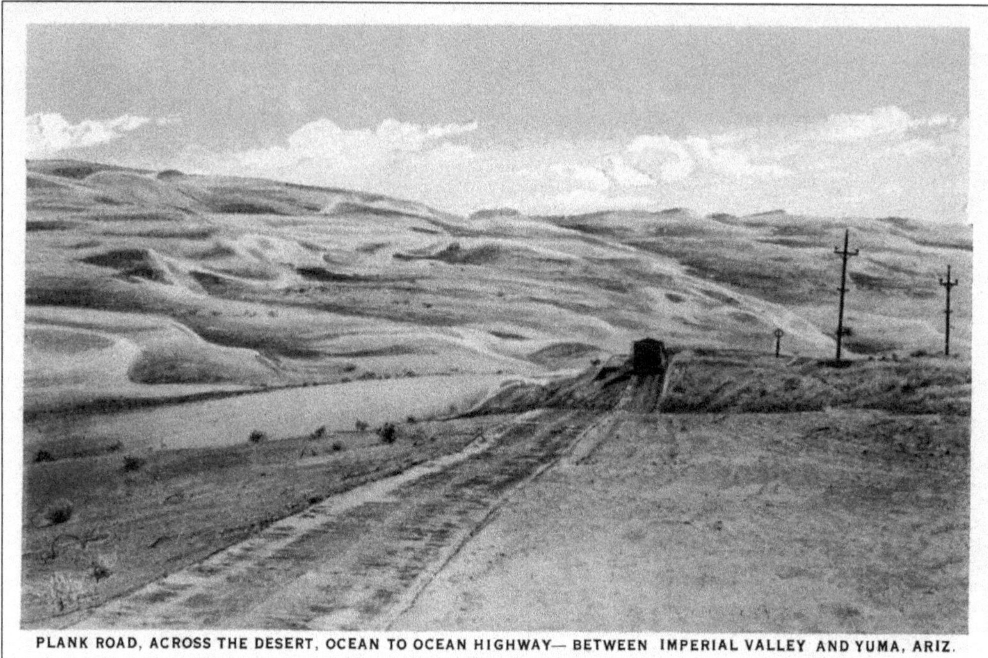

PLANK ROAD, ACROSS THE DESERT, OCEAN TO OCEAN HIGHWAY – BETWEEN IMPERIAL VALLEY AND YUMA, ARIZ. The first Plank Road lasted for only a year. Completion of the Ocean to Ocean Highway Bridge over the Colorado River at Yuma in 1915 increased road traffic. An improved and permanent version was constructed in 1916. The new version consisted of eight-foot-wide railroad ties dipped in tar and placed next to each other, lengthwise. The road was made up of eight-foot-wide by twelve-foot-long sections that weighed 1,500 pounds each and were held in place by iron bars bolted to the tie. It was necessary to have turnouts every quarter mile to allow passage of vehicles going in the opposite direction.

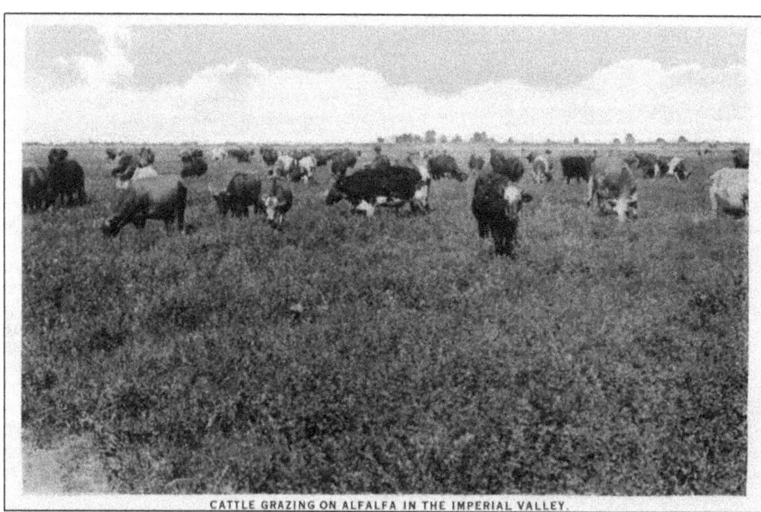

CATTLE GRAZING ON ALFALFA IN THE IMPERIAL VALLEY. As of 1999, there were 325,000 head of cattle in feedlots located in the Imperial Valley. The cattle had a gross value of $167 million. This area has the largest feedlot and fed-cattle capacity in California.

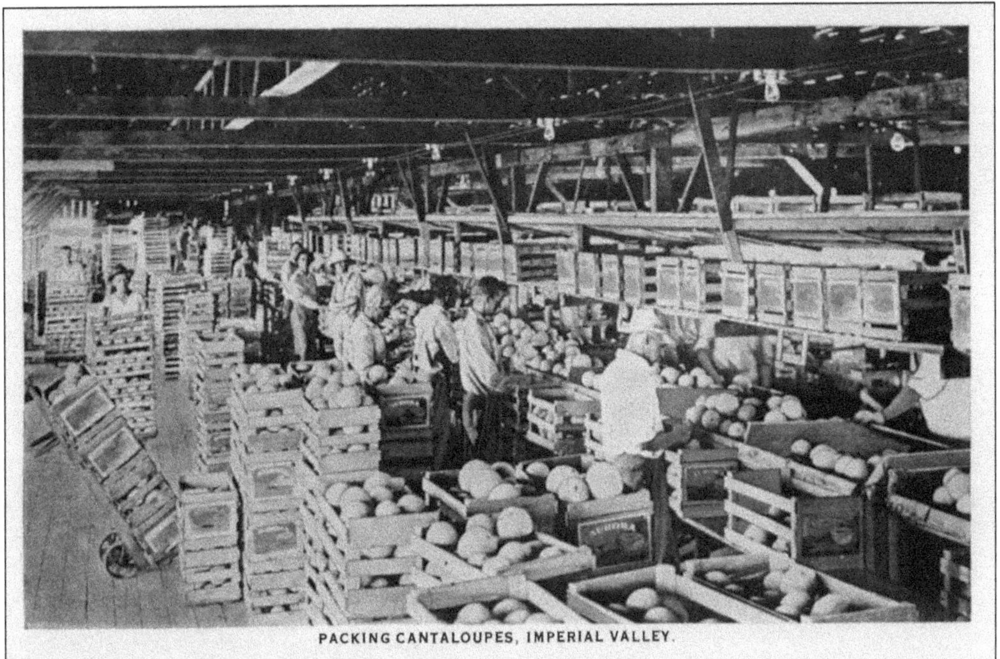
PACKING CANTALOUPES, IMPERIAL VALLEY.

PACKING CANTALOUPES, IMPERIAL VALLEY. Referring to the Imperials Valley, an identical postcard reads, "The Richest Producing Area in the World. One of the principal industries in the Valley is cantaloupe growing. Over 14,000 crates are annually shipped out of this section."

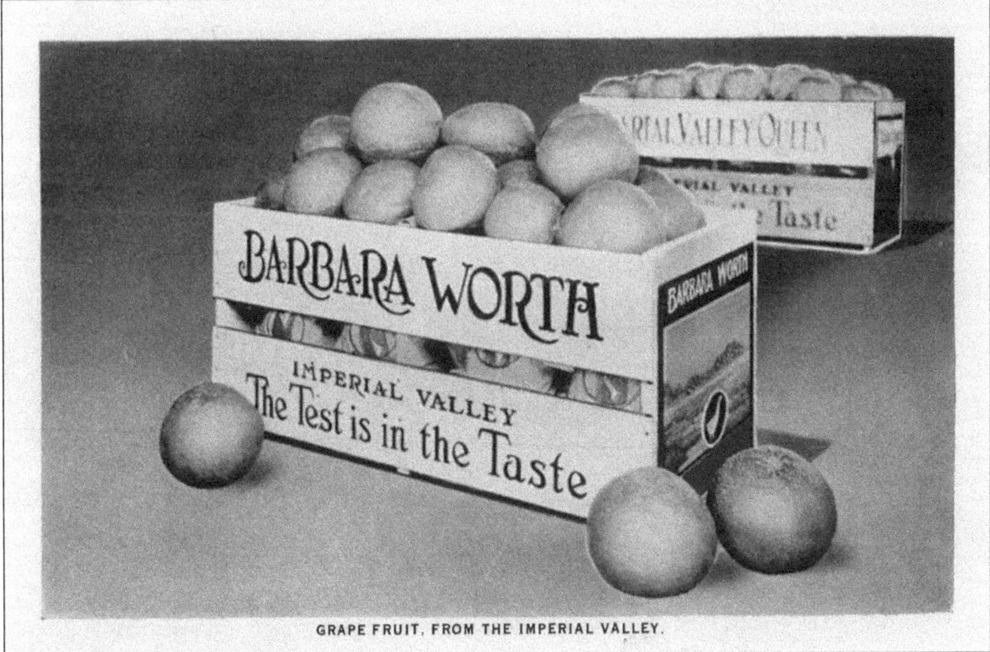

GRAPE FRUIT, FROM THE IMPERIAL VALLEY.

GRAPE FRUIT, FROM THE IMPERIAL VALLEY. Grapefruit prospers in a warm subtropical climate. Temperature differences affect the length of time from flowering to fruit maturity. At Riverside, California, the period is 13 months; at warmer Brawley in the Imperial Valley, it takes only 7 to 8 months.

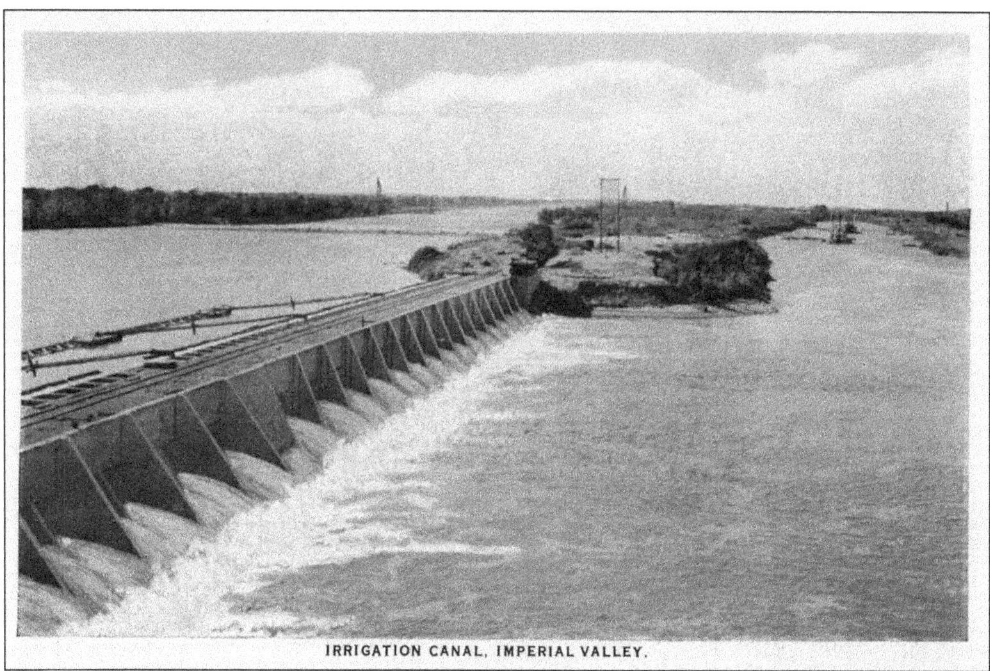

IRRIGATION CANAL, IMPERIAL VALLEY. The Imperial Irrigation District (IID) provides water primarily for agricultural use in Southern California's Imperial Valley. This entity is the largest irrigation district in the United States. It maintains approximately 3,000 miles of canals and drains, including the All-American Canal.

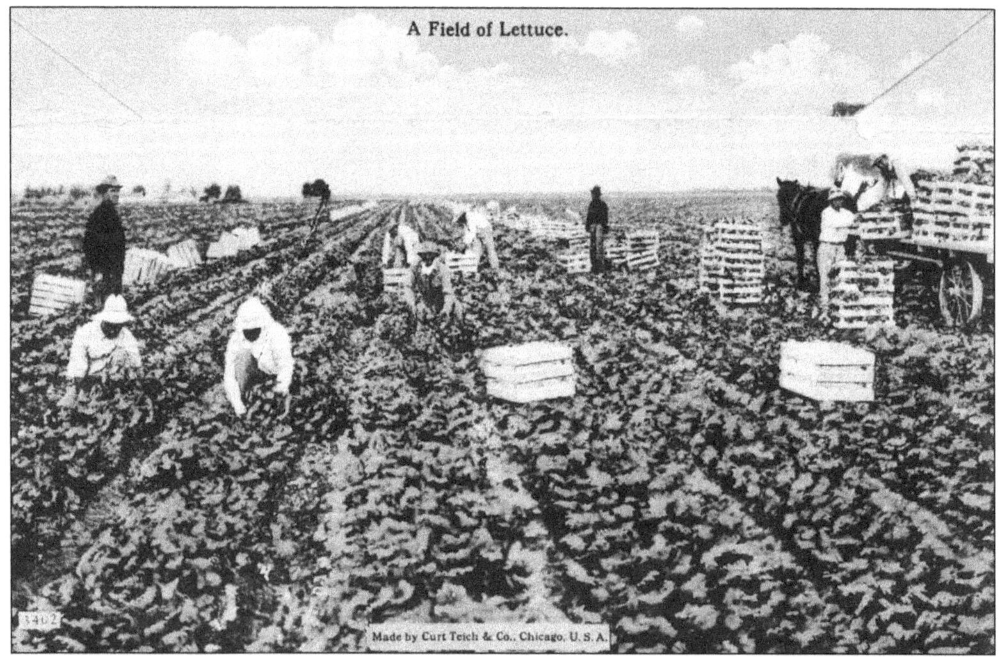

A FIELD OF LETTUCE. The Imperial Valley is well known for midwinter salad vegetables. Shipments of crisp head and leaf lettuce start in December and continue until March.

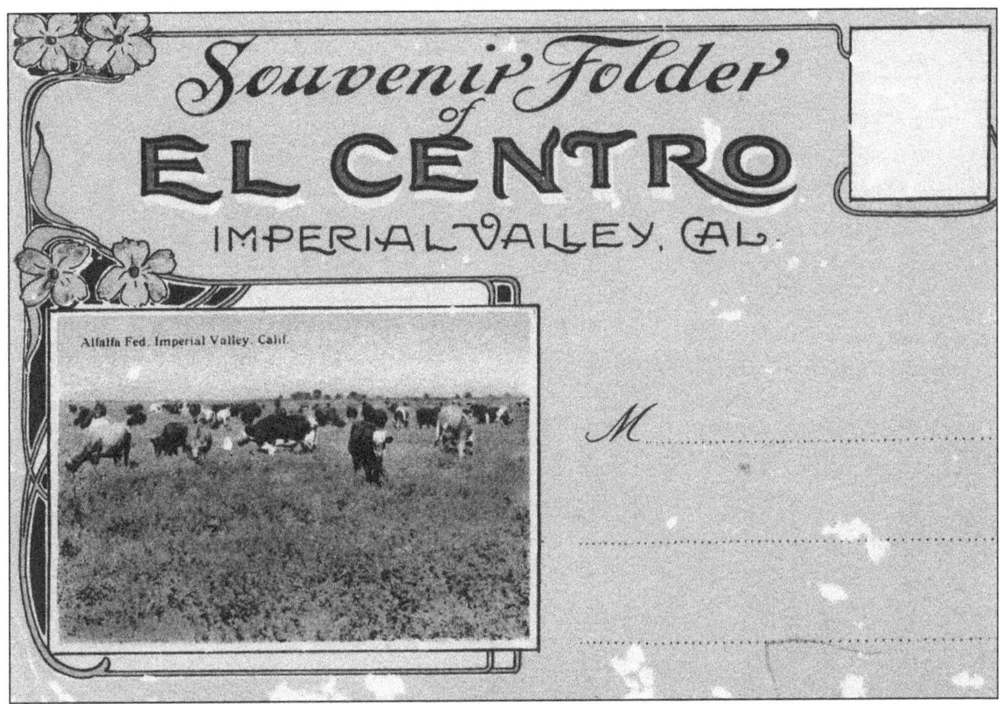

SOUVENIR FOLDER OF EL CENTRO, IMPERIAL VALLEY, CAL. This book of 22 postcards includes a back inside page featuring Imperial Valley, California, the desert that is "Blossoming as the Rose."

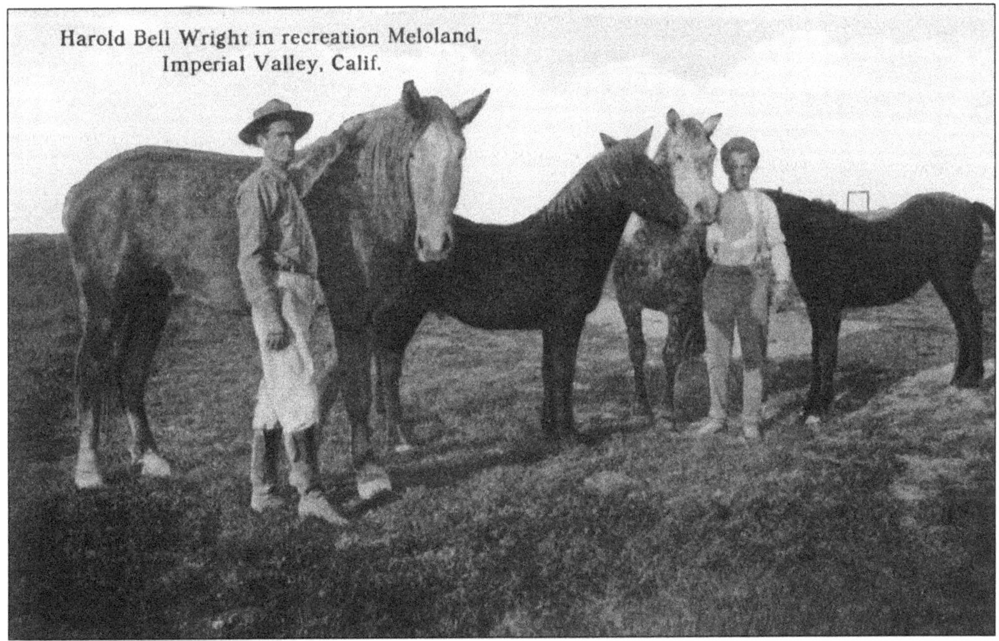

HAROLD BELL WRIGHT IN RECREATION MELOLAND, IMPERIAL VALLEY, CALIF. Wright moved from Branson, Missouri, to the Tecolote Rancho in a little area he named Meloland, just to the east of El Centro.

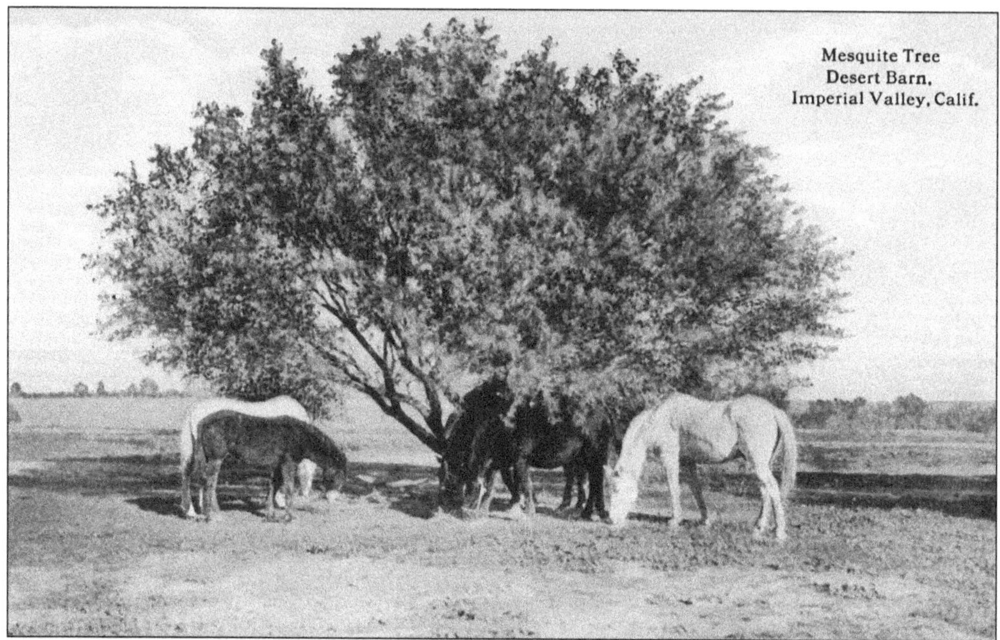

MESQUITE TREE DESERT BARN, IMPERIAL VALLEY, CALIF. Traditional livestock barns were not commonplace in the Imperial Valley. Horses would seek relief from the hot sun under the shade of a mesquite tree.

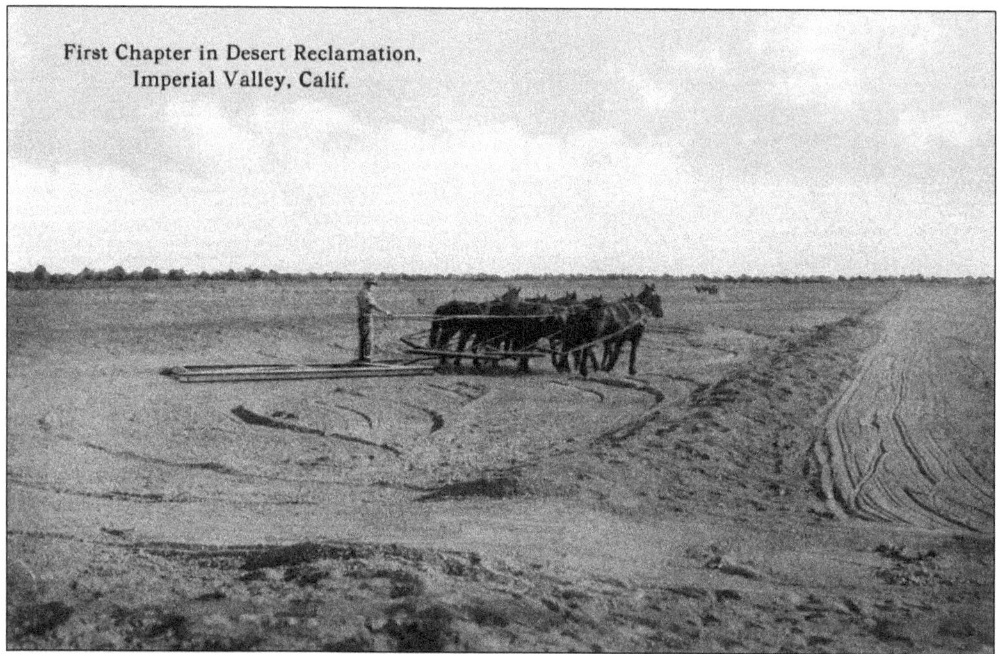

FIRST CHAPTER IN DESERT RECLAMATION, IMPERIAL VALLEY, CALIF. The Imperial Valley contains about 500,000 acres that was government property. Federal law permitted that property rights could be transferred to individuals who were willing to cultivate the land. The Desert Act allowed sale of the land for $1.25 per acre. Under the Homestead Act, the government was allowed to donate parcels large enough to support a family.

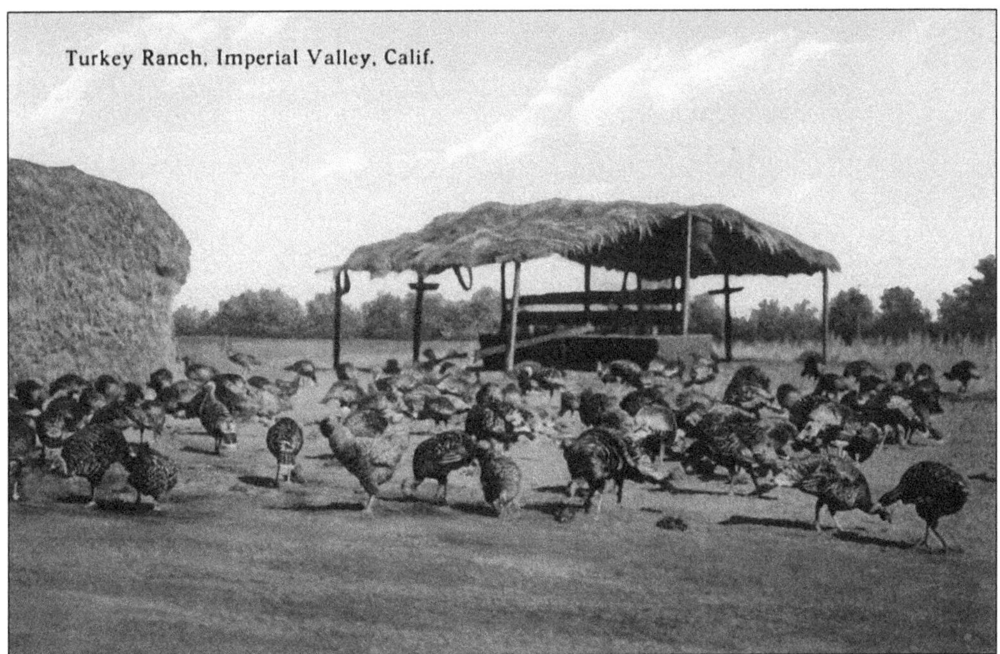

TURKEY RANCH, IMPERIAL VALLEY, CALIF. Imperial Valley leads in raising turkeys. There is no rain and there are no cold, damp days, so housing the turkeys isn't necessary. Plenty of forage in the alfalfa and barley fields makes the expense of raising turkeys very low.

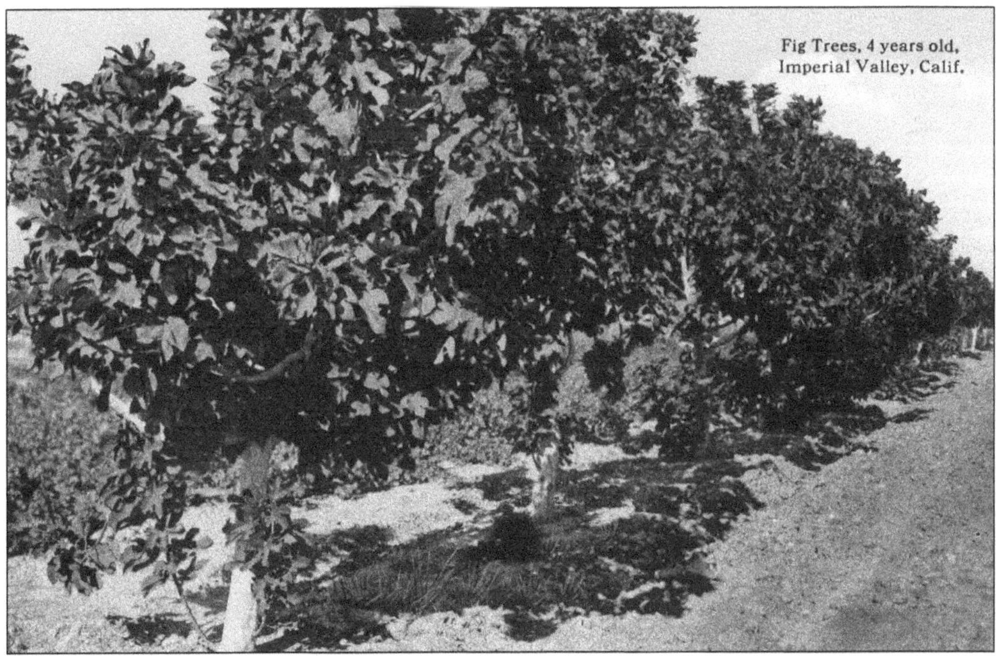

FIG TREES, 4 YEARS OLD, IMPERIAL VALLEY, CALIF. An identical postcard reads, "From Desert to Garden in twelve years. Trees and its fruits are among the most wonderful products."

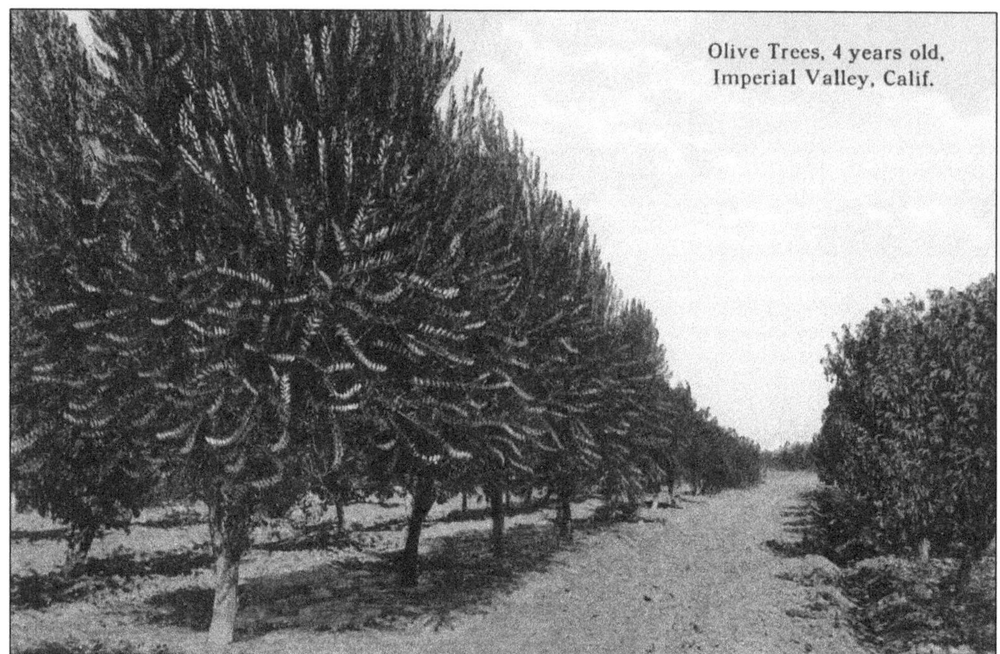

OLIVE TREES, 4 YEARS OLD, IMPERIAL VALLEY, CALIF. A separate printing of the same card reads, "From Desert to Garden in twelve years. Trees and its fruits are among its most wonderful products."

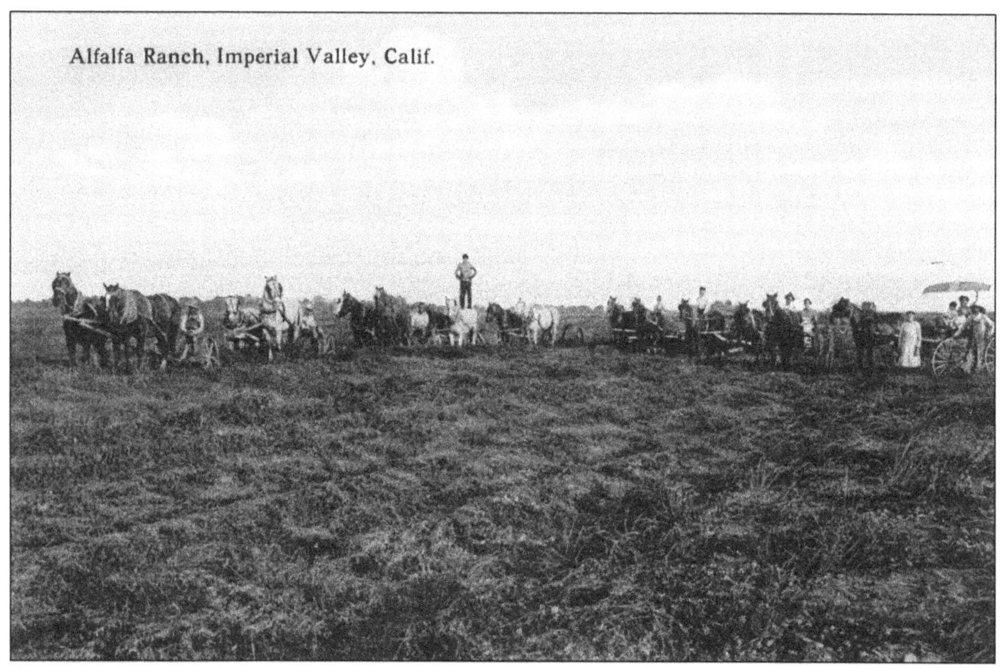

ALFALFA RANCH, IMPERIAL VALLEY, CALIF. An identical postcard indicates that "100,000 acres of alfalfa cut from five to eight times to the acre."

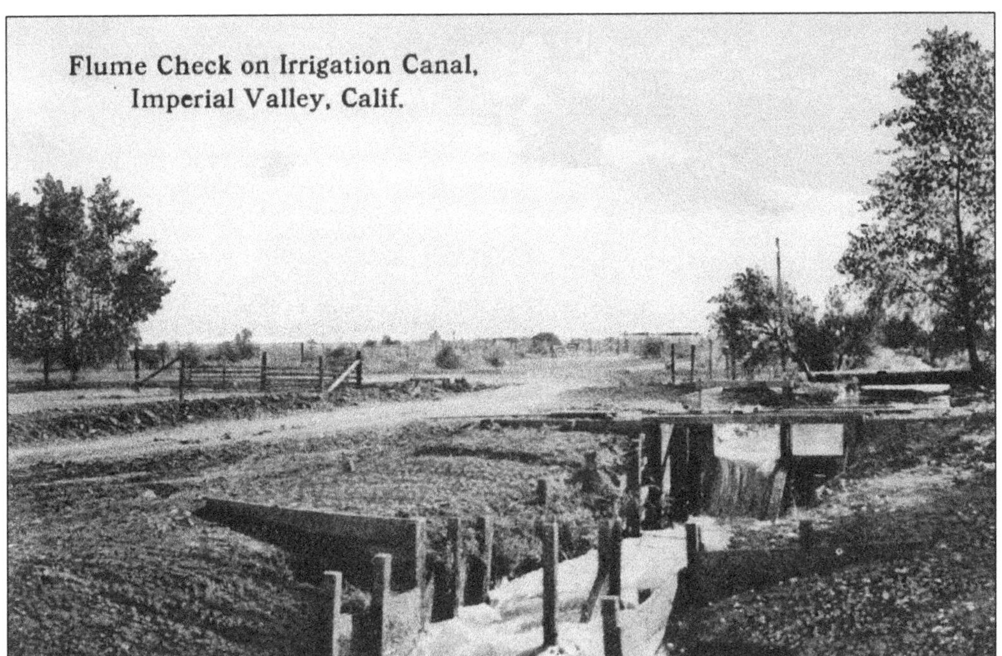

FLUME CHECK ON IRRIGATION CANAL, IMPERIAL VALLEY, CALIF. An identical postcard stated that the "Imperial Valley, California, is 60 miles long, 45 miles wide, watered from the Colorado River. It is the largest irrigation section in America. With soil of miraculous fertility, the crops are earliest in market."

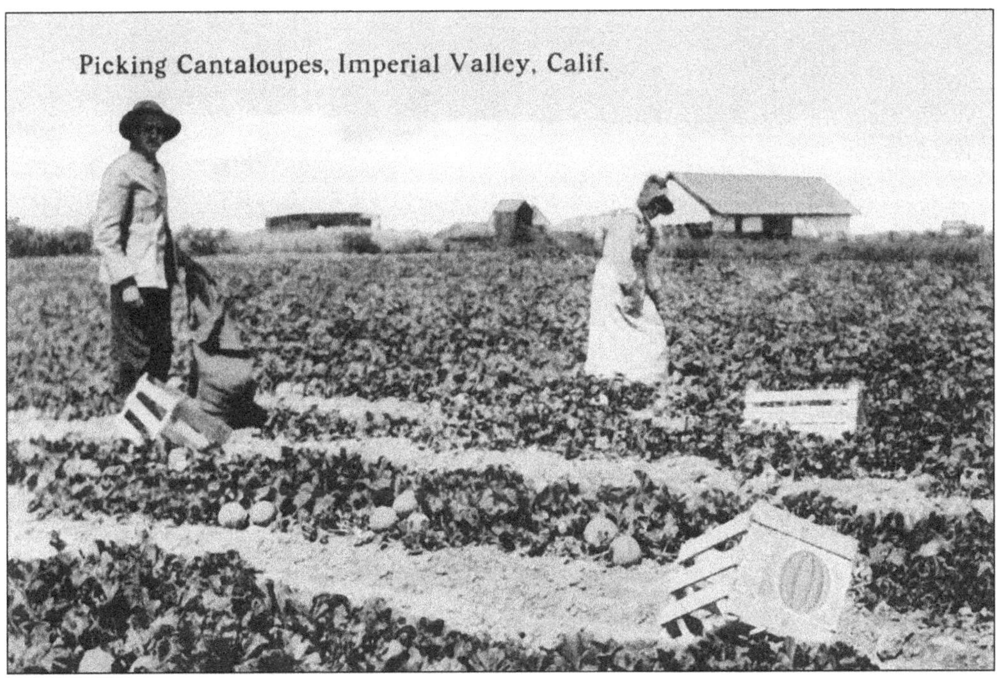

PICKING CANTALOUPES, IMPERIAL VALLEY, CALIF. An identical card states that Imperial Valley cantaloupes "reach the eastern markets weeks ahead of others and command highest prices."

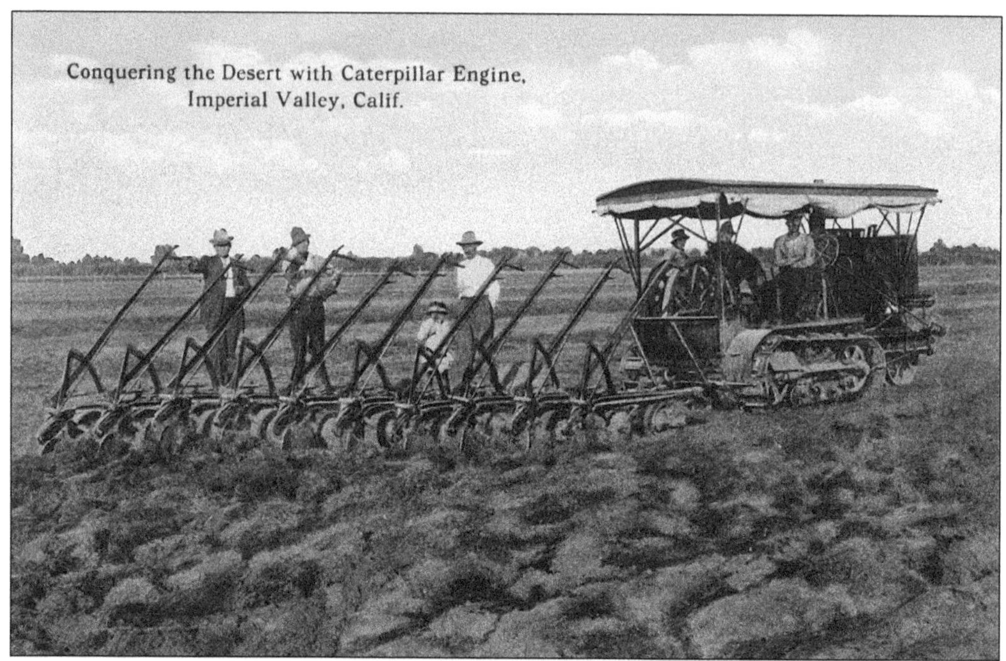

CONQUERING THE DESERT WITH CATERPILLAR ENGINE, IMPERIAL VALLEY, CALIF. In 1925, the Holt Manufacturing Company, the inventor of the crawler tractor, and the C.L. Best Tractor Company merged, creating a new entity, the California-based Caterpillar Tractor Company.

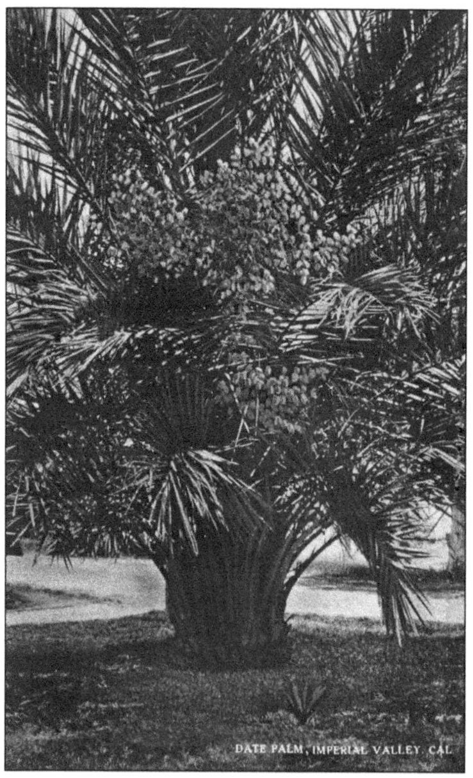

DATE PALM, IMPERIAL VALLEY, CAL. Dates produced in the Coachella and Imperial Valleys account for 85 percent of the production for the entire nation.

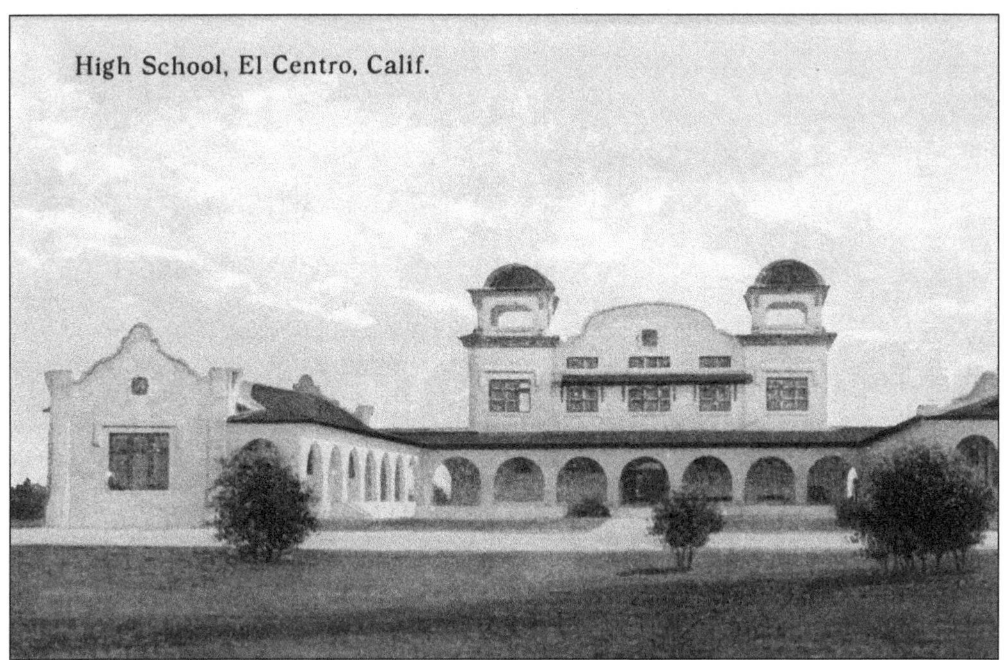

HIGH SCHOOL, EL CENTRO, CALIF. Today, El Centro has 11 elementary schools, 3 middle or junior high schools, and 3 high schools.

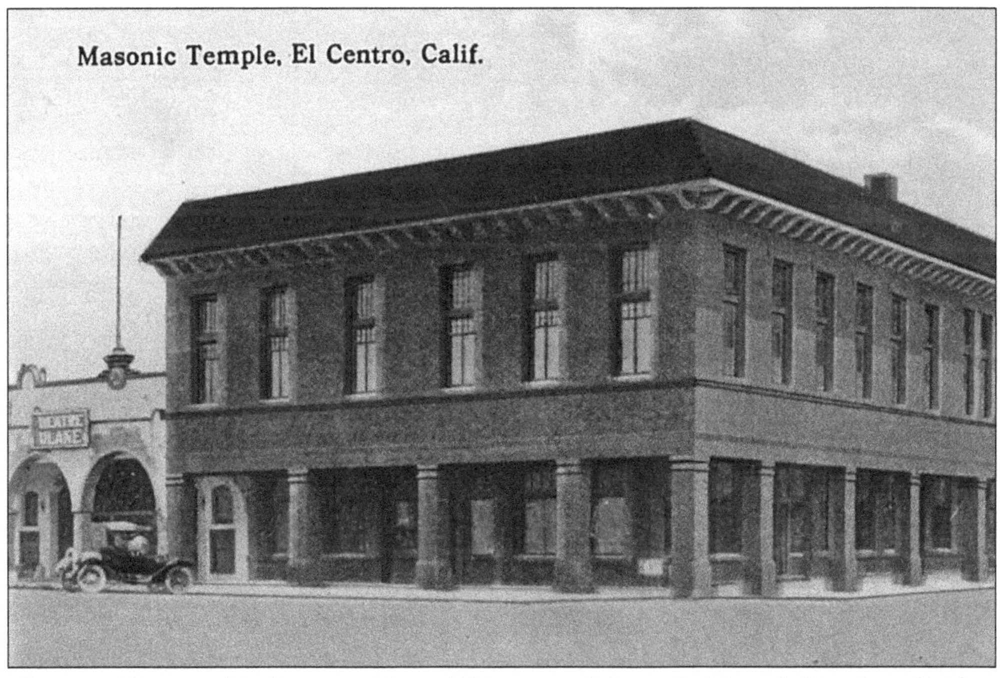

MASONIC TEMPLE, EL CENTRO, CALIF. This postcard shows the Masonic Temple and Tulare Theatre around 1914. The photograph suggests that El Centro was sparsely populated. However, historians recall that from 1910 to 1920, El Centro was one of the fastest growing cities in Southern California, nearly tripling in population, from 1,610 to 5,646, in a single decade.

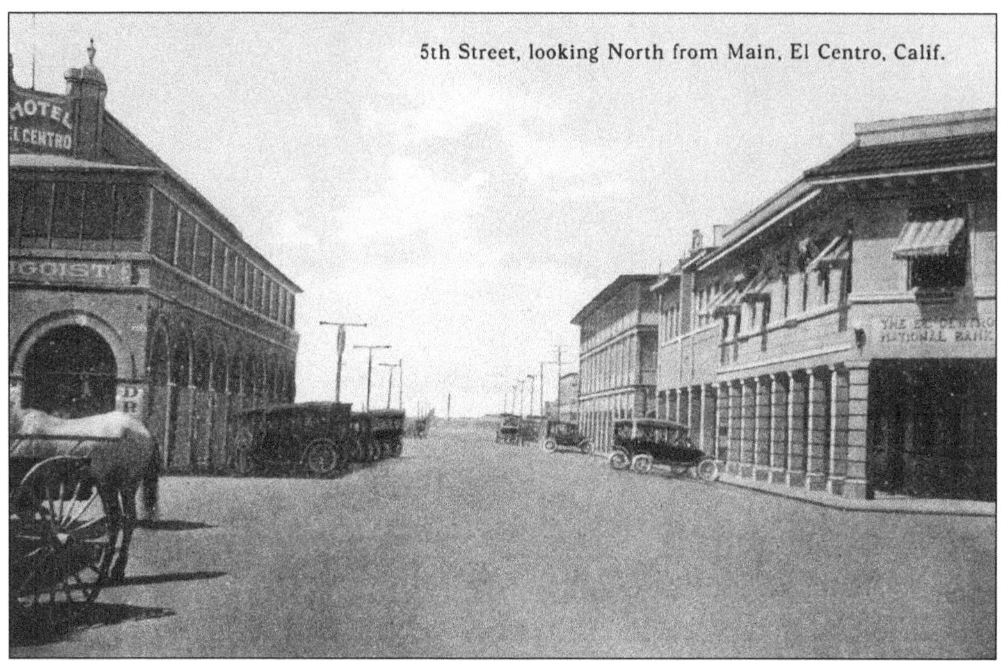

5th Street Looking North from Main, El Centro, Calif. El Centro is the largest city as well as the county seat of Imperial County. It is also the largest American city to lie entirely below sea level (-50 feet).

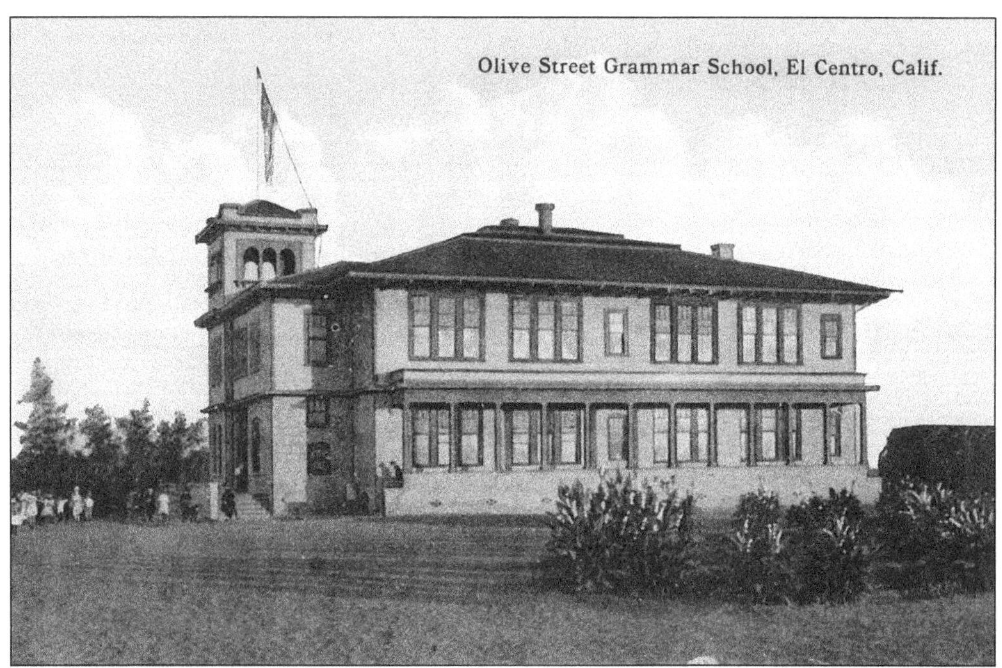

Olive Street Grammar School, El Centro, Calif. The 2000 census listed the population of El Centro as 37,835.

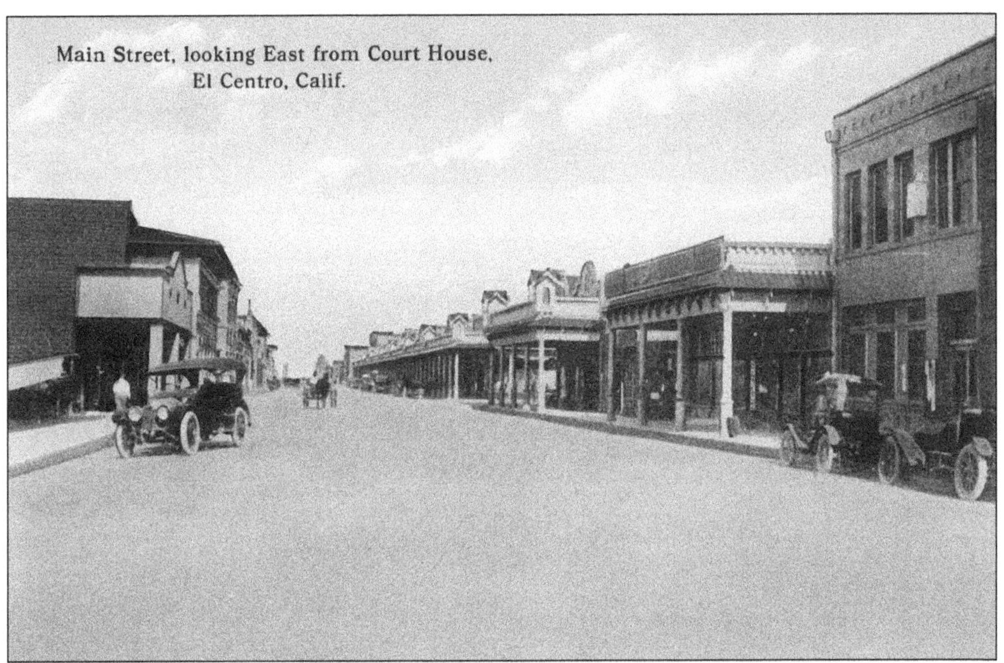

MAIN STREET, LOOKING EAST FROM COURT HOUSE, EL CENTRO, CALIF. In August 2010, El Centro had the highest unemployment rate among American cities, at 30.4 percent.

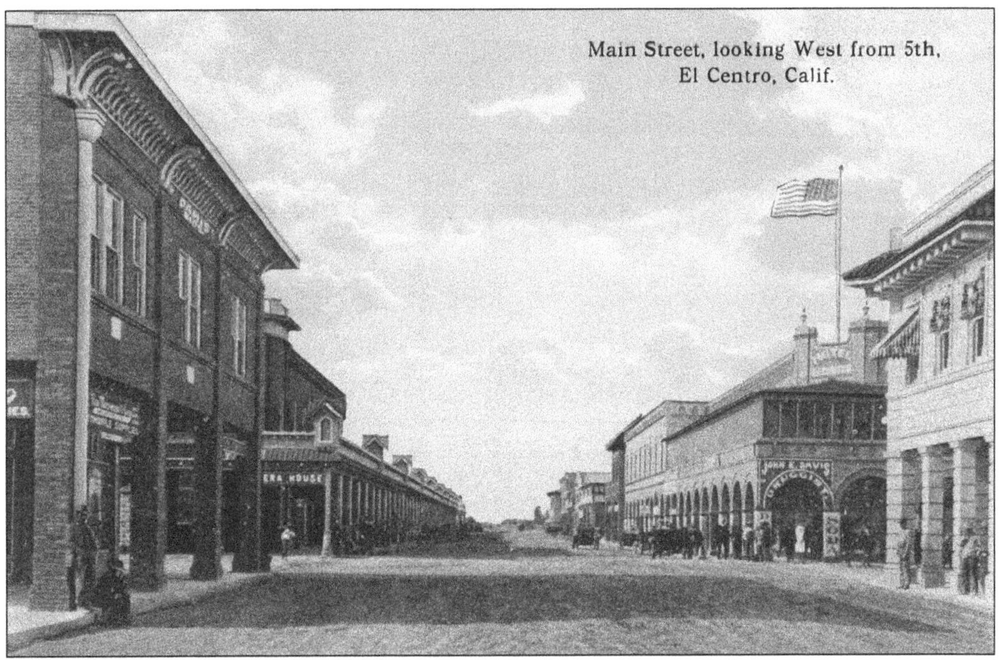

MAIN STREET, LOOKING WEST FROM 5TH, EL CENTRO, CALIF. El Centro is surrounded by thousands of acres of farmland that have transformed the desert into one of the most productive farming regions in California, with an annual crop production of over $1 billion.

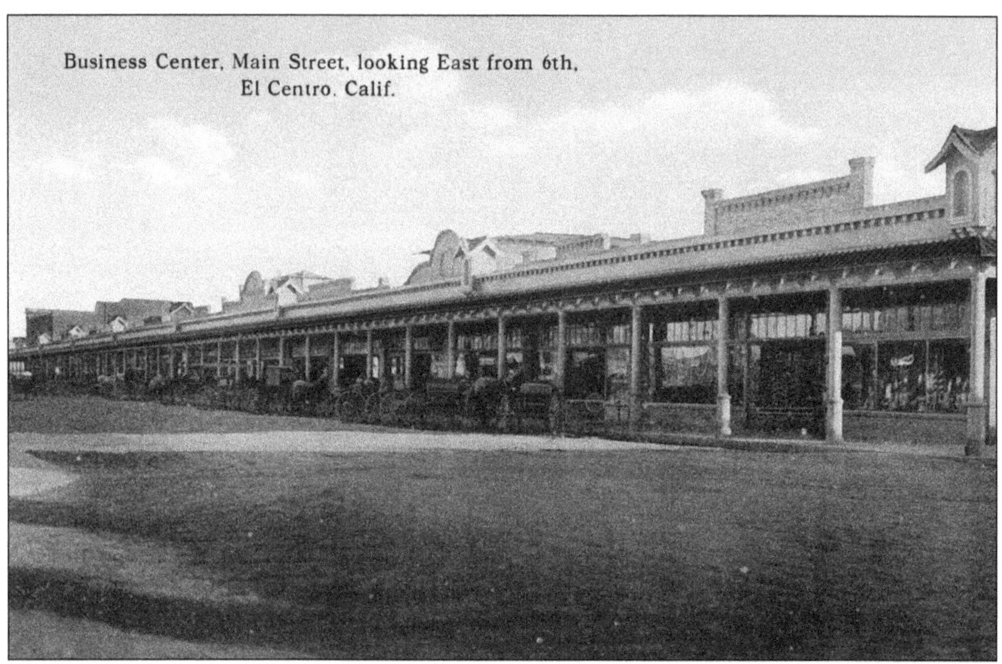

Business Center, Main Street, looking East from 6th, El Centro, Calif. Agriculture is the largest industry in Imperial County and accounts for 48 percent of all employment.

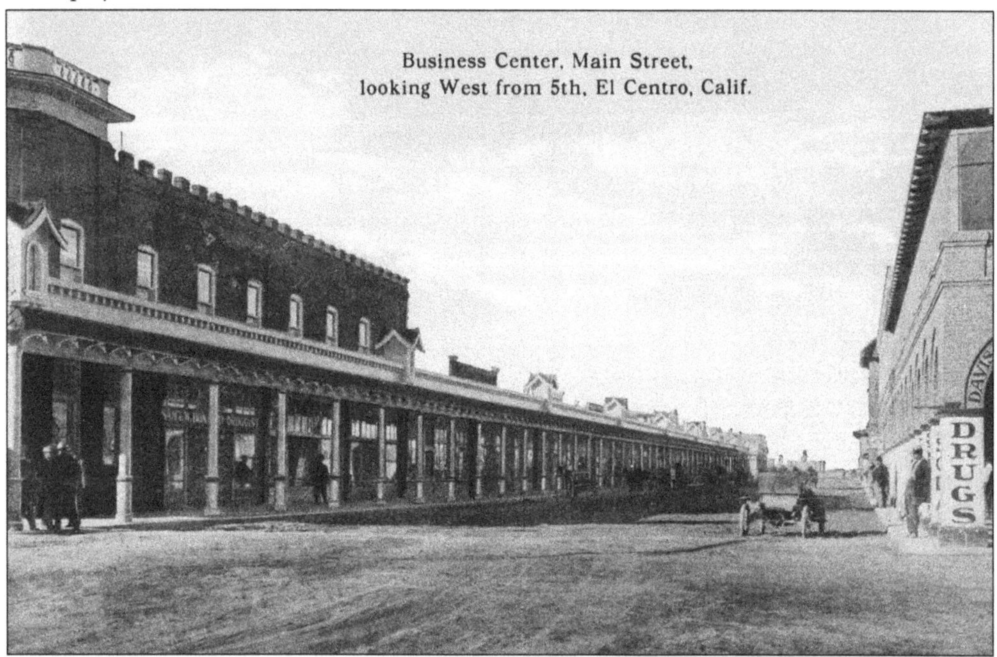

Business Center, Main Street, looking West from 5th, El Centro, Calif. Due to its desert environment and proximity to Los Angeles, movies are sometimes filmed in the sand dunes outside the agricultural portions of El Centro and Imperial County. These have included *Return of the Jedi*, *Stargate*, *The Scorpion King*, and *Into the Wild*. Portions of the 2005 film *Jarhead* were filmed here because of its similarity to the desert terrain of Iraq.

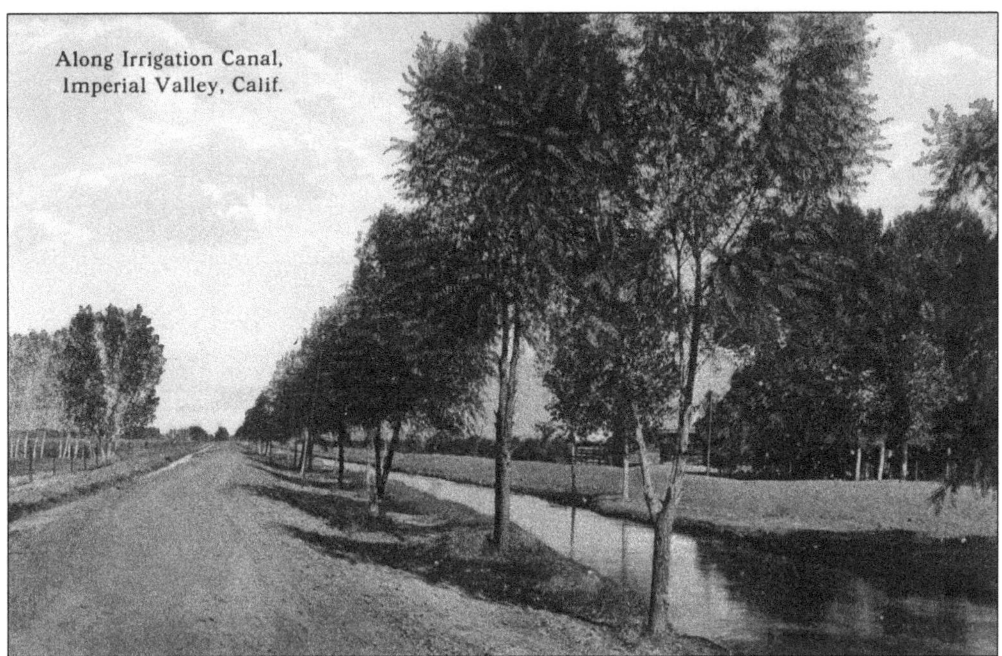

Along Irrigation Canal, Imperial Valley, Calif. The original Alamo Canal extended into Mexico. The All-American Canal was completed in 1942 and flowed solely through US territory.

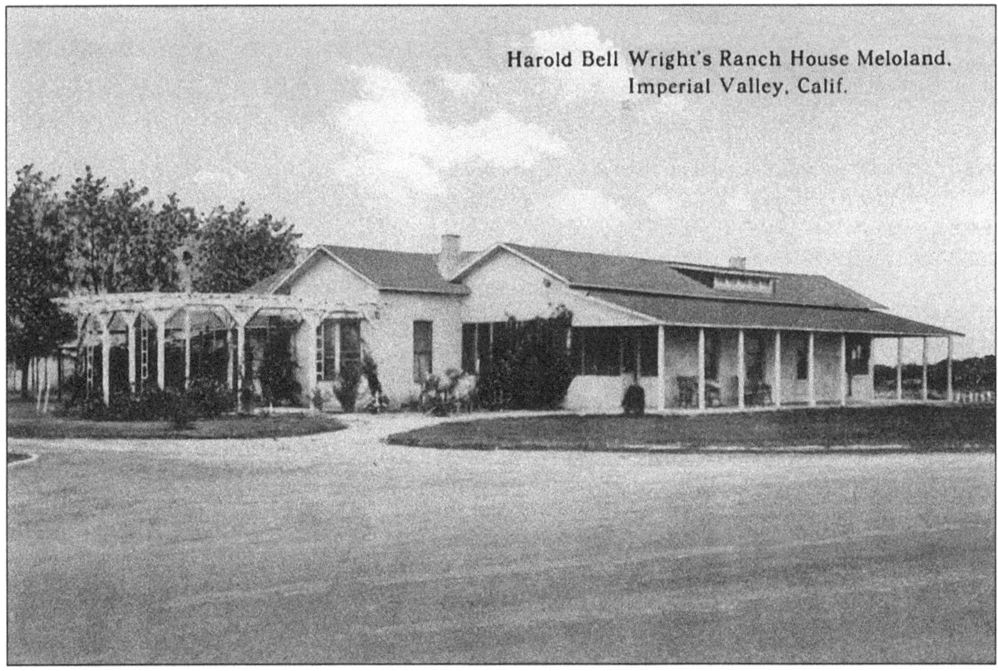

Harold Bell Wright's Ranch House Meloland, Imperial Valley, Calif. A separate print of the same card reads, "Harold Bell Wright, the author of *The Winning of Barbara Worth*, the romance of Imperial Valley, is one of the strongest believers in its agricultural future, and is largely interested in its lands."

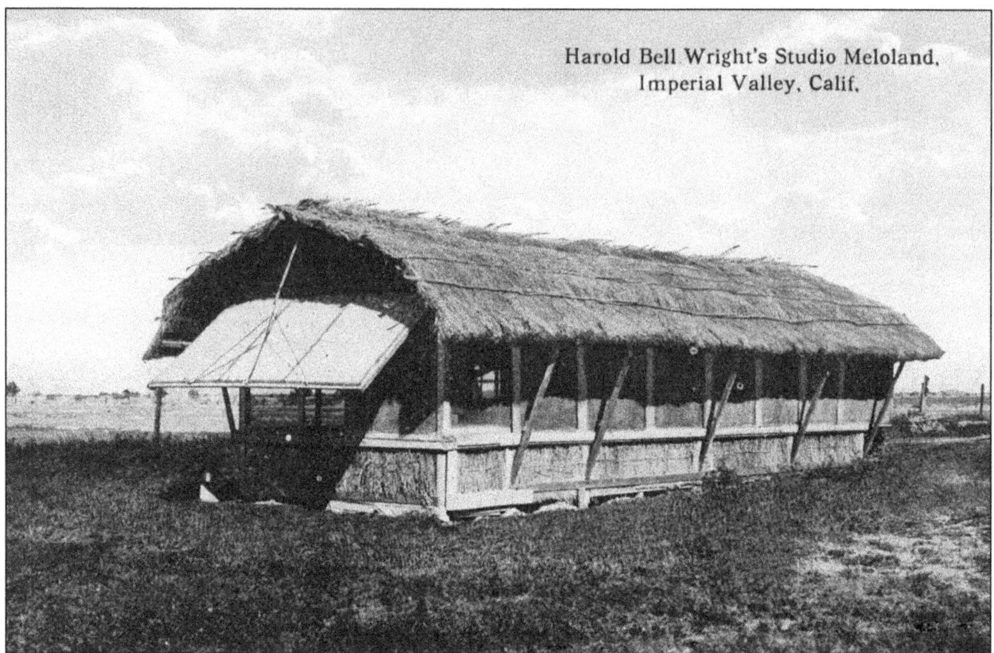

HAROLD BELL WRIGHT'S STUDIO, MELOLAND, IMPERIAL VALLEY, CALIF. Today, Wright's house, studio, and horse stables are gone. The property is now a cultivated field on Barbara Worth Road.

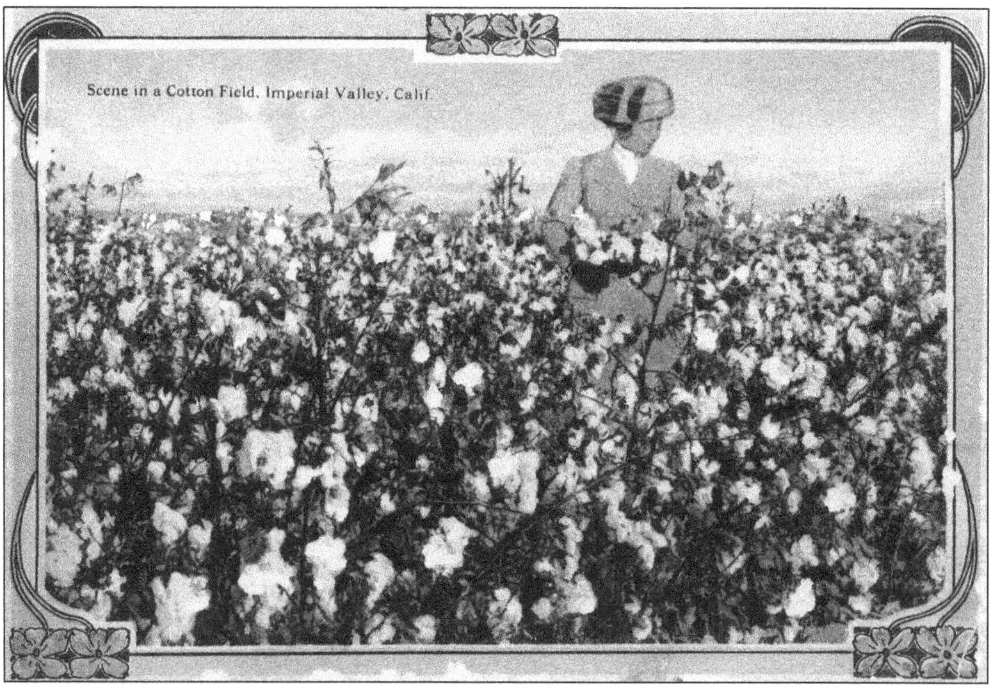

SCENE IN A COTTON FIELD, IMPERIAL VALLEY, CALIF. This cotton field scene of the Imperial Valley portrays an age of innocence and romance of a bygone era. Today, the thought of working in a cotton field suggests poverty, oppression, and hopelessness.

Four

Resorts and Attractions of the Salton Sea

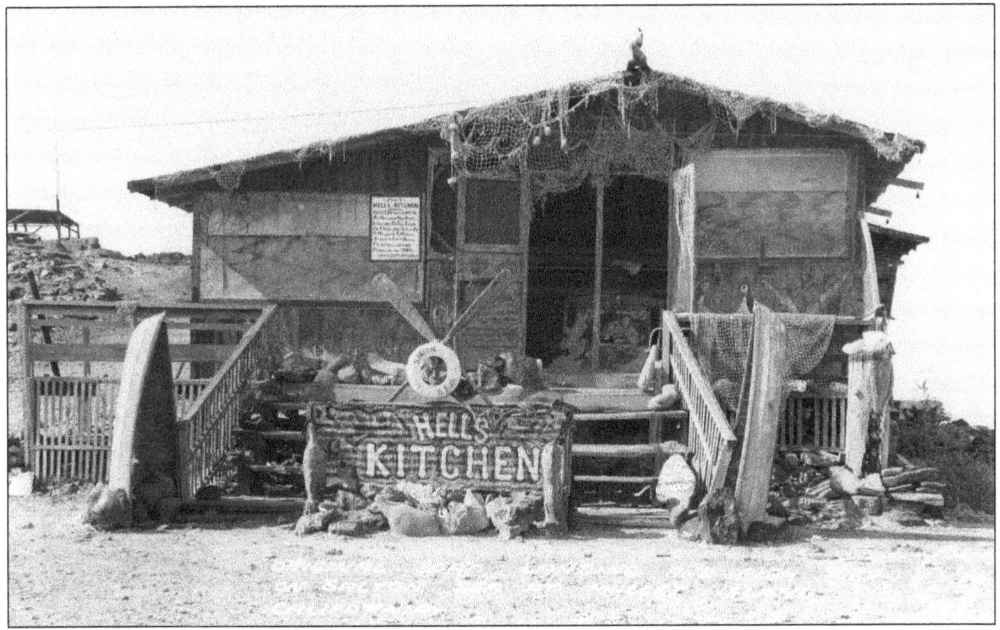

Original Boat Landing and Fish Pier on Salton Sea at Mullet Island, California. There are five buttes around the Salton Sea's southeast shoreline thought to be extinct volcanoes. In 1898, Capt. Charles E. Davis made camp on one of the dead volcanic buttes known as Mullet Island. He was fascinated with the idea of living on a dead volcano 200 feet below sea level. Captain Davis acquired the butte and began construction of his cabin. A hand-painted sign propped against the building proclaimed that this was Hell's Kitchen. Unused photo card. (Frashers Fotos Pomona, Calif.)

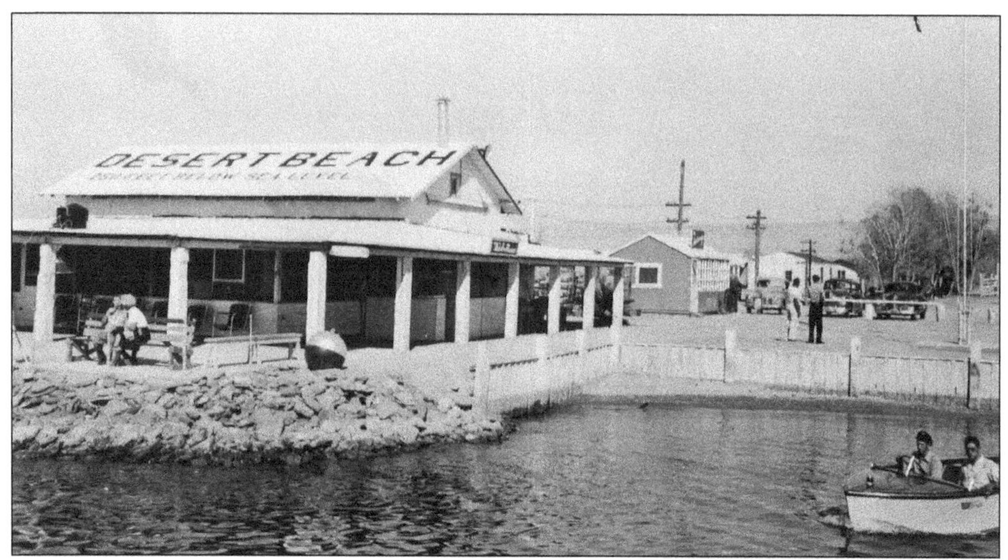

OUTWARD BOUND—DESERT BEACH ON SALTON SEA; E-4321. The Date Palm Beach Resort, later renamed the Desert Beach, was conceived by Gus Eilers and with John Goldthwaite, a Bay Area promoter. They acquired land form the Southern Pacific Railroad on the north shore, toward the Salton Sea from the old train stop at Mortmar. The land was 250 feet below sea level. Unused photo card.

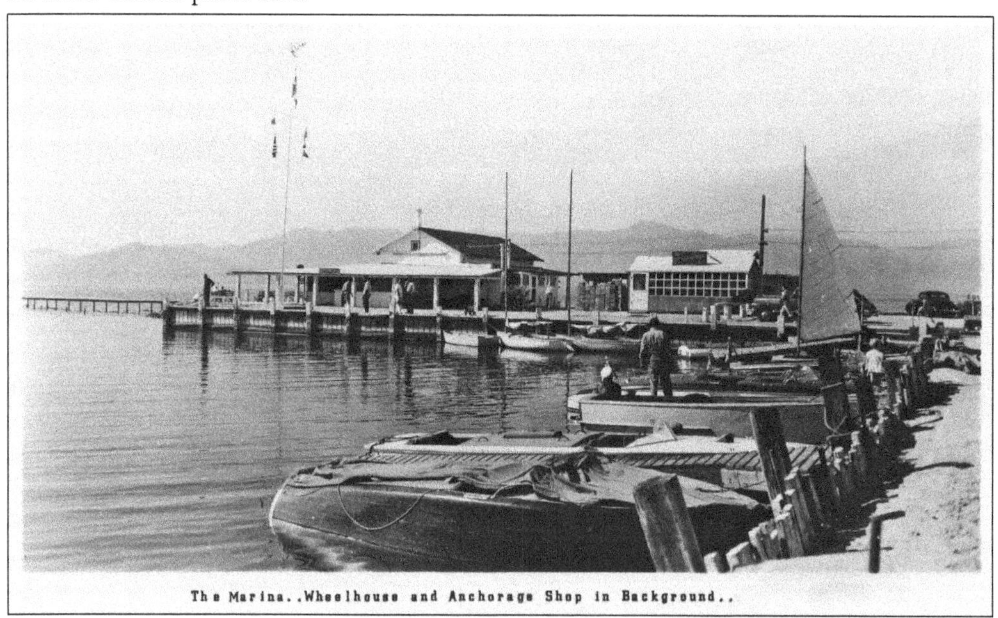

THE MARINA . . WHEELHOUSE AND ANCHORAGE SHOP IN BACKGROUND . . DESERT BEACH ON SALTON SEA; E-4322. In 1946, Gus Eilers sold the Desert Beach to C. Roy Hunter. As a young man, Hunter had sailed with Teddy Roosevelt's Great White Fleet. After his purchase of the Date Palm Beach resort (which he later renamed Desert Beach), he was on a shopping trip to San Francisco and was asked if he would like to buy an old wheel from a US battleship. As fate happened, the wheel was from the *Nebraska*, on which Hunter sailed around the world. Hunter purchased the wheel, and after installing it in the clubhouse, renamed it the Wheelhouse. Unused photo card.

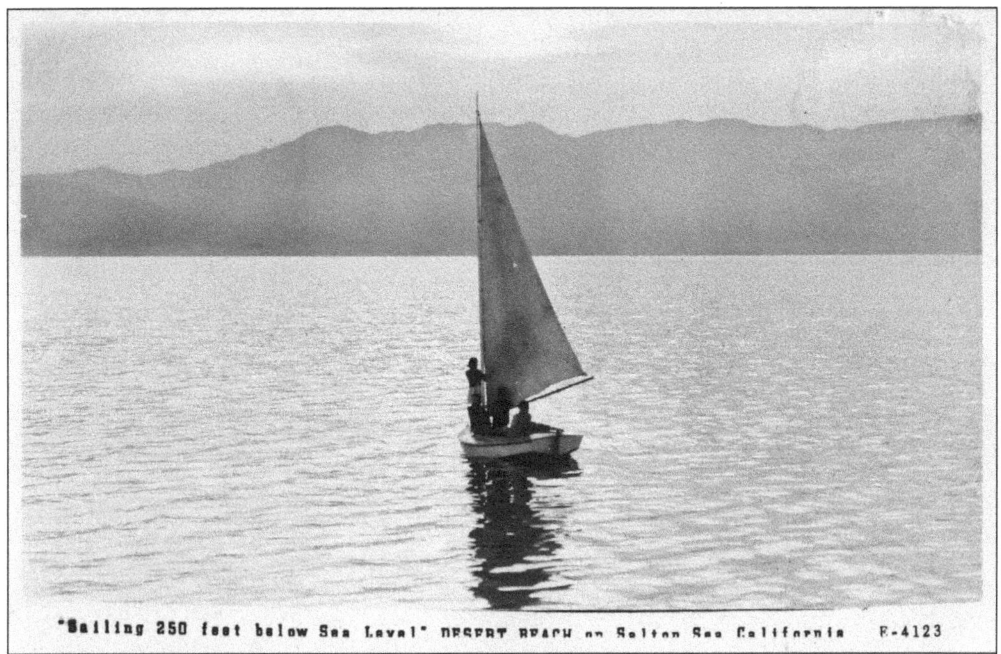

"SAILING 250 FEET BELOW SEA LEVEL!" DESERT BEACH ON SALTON SEA, CALIFORNIA; R-41232. According to a 1950 article in *National Motorist* magazine, "Low barometric pressure and greater water density make the Salton Sea the fastest body of water in the world for speedboat racing." There were sailboat regattas, powerboat races, Hawaiian luaus, and fishing tournaments derbies that attracted thousands of people, including the rich and famous, such as Frank Sinatra, Dwight Eisenhower, and Desi Arnaz. Mailed 1948 to Franklin, Massachusetts.

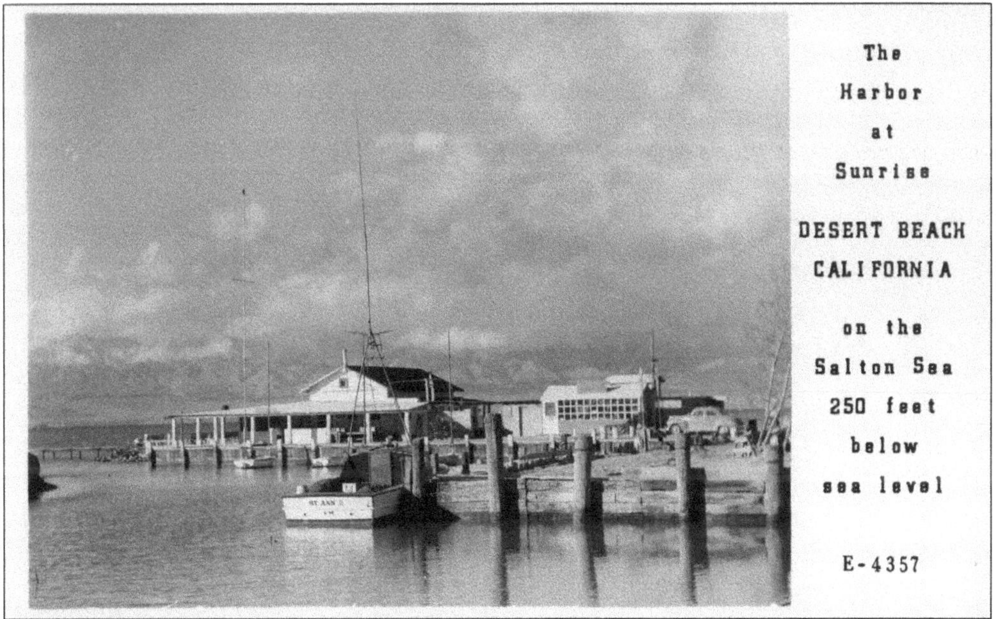

THE HARBOR AT SUNRISE, DESERT BEACH, CALIFORNIA, ON THE SALTON SEA 250 FEET BELOW SEA LEVEL; E-4357. The tranquil sea and peaceful harbor are reminiscent of the postwar charm of Southern California. Unused photo card.

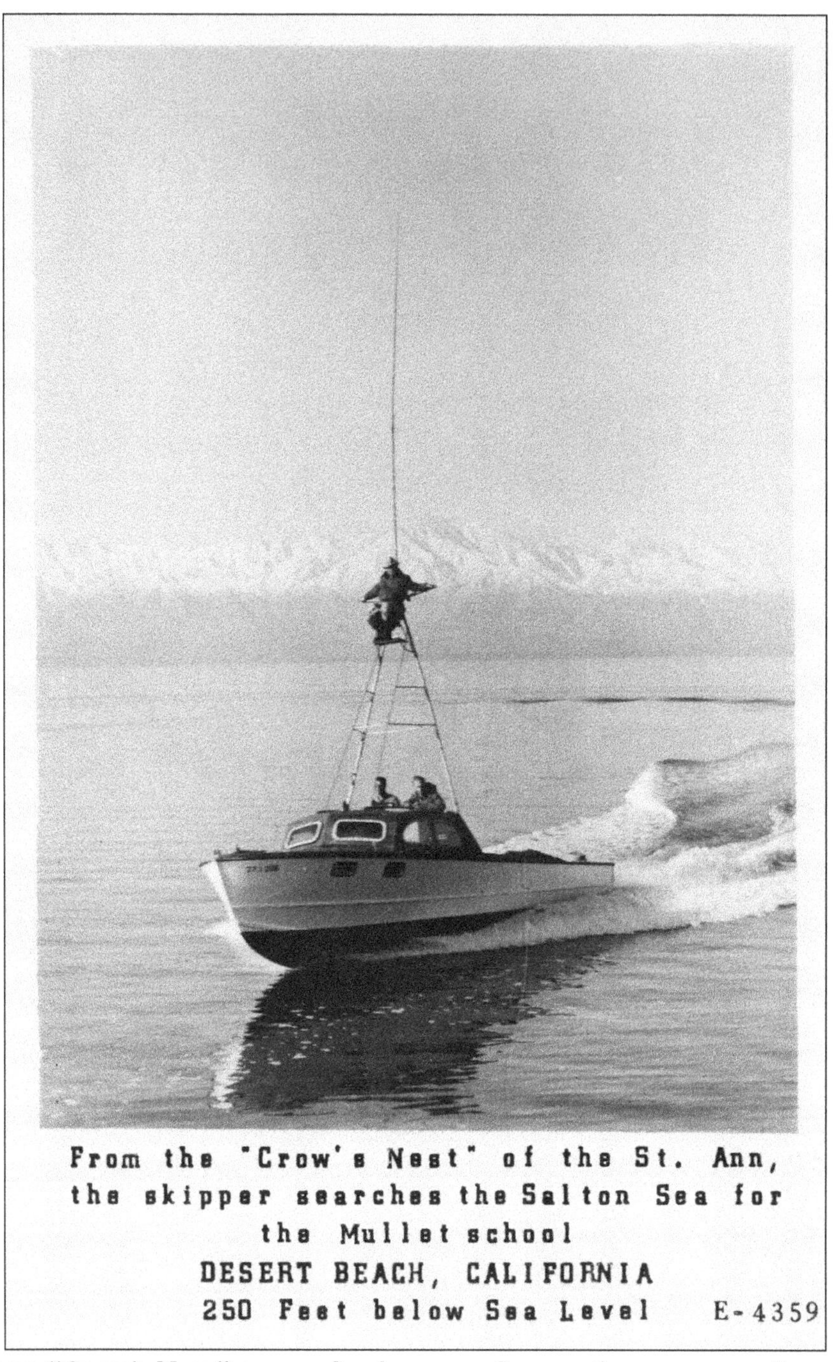

FROM THE "CROW'S NEST" OF THE ST. ANN, THE SKIPPER SEARCHES THE SALTON SEA FOR THE MULLET SCHOOL, DESERT BEACH, CALIFORNIA, 250 FEET BELOW SEA LEVEL. In 1948, the elevation of the lake began to rise. By 1953, C. Roy Hunter's improvements at Desert Beach were awash in water. He filed a lawsuit against the Coachella Valley Water District and Imperial Irrigation District for the rise in sea level and resulting damage to his resort. In 1960, Judge Bertram Janes awarded $188,000 to the Desert Beach owners. The national press later referred to the Salton Sea as "the Cruel Sea." Unused photo card. (E-4359).

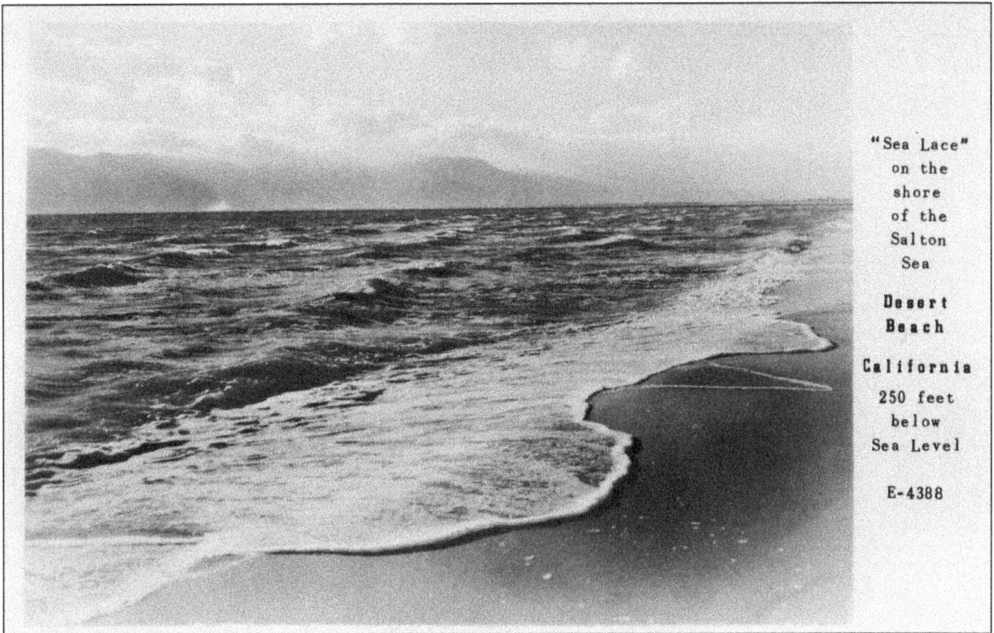

"Sea Lace" on the Shore of the Salton Sea, Desert Beach, California, 250 Feet below Sea Level. Sea lace, or dead man's rope, is brown seaweed that grows on stones under sandy bottoms and produces chord-like fronds up to 28 feet long. Unused photo card. (E-4388). (Frashers Foto Card, Scenic Photos of the West.)

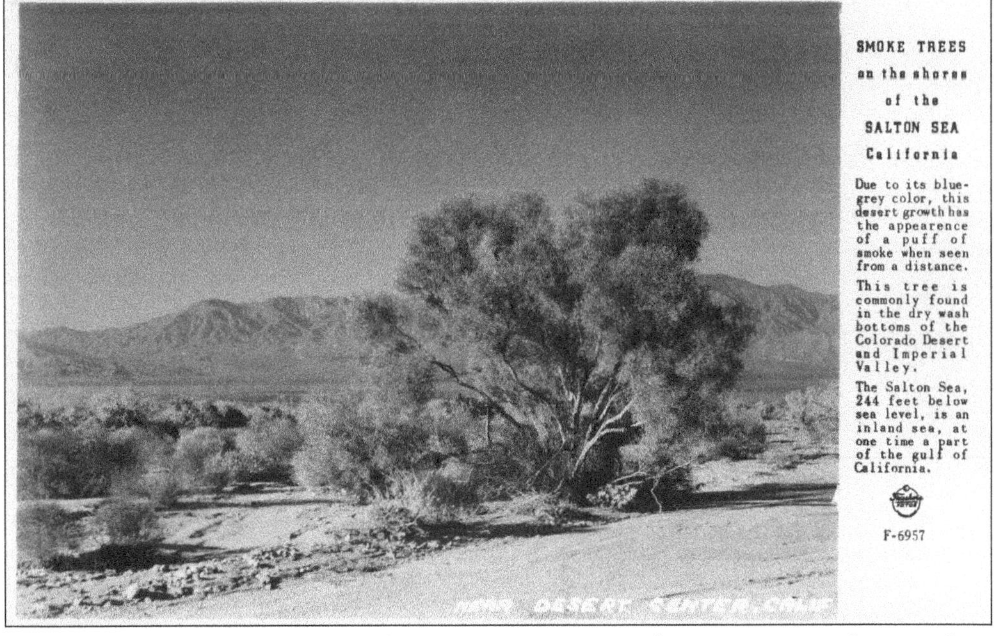

Near Desert Center, Calif., Smoke Trees on the Shores of the Salton Sea, California. Due to its blue-grey color, this desert growth has the appearance of a puff of smoke when seen from a distance. This tree is commonly found in the dry-wash bottoms of the Colorado Desert and Imperial Valley. The Salton Sea, 244 feet below sea level, is an inland sea, at one time a part of the gulf of California. Unused. (Frashers Foto Card F-6957.)

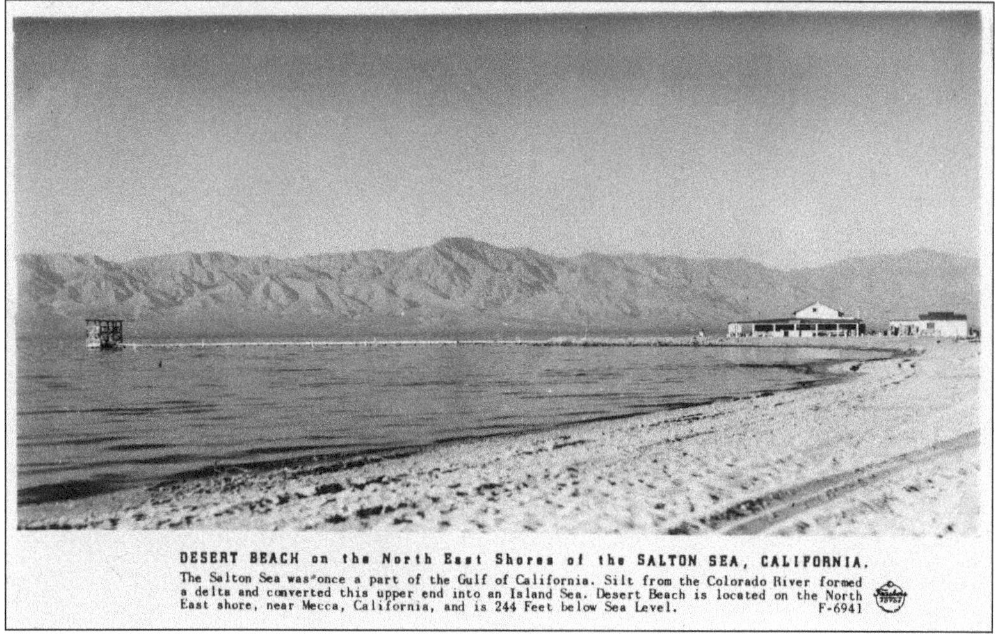

Desert Beach on the North East Shores of the Salton Sea, California. "The Salton Sea was once a part of the Gulf of California. Silt from the Colorado River formed a delta and converted this upper end into an island sea. Desert Beach is located on the northeast shore, near Mecca, California, and is 244 feet below sea level." (Frashers Foto Card F-6941.)

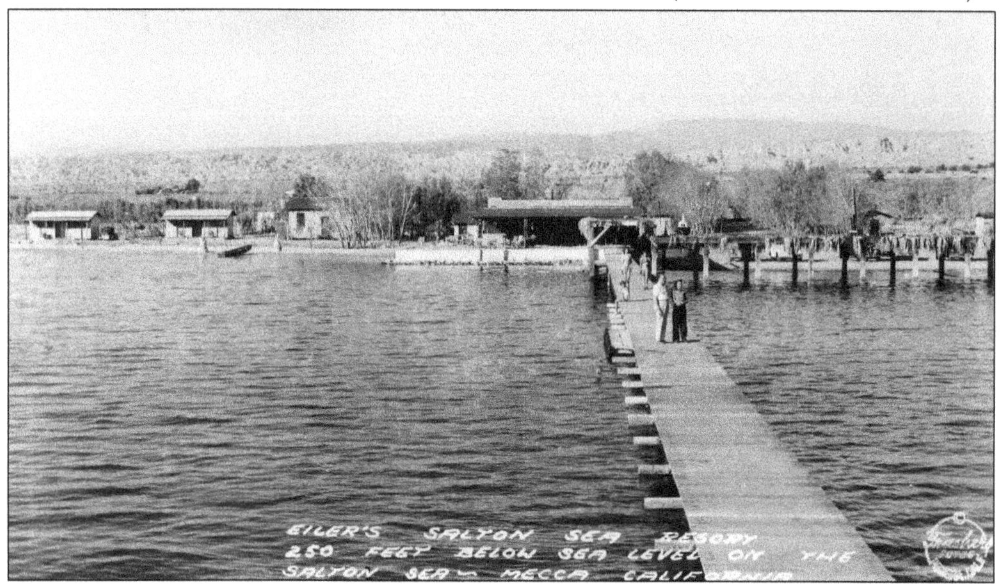

Eiler's Salton Sea Resort, 250 Feet below Sea Level on the Salton Sea – Mecca, California. In 1926, Gus Eilers came to the Salton Sea with a dream. He and John Goldthwaite acquired land on the north shore from the Southern Pacific Railroad. He built a small building and pier. His partnership with Goldthwaite ended as a result of the 1929 stock market crash. Undaunted by the economic downturn, Eilers purchased two cottages from the 1932 Olympic village in Los Angeles and constructed a 200-foot pier where motorboats could be moored throughout the year. Unused photo card. (Frashers Fotos, Pomona, California.)

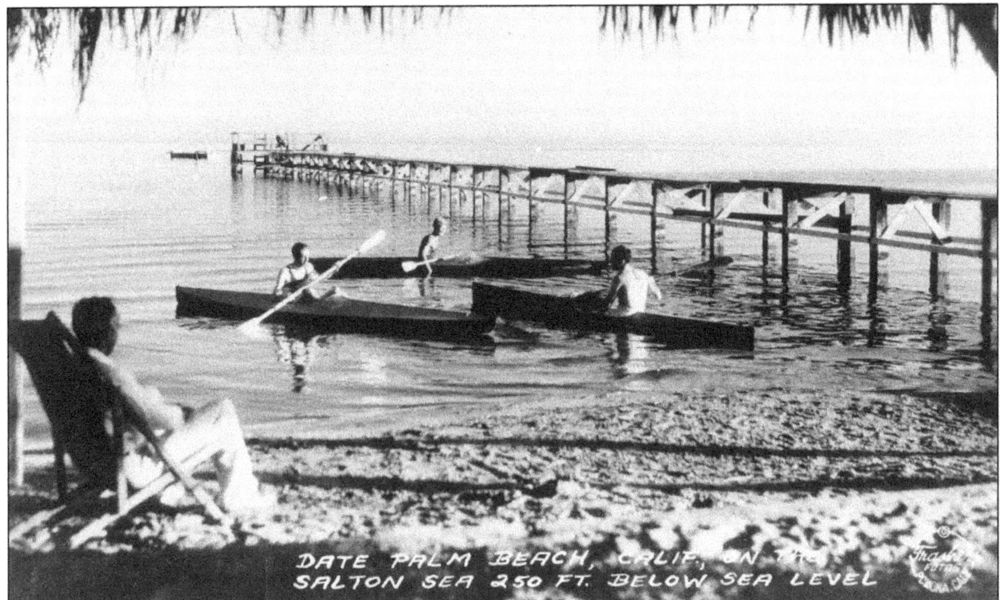

DATE PALM BEACH, CALIF. SALTON SEA, 250 FT. BELOW SEA LEVEL. The Date Palm Resort was very busy during the war years, when soldiers stationed at nearby Camp Young were offered a free swim. More than 150,000 soldiers took advantage of the offer. General Patton often visited the resort. Unused photo card. (Frashers, Pomona, Califiornia.)

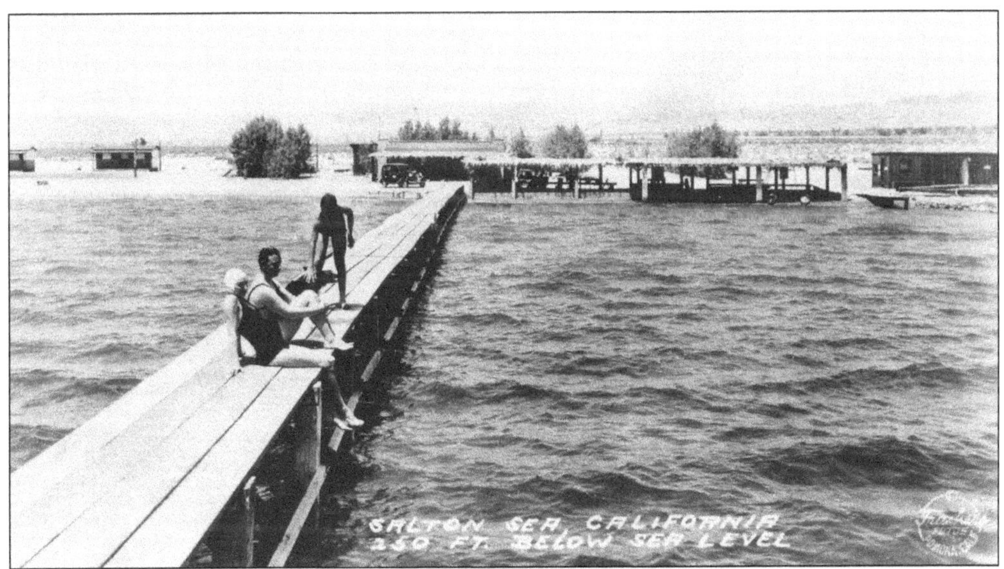

SALTON SEA, CALIFORNIA, 250 FT. BELOW SEA LEVEL. For many years, the Salton Sea seemed destined to develop into one of the major leisure destinations in California. Resorts were built, and the lake became a popular location for sunbathing, swimming, boating, water skiing, and fishing. However, there is no outlet channel, and the water gradually became more saline. Minerals leached from the hills, and pollution from dissolved pesticides and sewage washed into the lake from Mexico via the New and Alamo Rivers. Unused photo card. (Frashers Fotos, Pomona, California.)

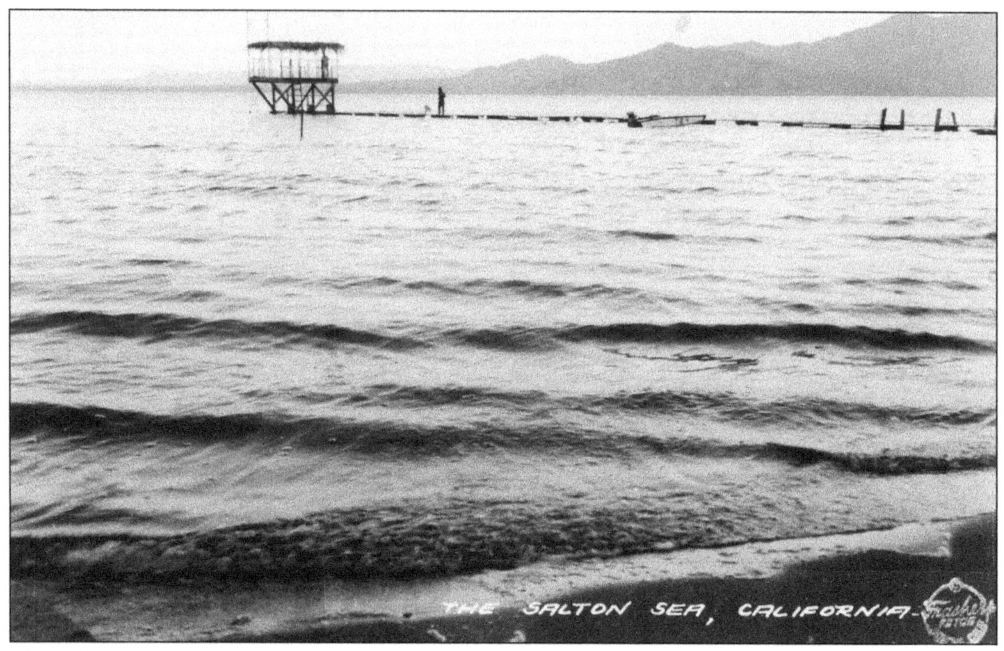

The Salton Sea, California. "Dear Friend—Here I am in sunny Calif. Having a fine time and like it here very much. It's so nice and warm here. Flowers blooming everywhere, and so much to see." The photographer Burton Frasher lived from 1888 until 1955. His photo postcards often have an imprint on the front that reads, "Frashers, Inc., Pomona, Calif." and there are a variety of imprints on the backs, such as "Frashers Foto Card." Frasher was known as the postcard king of the west. The Pomona Library was given Frasher's collection of about 60,000 photos and postcards. Mailed February 18, 1947, to Montgomery, Minnesota. (Frashers Fotos, Pomona, California.)

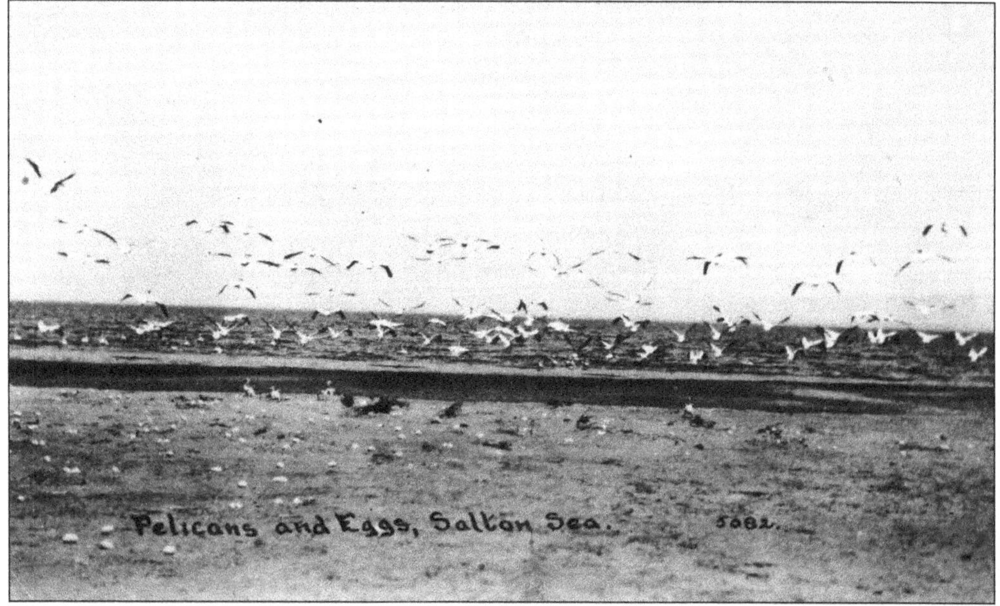

Pelicans and Eggs, Salton Sea; 5082. The Salton Sea supports 30 percent of the remaining population of the American white pelican. Unused photo card.

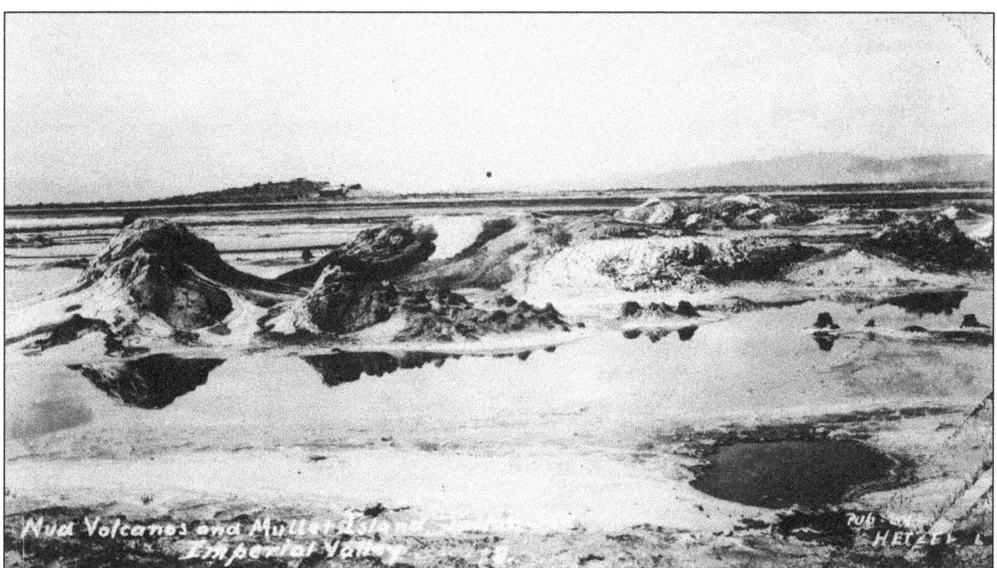

Mud Volcanoes and Mullet Island Salton Sea Imperial Valley 8. Marcia Rittenhouse Winn lived on Mullet Island during the 1920s. She stated that "the hissing of steam and the gurgling that came up from some mysterious subterranean discontent were to be an ever present reminder that we were sitting on top of volcanic ground, whose steam vents man could not turn off." The geysers kept a thin layer of moisture on top of the surrounding silt in all seasons. Occasionally, there were visits from geologists, scientists, Boy Scout groups, and others who came to marvel at the paint (mud) pots and the steaming mud geysers. (Published by Hetzel.)

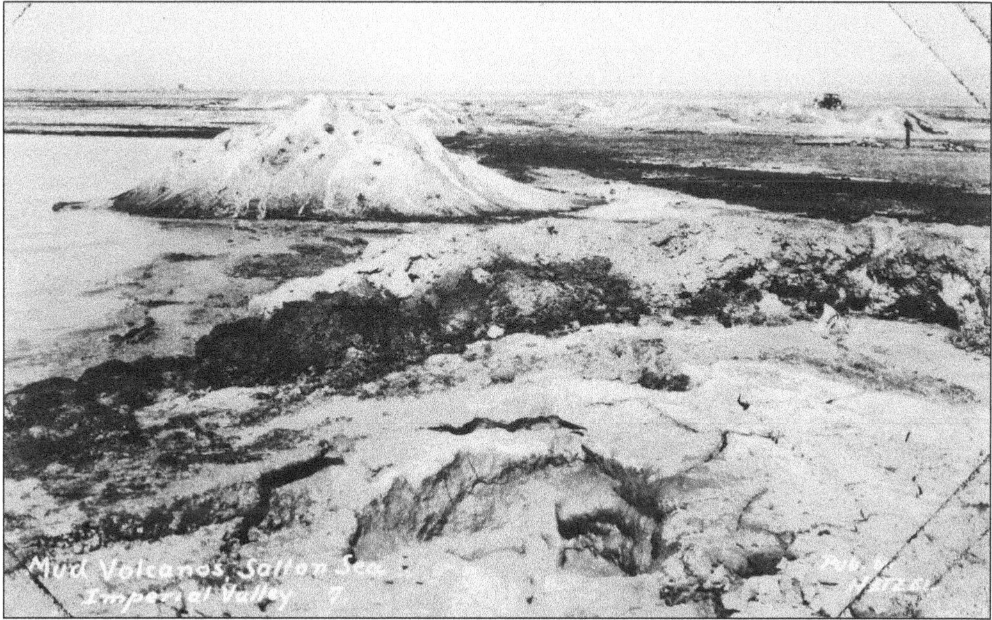

Mud Volcanos, Salton Sea, Imperial Valley 7. The terms "mud volcano" and "mud dome" refer to formations created by geo-excreted liquids and gases. Hot water mixes with mud and surface deposits. The mud eruptions are warm to the touch. Unused photo card. (Published by Hetzel.)

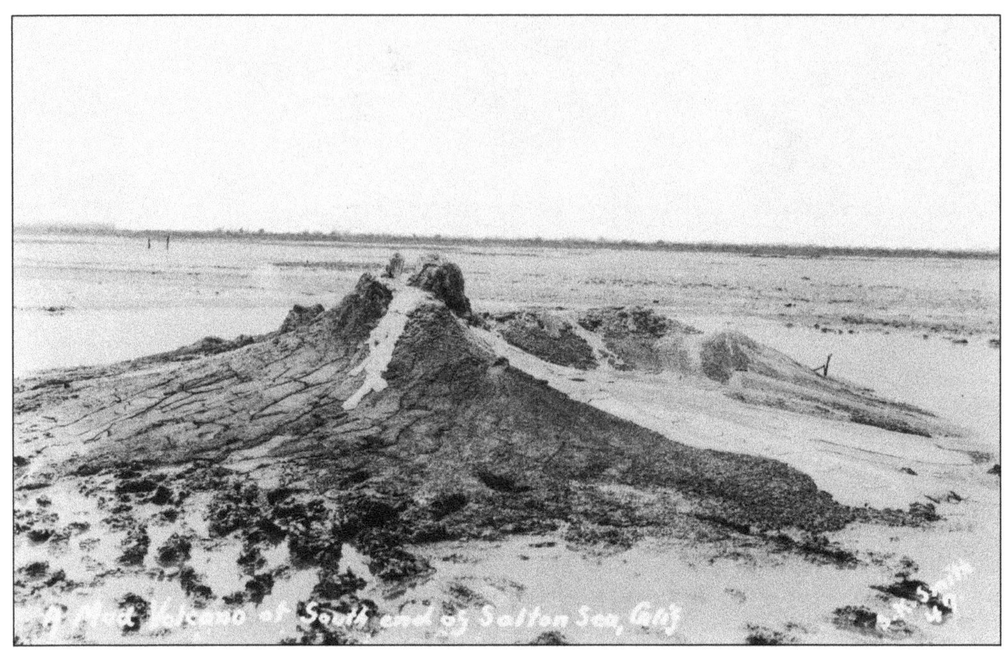

A Mud Volcano at South End of Salton Sea, Calif. Mud geysers or volcanic domes lie near of bottom of the depression that is the northern extension of the Gulf of California. They are located at the intersection of Davis and Schrimpf Road, near Calipatria, California. Unused photo card. (S.K. Smith 47.)

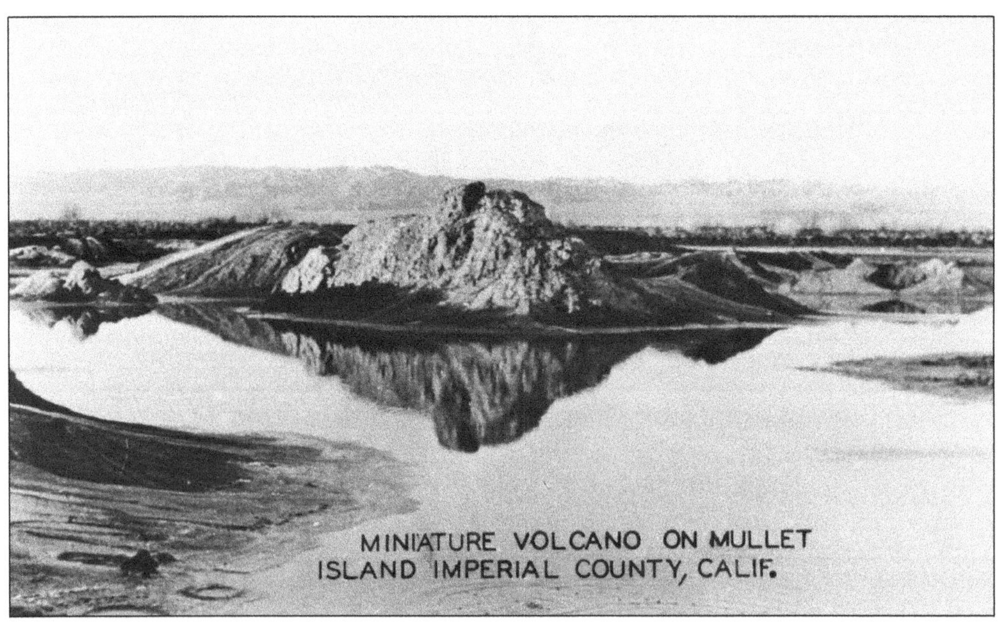

Miniature Volcano on Mullet Island Imperial County, Calif. Unused photo card.

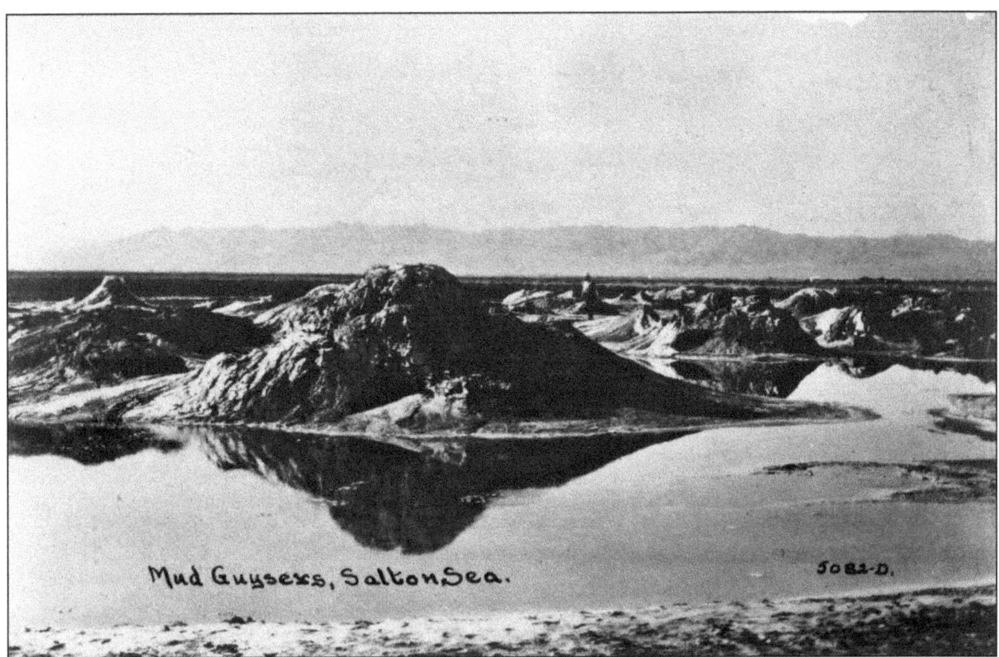

MUD GUYSERS [*SIC*], SALTON SEA. The bubbling mud pots are powered by carbon dioxide gas of hydrothermal origin. The fluids are mixed with brines nearer the surface, so they are generally warm rather than hot. Unused photo card. (50 B2-D.)

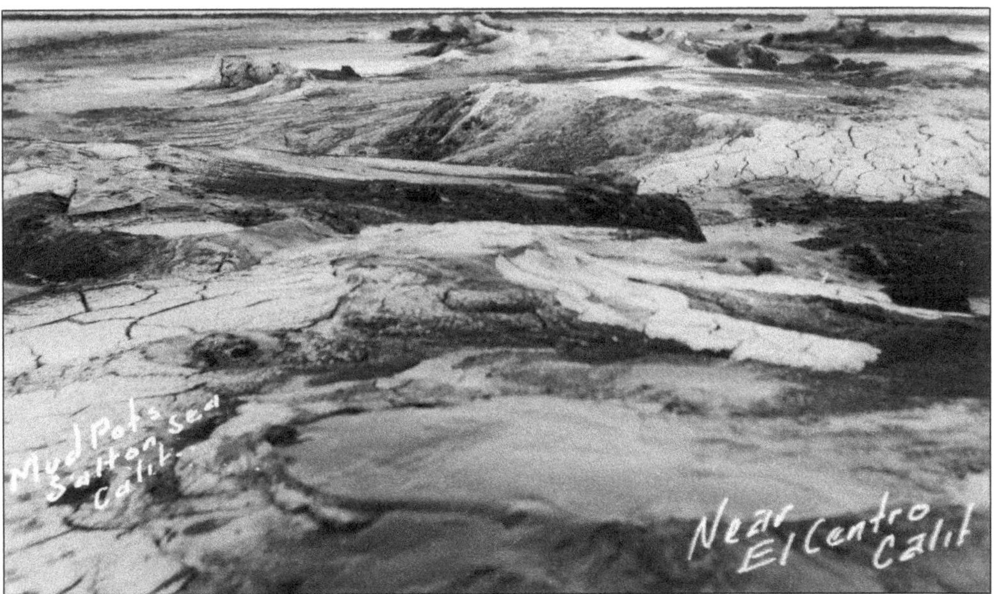

MUD POTS, SALTON SEA, CALIF. NEAR EL CENTRO, CALIF., ELC3. Visitors can experience the bubbling sights and sounds and feel the warm mud as it flows from within the Earth. Unused photo card.

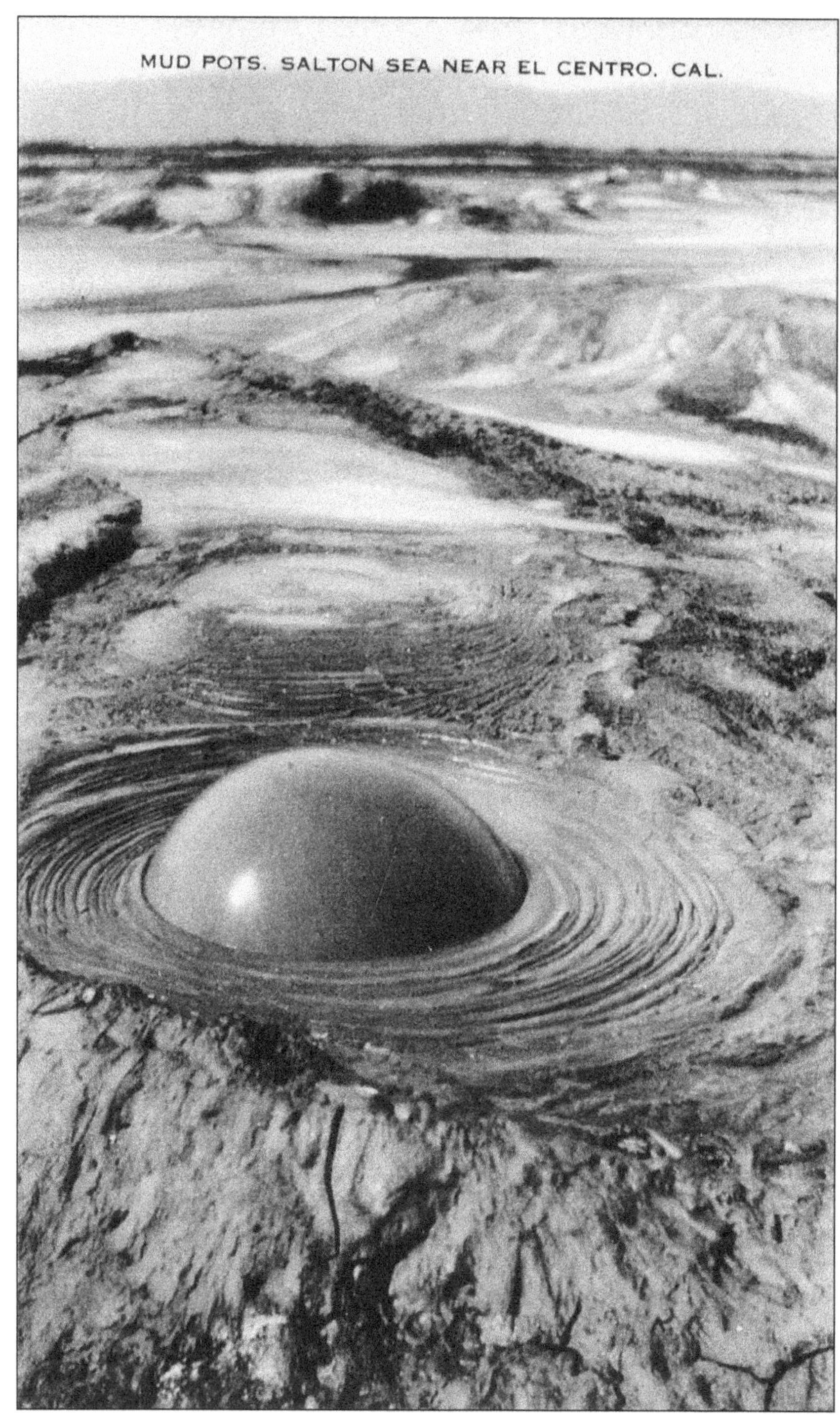

MUD POTS. SALTON SEA, NEAR EL CENTRO, CAL. Approximately 1,100 mud volcanoes have been identified on land and in shallow water. It has been estimated that well over 10,000 may exist on continental slopes and abyssal plains. Unused photo card. (Published by Artvue Post Card Co., 225 Fifth Avenue, New York, New York.)

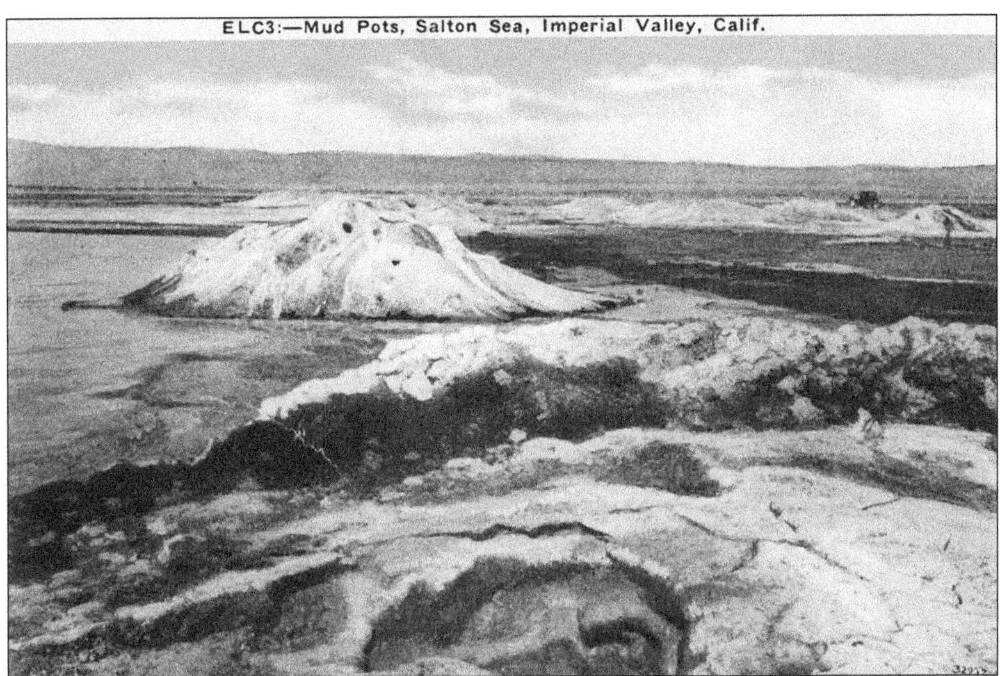

ELC3; Mud Pots, Salton Sea, Imperial Valley, Calif. Mud pots are located in proximity to geothermal energy resources. As of 2001, there were 15 geothermal plants located on the southeast side of the Salton Sea, near the cities of Niland and Calipatria. CalEnergy owns about half of the plants, and the rest are owned by other companies. The plants have a combined capacity of about 570 megawatts. One megawatt is equal to one million watts, and 570 megawatts can power 570,000 homes. ; Unused. (Published by M. Kashower Co., Los Angeles, California.)

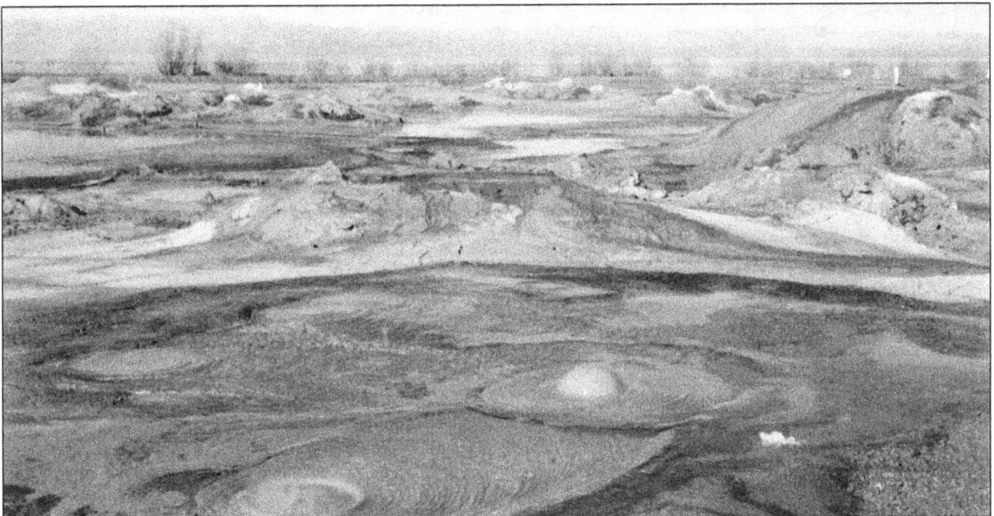

Boiling Mud Pots of the South End of Salton Sea Erupt Steam and Gases Accompanied by Mud. "Upon approaching them, the rush of steam and the sound of boiling mud can be heard. For several years the 'mud volcanoes' were covered by the Sea, but as it receded the mud pots emerged to view." Unused photo card. (Union Oil Company's Natural Color Scenes of the West.)

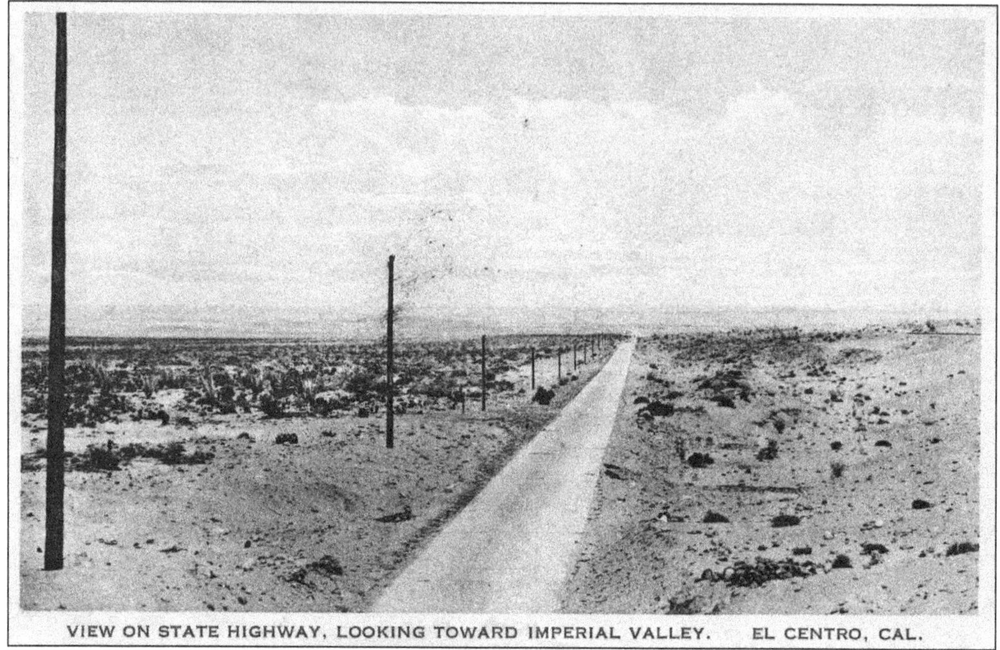

VIEW ON STATE HIGHWAY, LOOKING TOWARD IMPERIAL VALLEY, EL CENTRO, CAL. State Highway 111 extends from Interstate 10 at Whitewater through Palm Springs, along the eastern corridor of the Salton Sea, and through North Shore, Bombay Beach, and Niland to Calexico. Highway 86 is so dangerous that it has been nicknamed "the killer highway" by area residents. In fact, since 1977 there have been over 200 fatalities in car-related accidents on this 93-mile stretch of highway, much of which is a dusty, unlit, two-lane road. The highway runs from Indio through Desert Shores and Salton City, along the western side of the Salton Sea to Calexico. Unused photo card. (Published by Francis Drug Co., Post Cards of Quality—the Albertype Co., Brooklyn, New York.)

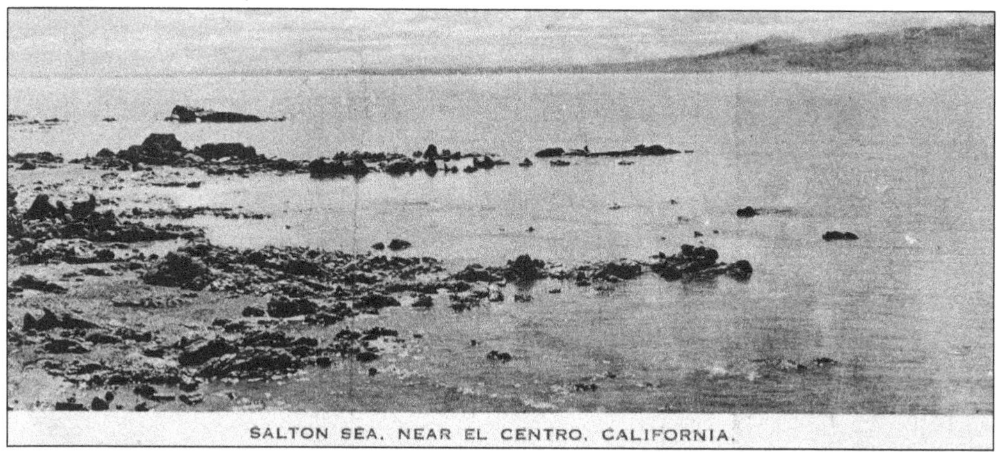

SALTON SEA, NEAR EL CENTRO, CALIFORNIA. The southern portion of the Salton Sea is known for its wide array of migratory birds, large farms, and a few small communities. When traveling through El Centro, Niland, Calipatria, Holtville, and other small towns, the buildings are worn and from another era. The promise of a good life seems much more elusive than elsewhere in southern California. Unused photo card. (Published by Francis Drug Co., Post Cards of Quality—The Albertype Co., Brooklyn, New York.)

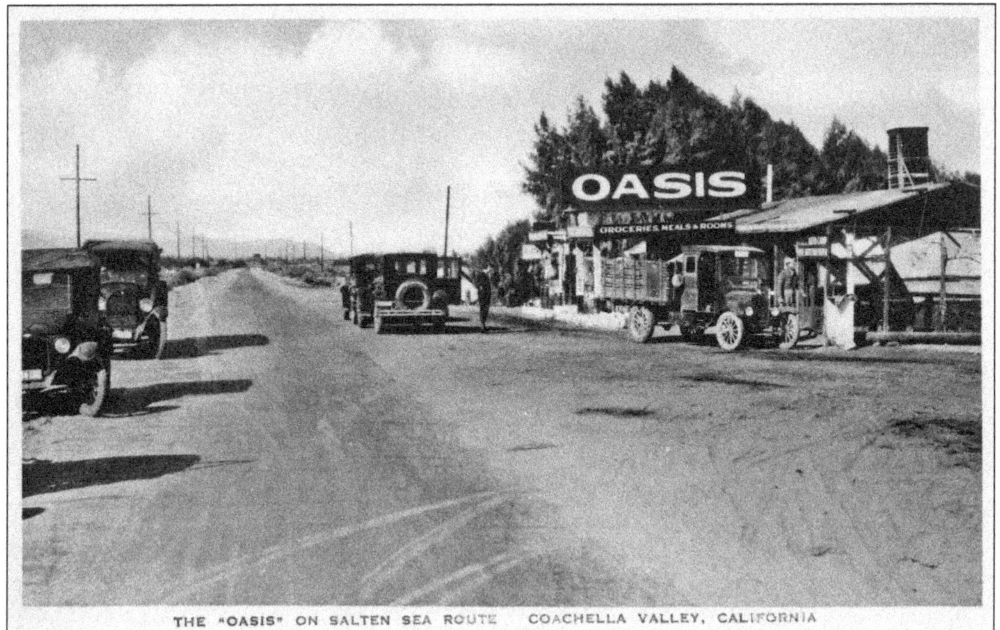

THE "OASIS" ON SALTEN [*SIC*] SEA ROUTE, COACHELLA VALLEY, CALIFORNIA. The Oasis Date Gardens was established in 1912 by Ben and Lucy Laflin. It is a 175-acre working date ranch. Oasis and its sister company, Winterhaven Ranch, produce about 1,300,000 pounds of Medjool dates and another 100,000 pounds of other varieties. In 1997, the ranch was acquired by Chris and Marlene Nielsen and Jim and Judy Freimuth. Unused photo card. (Published by Bisbee & Sons, Oasis Station, Thermal, California; Post Cards of Quality, the Albertype Co., Brooklyn, New York.)

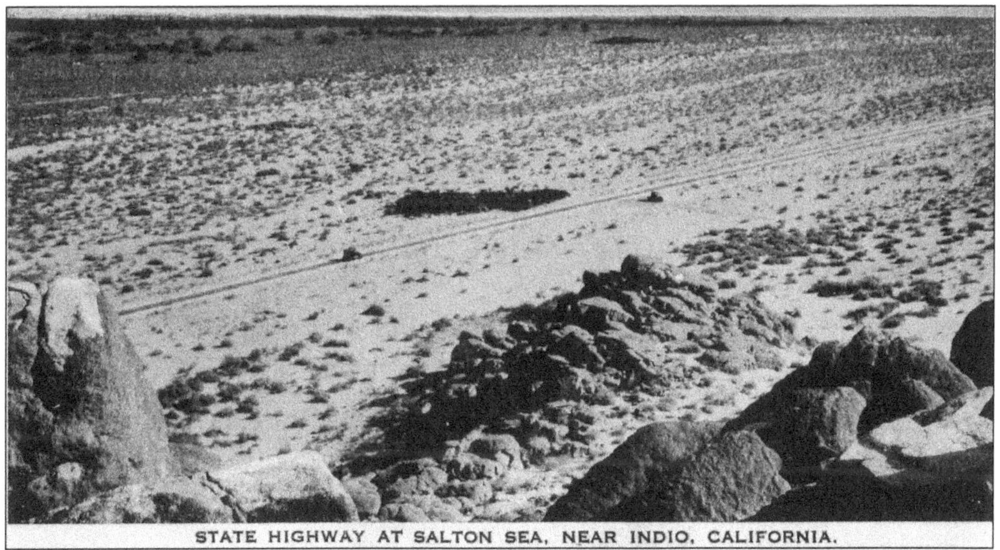

STATE HIGHWAY AT SALTON SEA, NEAR INDIO, CALIFORNIA. "Dear old reprobate. We are about 135 miles SE of Los Angeles and going fine. Have not met any speed cops to date. 18 ft. concrete road in picture, which we went over this afternoon. Got off the road to take picture and got stuck in sand for about an hour. Regards Ed." Mailed November 24, 1927, to Bedford, Oregon. (Published by W.B Burnham, Druggist, Indio, California.)

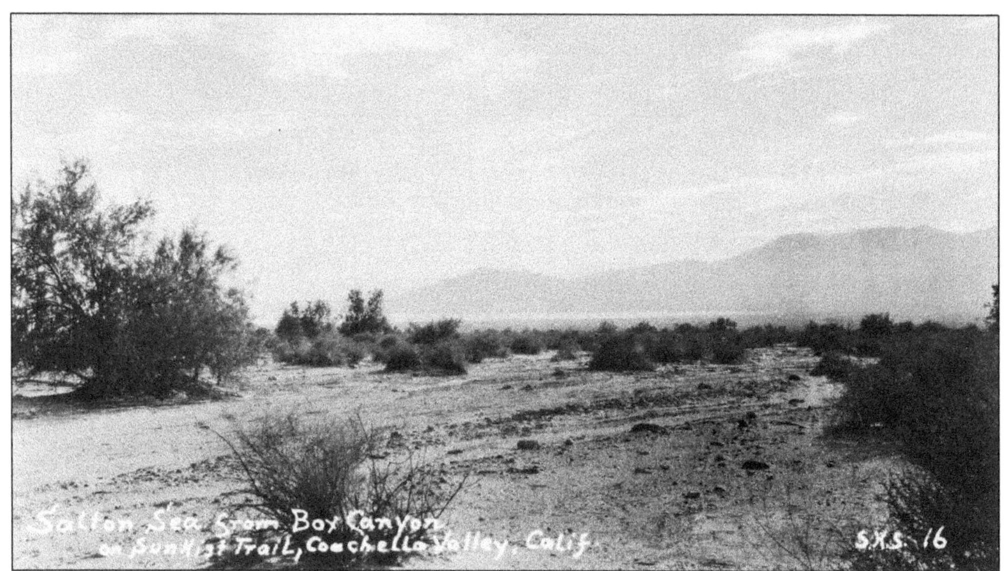

Salton Sea from Box Canyon on Sunkist Trail, Coachella Valley, Calif. S.X.S. 16. Box Canyon is located on State Highway 195. The road runs through the ravine, linking State Highway 111 with Interstate 10 and continuing into Joshua Tree National Park. Plant life is limited to scattered bushes and Palo Verde trees along the sandy floor, with jagged rock walls that are completely bare. The surrounding hills contain narrow ravines, including slot canyons, and springs, oases, and a large area of vividly colored badlands. Mailed March 5, 1930, to Glendora, California.

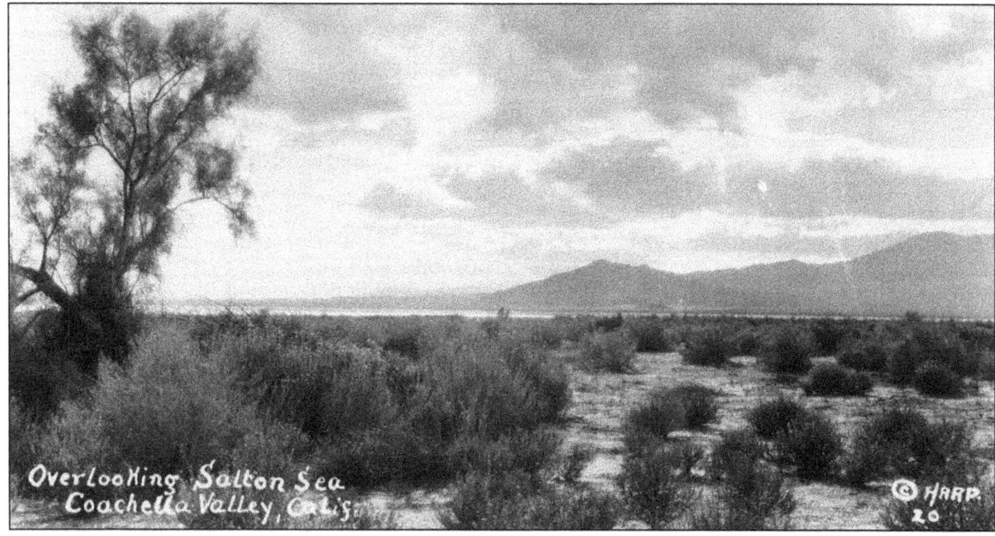

Overlooking Salton Sea, Coachella Valley, Cal. A trip to the Salton Sea shows an extreme contrast of America. The greater Palm Springs area is home to approximately 25 percent of the nation's wealth during March. The lower Coachella Valley and Imperial County have some of the most impressive farms in the nation. However, about 29 percent of the residents of the lower Coachella Valley and Imperial County are below the poverty line. Although a visible majority of the buildings and homes around the lake are abandoned, underwater, or decayed, the Salton Sea retains a rare and austere beauty. Mailed April 2, 1930, to Pasadena, California. (© Harp 20.)

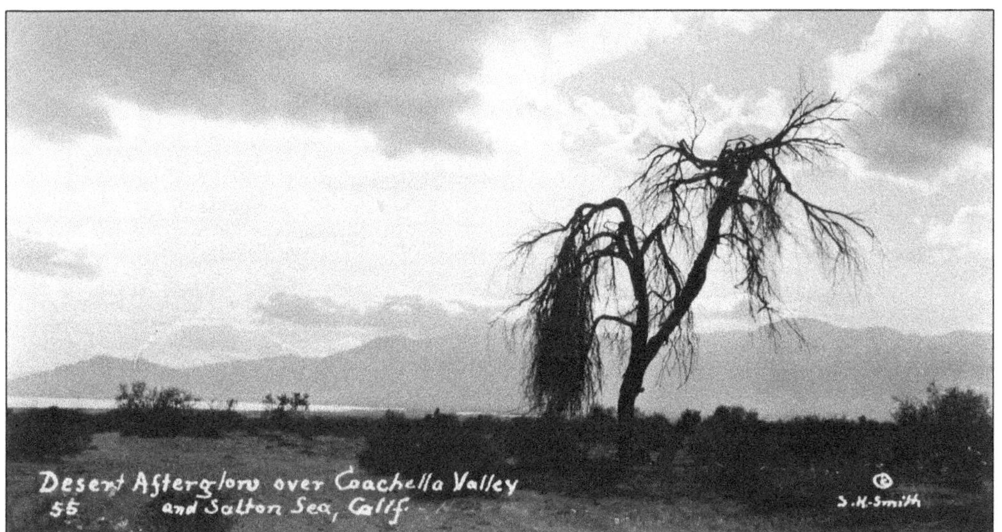

Desert Afterglow over Coachella Valley and Salton Sea, Calif. Sunsets over the Salton Sea are quite amazing. The entire lake turns orangey red when the sun sets. The lake is also a favorite destination for stargazers because of the clear skies and darkness of its evenings. Unused photo card. (© S.K. Smith.)

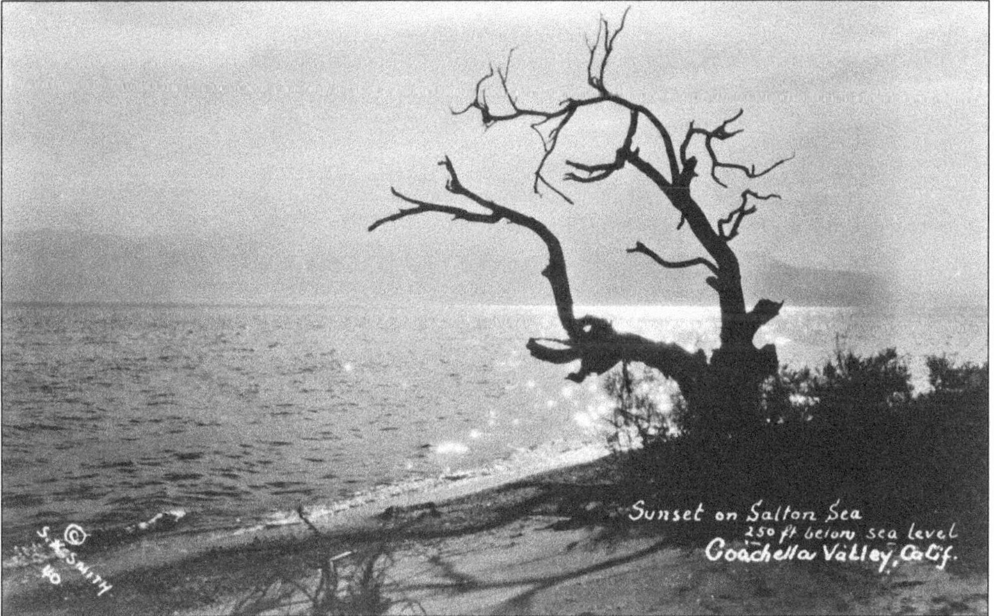

Sunset on Salton Sea, 250 Ft. below Sea Level, Coachella Valley, Calif. According to the Salton Sea Authority, the Salton Sea is California's largest lake. At a surface elevation of 227 feet below sea level, it has an area of 243,718 acres or 381 square miles. The maximum depth of the sea is about 51 feet, and the average depth is 31 feet. The annual inflow to the sea averages about 1,300,000 acre-feet, carrying approximately 4,000,000 tons of dissolved salt. Below an elevation of -220 feet, the federal government has designated the Salton Sea as a repository for agricultural drainage. Without this use of the sea, land in the Imperial and Coachella Valleys would be either too waterlogged or too saline (or both) for agriculture. Unused photo card. (© S.K. Smith 40.)

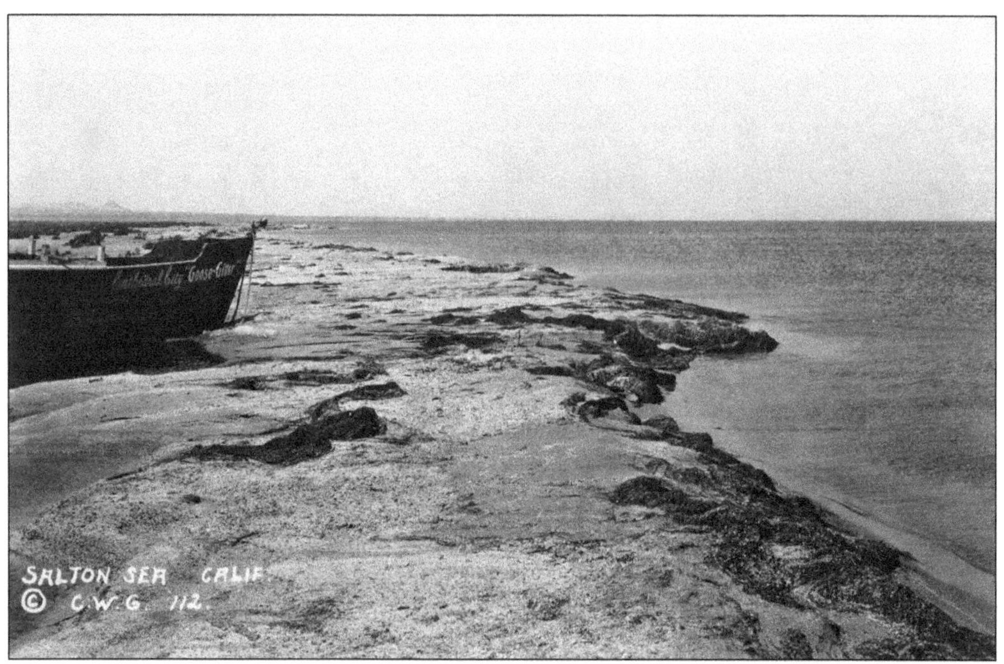

SALTON SEA, CALIF. On January 24, 2008, the California Legislative Analysis Office released a report entitled "Saving the Salton Sea." The preferred alternative plan calls for spending a total of almost $9 billion over 25 years and proposes a smaller but more manageable Salton Sea. The amount of water available for use by humans and wildlife would be reduced by 60 percent, from 365 square miles to about 147 square miles. (© C.W.G. 112.)

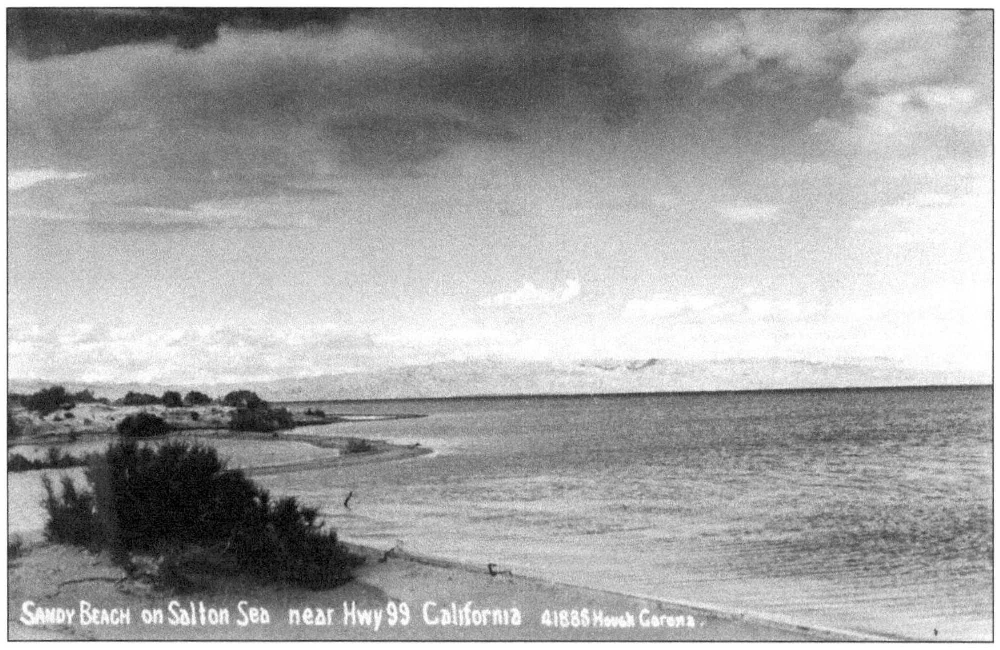

SANDY BEACH ON SALTON SEA, NEAR HWY 99, CALIFORNIA. Salton Sea Wildlife Refuge is located at a point previously designated as Sandy Beach. Unused photo card. (41885 Houck Corona.)

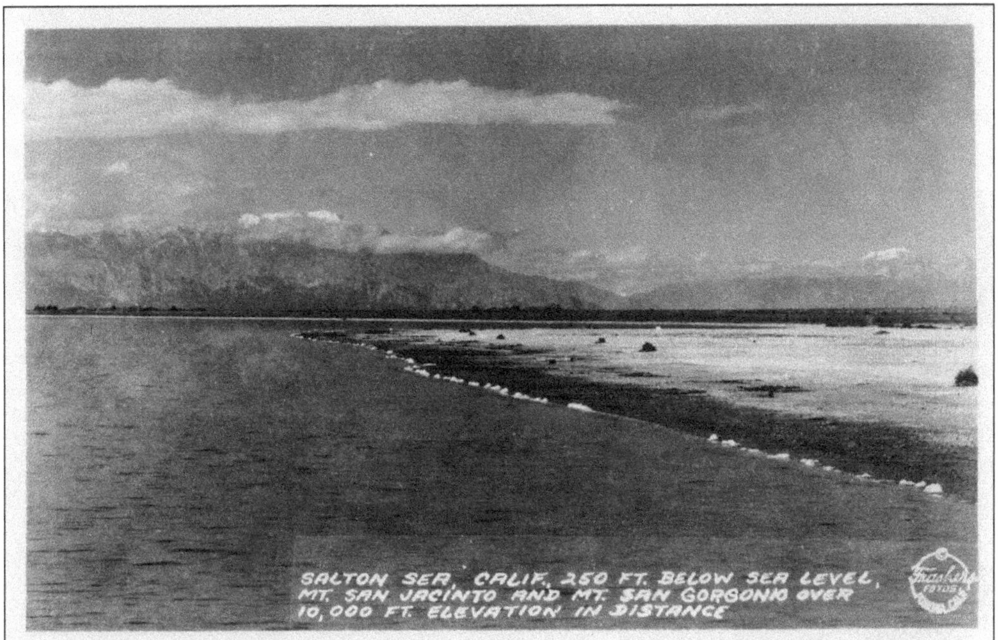

Salton Sea, Calif., 250 Ft. below Sea Level, Mt. San Jacinto and Mt. San Gorgonio, over 10,000 Ft. Elevation in Distance. The tallest mountain peaks in Southern California are Mount San Gorgonio (11,502 feet) and Mount San Jacinto (10,804) feet. The Salton Sea is about 50 miles away and can be viewed from both peaks. Unused photo card. (Frashers, Pomona, Calif.)

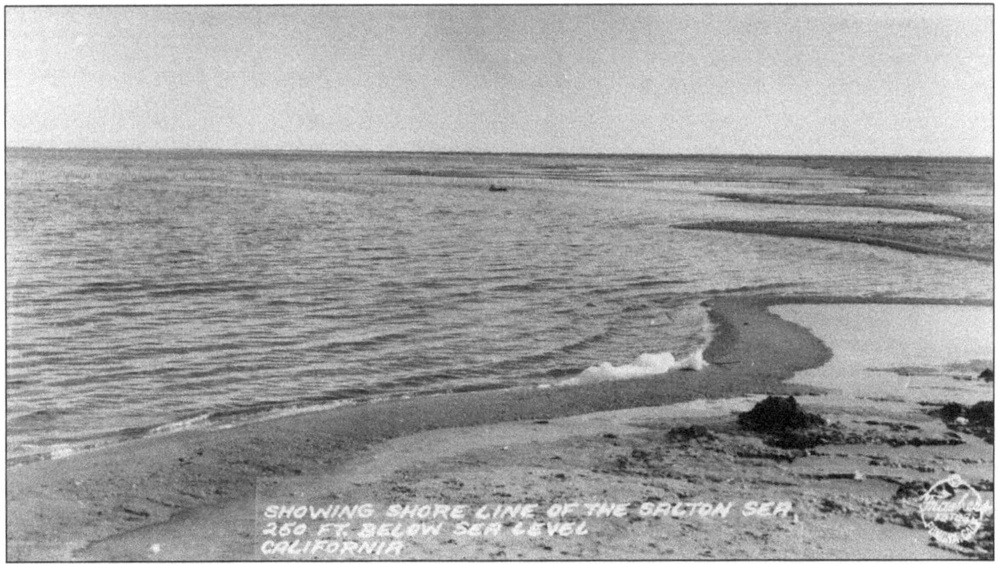

Showing Shore Line of the Salton Sea, 250 below Sea Level, California. As the Salton Sea's water level drops in coming years, approximately half of the lakebed that is exposed may cause major air-quality problems for the Salton Sea as well as the Imperial and Coachella Valleys. Studies show that where water has already receded, the surface areas contain a salty mix of sediments that can change from a hardened salt crust to a fluffy soft layer of dust depending upon the season. Unused photo card. (Frashers, Pomona, Calif.)

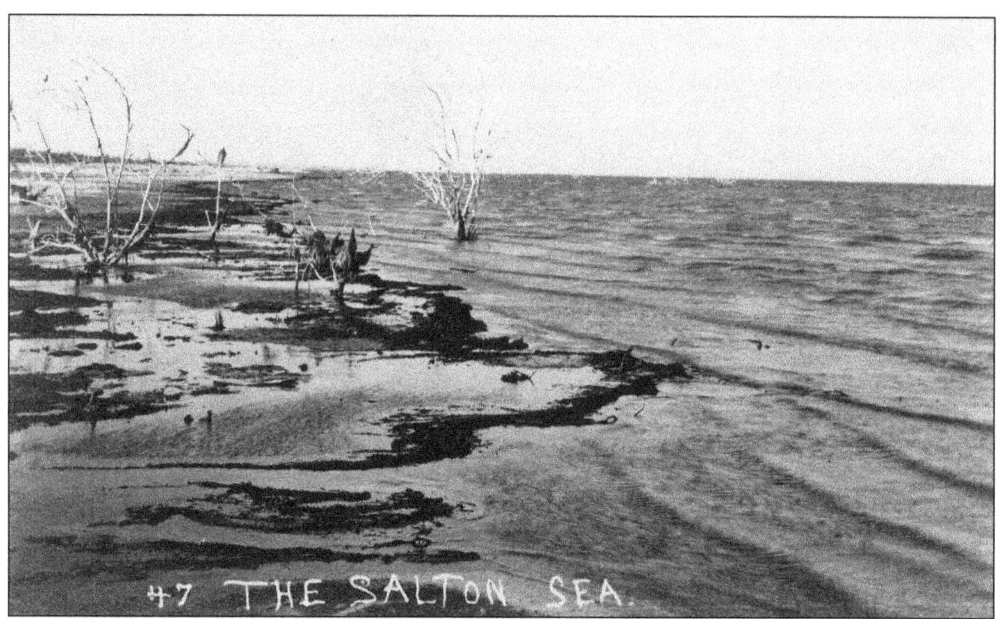

47 The Salton Sea. This postcard is as an early Stephen Willard black-and-white photograph. His former Palm Springs residence is located on the grounds of the present-day Moorten Botanical Gardens. Also, the Stephen H. Willard Photography Collection and Archives is on display at the Palm Springs Art Museum. Unused photo card. (S.H. Willard Photo, Corona, Cal.)

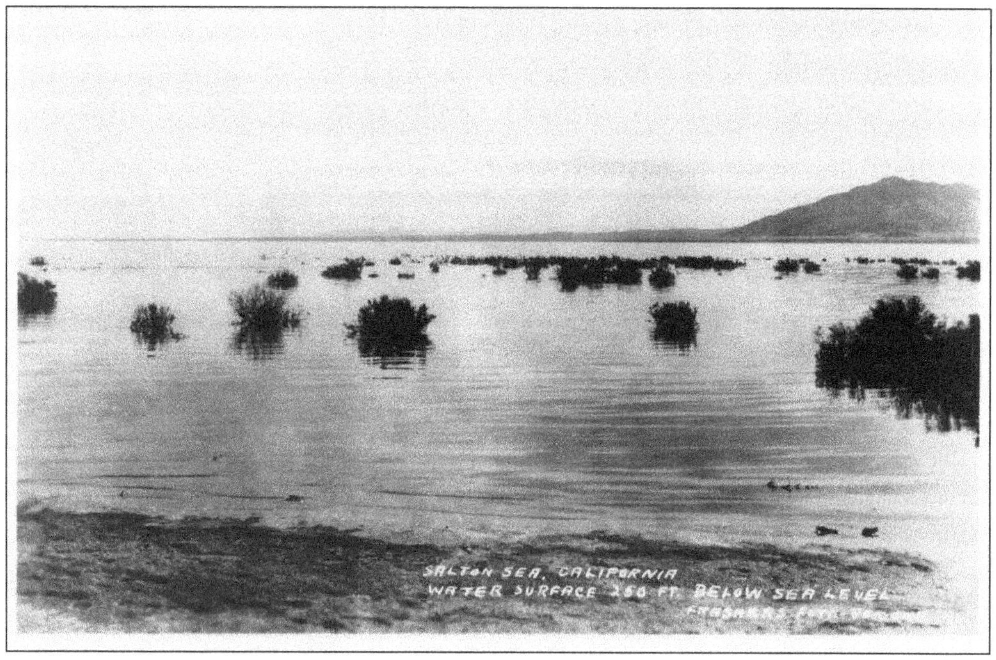

Salton Sea, California, Water Surface 250 Ft. below Sea Level. At 250 feet below sea level, the Salton Sea is the second lowest elevation in the United States. Death Valley, California, at 282 feet below sea level, has the lowest elevation. The Dead Sea has the lowest elevation in the world at 1,349 feet below sea level. Unused photo card. (Frashers Fotos, Pomona, Calif.)

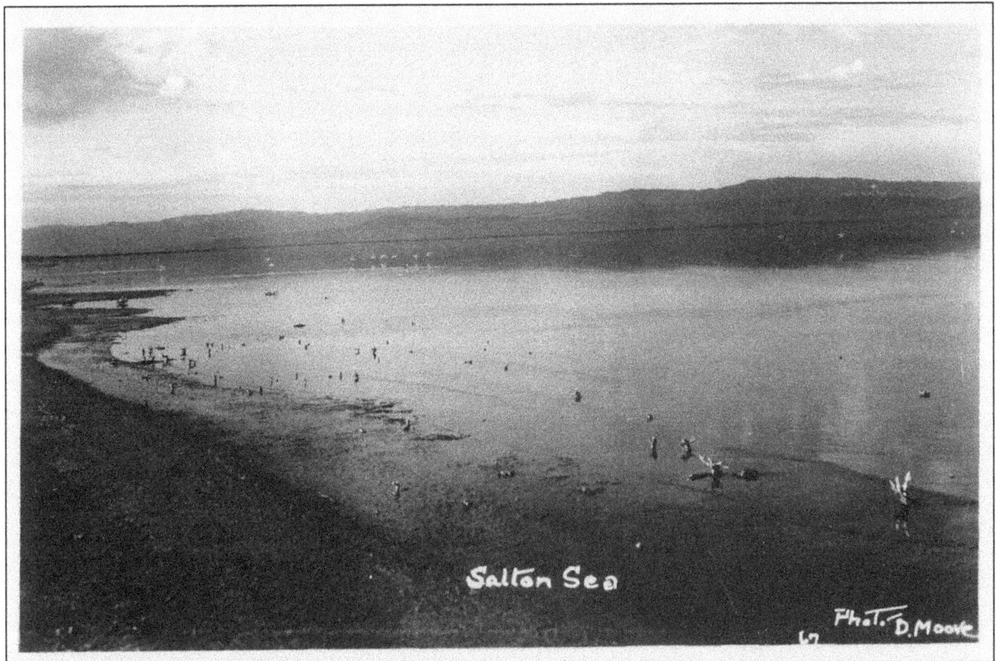

SALTON SEA. Little information is available about Dewey Moore. However, he was a desert photographer whose "Desert Lily in Coachella Valley" was featured on the March 1938 cover of the *Desert Magazine*. Unused photo card. (Photograph by D. Moore.)

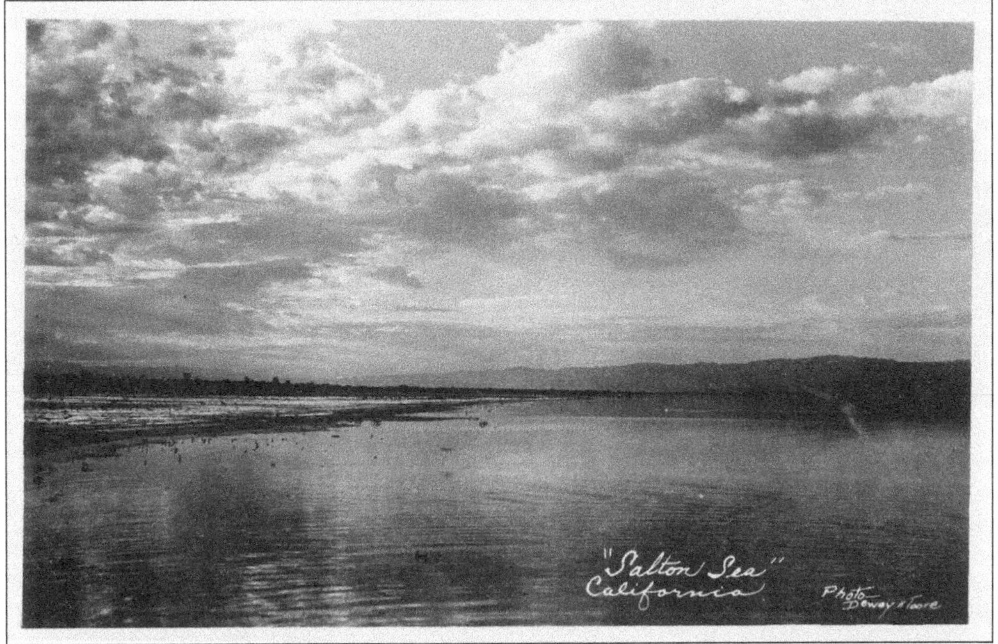

SALTON SEA, CALIFORNIA. Both of the Dewey Moore postcards in the author's collection are Salton Sea photographs with this name. Unused photo card. (Photograph Dewey Moore.)

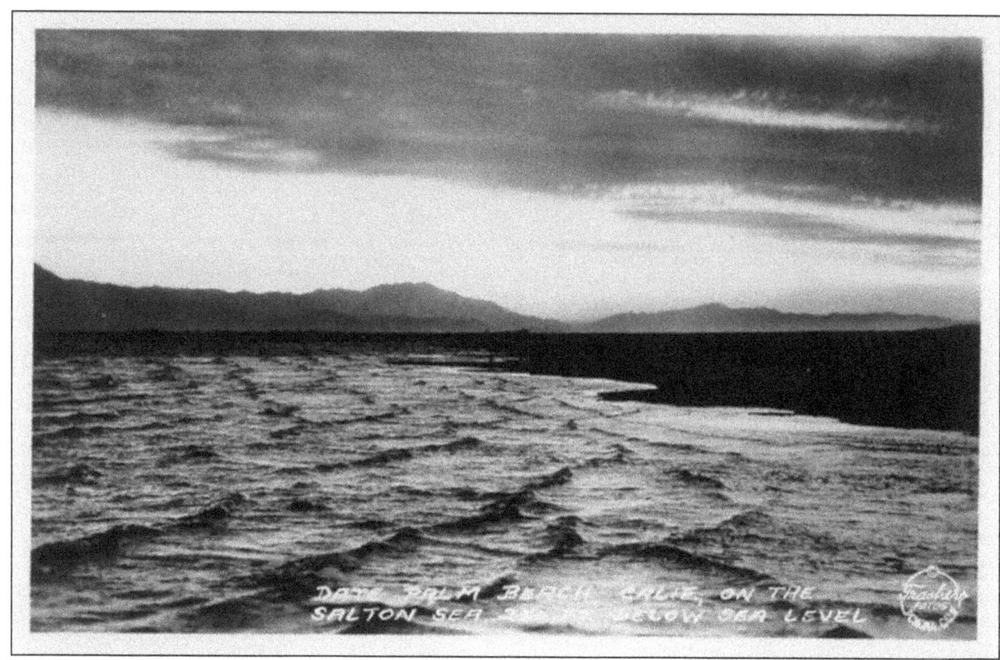

Date Palm Beach, Calif., on the Salton Sea, 250 Ft. below Sea Level. Date Palm Beach was previously known as Eiler's Salton Sea Resort. It is a faded community on the northeast shore of the lake, about a quarter mile south of the North Shore Marina and a mile north of the Salton Sea State Recreation Area entrance. The development is gated for residents only, and there is no public access. Unused photo card. (Frashers, Pomona, Calif.)

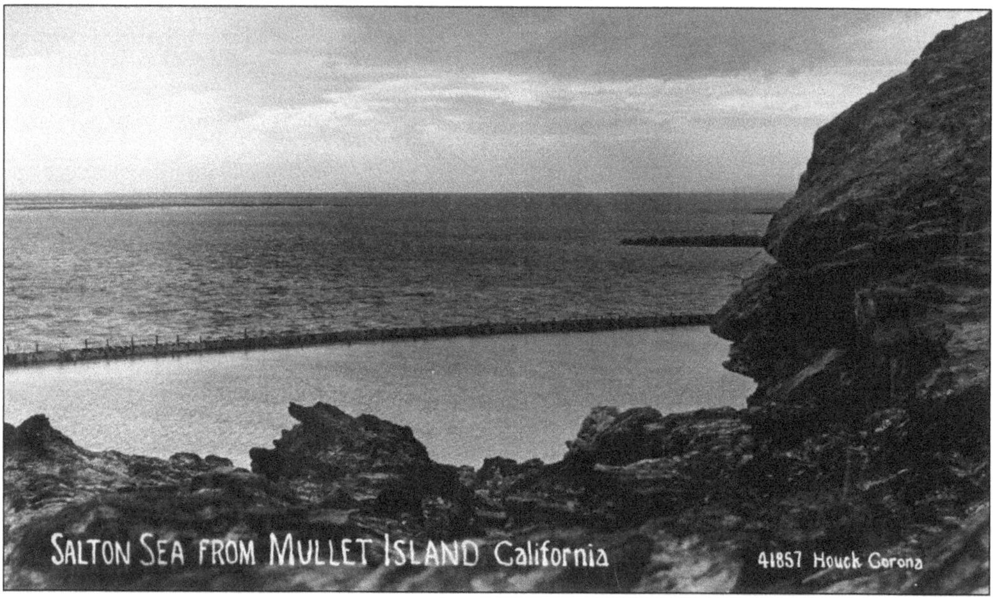

Salton Sea from Mullet Island California. Mullet Island is named after the mullet fish. Mullets are thick-bodied food fish of inshore waters that belong to a large family that lives in fresh or salt water. From 1941 to 1945, commercial fishermen used the Salton Sea to supply coastal fish markets after German submarines made ocean fishing hazardous. Unused photo card. (41857 Houck Corona.)

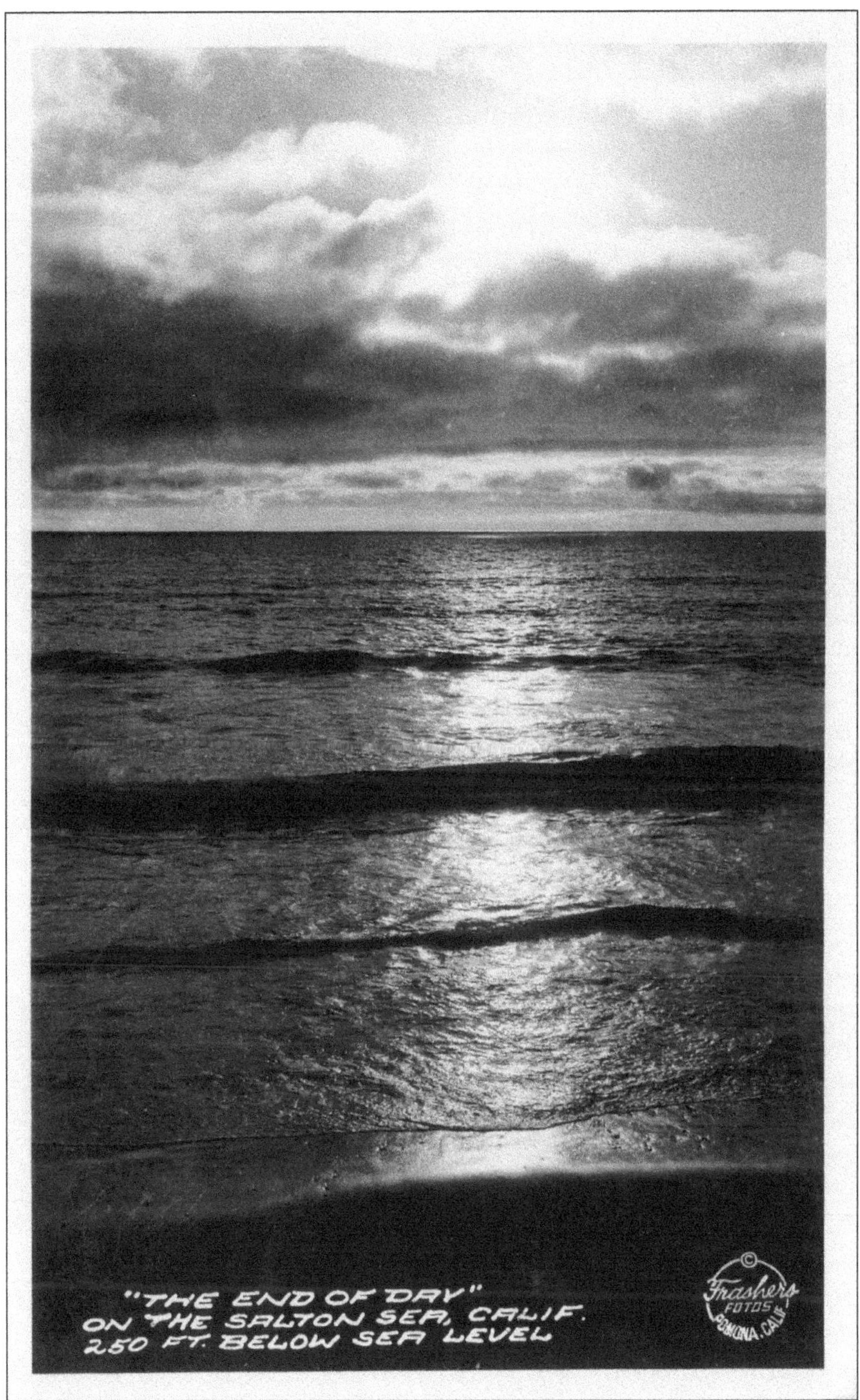

"The End of Day" on the Salton Sea, Calif., 250 Ft. below Sea Level. The Salton Sea is extremely quiet at the end of day. There is usually a nice breeze to break the heat. In addition, there is a noticeable lack of traffic, noise, or other people. Mailed May 14, 1943, to Bellevue, Michigan. (Frashers, Pomona, Calif.)

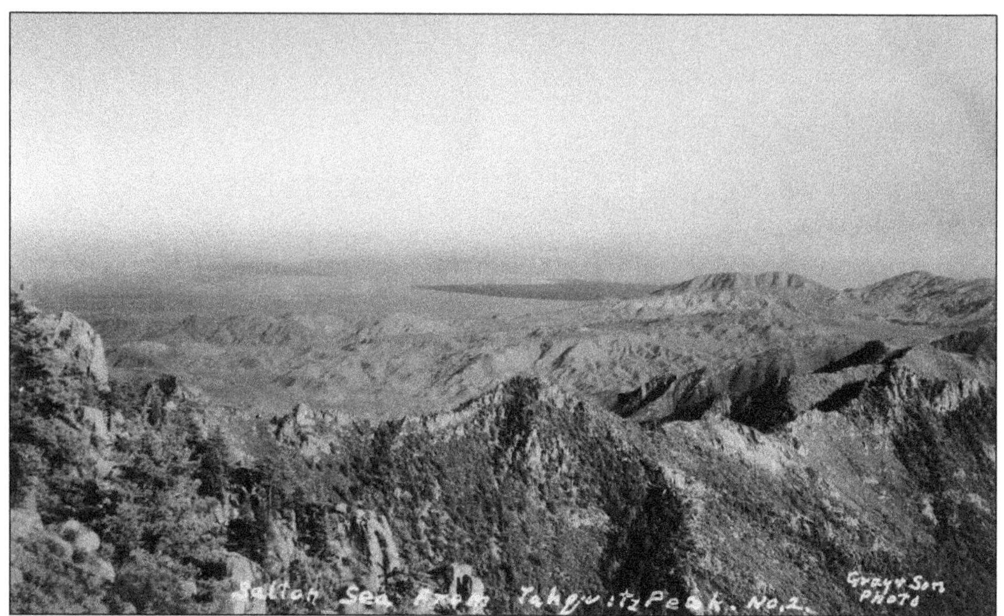

SALTON SEA FROM TAHQUITZ PEAK, NO. 2. Tahquitz Peak was a working fire lookout through 1993. It reopened to the public in October 1998. The 4.5-mile hike to the lookout through the San Jacinto Wilderness offers some of the most beautiful vistas in Southern California, including the Salton Sea. Tahquitz Peak Lookout, at an elevation of 8,828 feet, is the highest lookout in the San Bernardino National Forest. Unused photo card. (Gray & Son Photo.)

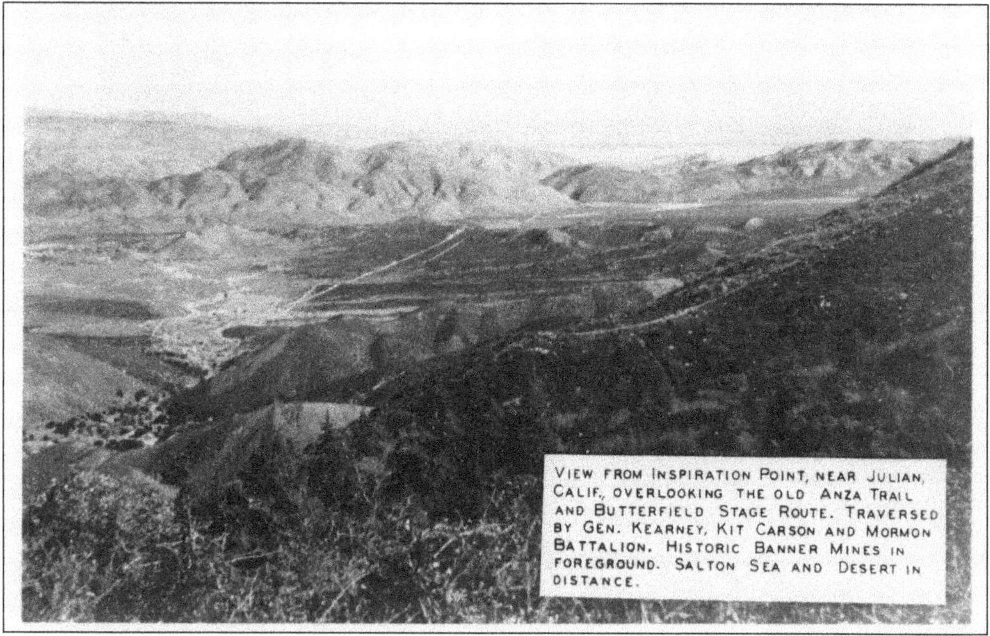

SALTON SEA AND DESERT IN DISTANCE DATED JANUARY 16, 1944. "View from Inspiration Point, near Julian, Calif., overlooking the Old Anza Trail and Butterfield Stage Route. Traversed by Gen. [Stephen W.] Kearny, Kit Carson and Mormon Battalion. Historic Banner Mines in foreground. Salton Sea and desert in distance. Unused photo card.

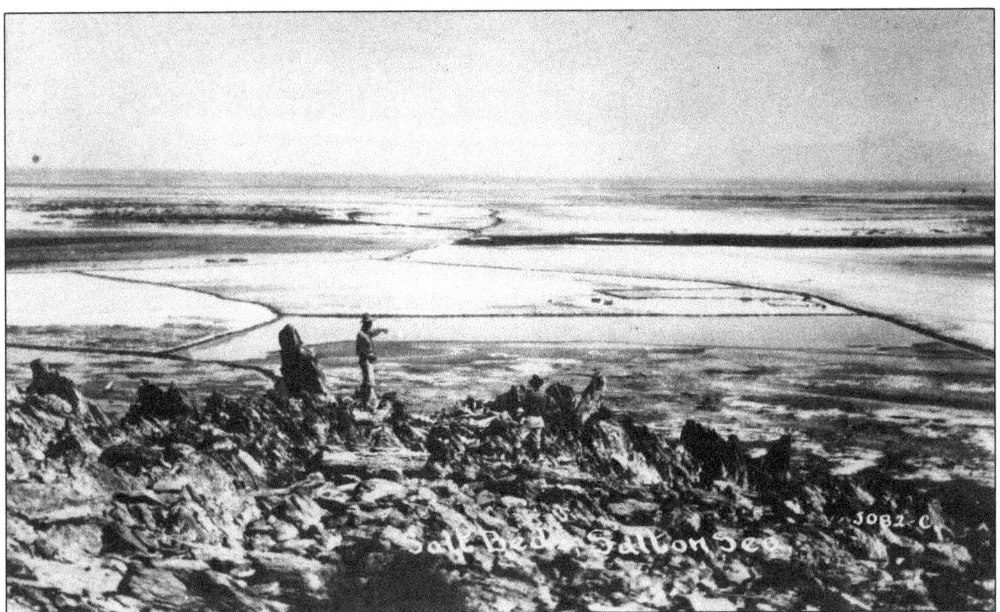

Salt Beds, Salton Sea. The New Liverpool Salt Company began operations in 1884. The vast salt deposits contained over 1,000 acres of pure rock salt. Cahuilla Indians provided the labor force and were capable of harvesting 700 tons per day. The salt beds seemed unending. As soon as one crop was worked, a new deposit would flow in from nearby saline springs. When the flow of the Colorado River moved north through the Salton Sink in 1905, the plant was soon covered by the newly formed Salton Sea. Unused photo card. (5082-C.)

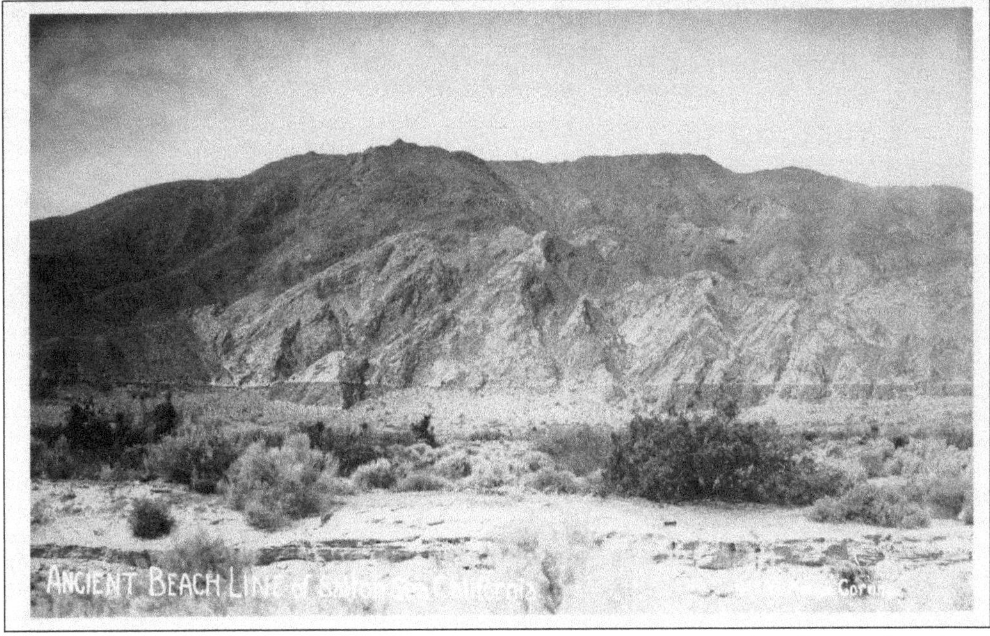

Ancient Beach Line of Salton Sea, California. Wave-cut shorelines and sand and gravel bars are found near Niland, left from the ancient beaches and strand lines. In most places, the beach line has a sand ridge a few feet high covered with an abundance of well-preserved freshwater shells. Mailed February 23, 1950, to a town in Kentucky.

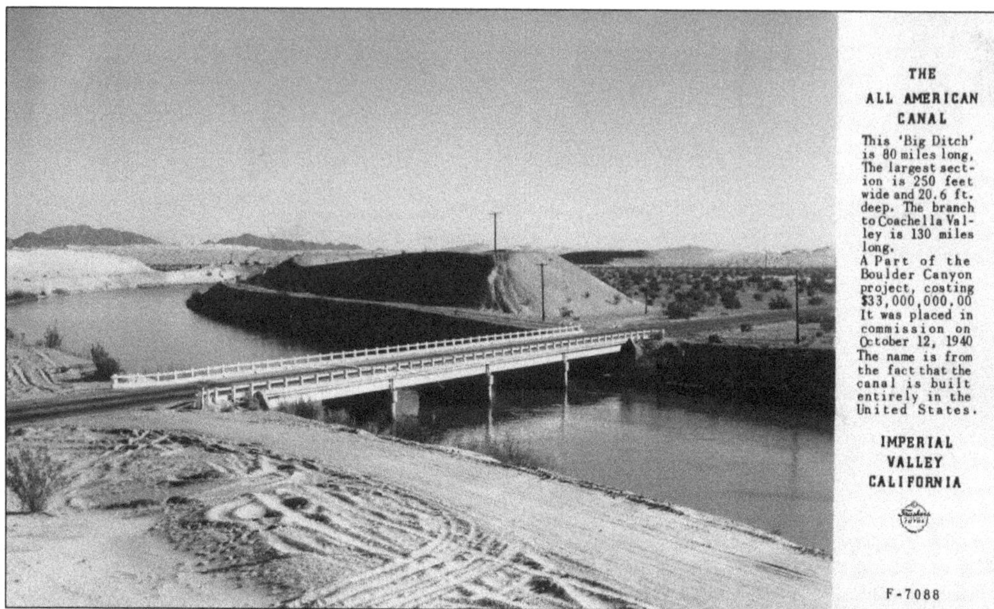

IMPERIAL VALLEY CALIFORNIA. The All-American Canal is 80 miles long. The largest section is 250 feet wide and 20.6 feet deep. The branch to Coachella Valley is 140 miles long. The canal was part of the Boulder Canyon Project, cost $33 million, and was placed in commission on October 12, 1940. The name was chosen because the canal was built entirely in the United States. The canal is an aqueduct that conveys water from the Colorado River to the Imperial Valley in California. It is the valley's only water source, and it replaced the Alamo Canal, which was located primarily in Mexico. Mailed February 6, 1949, to Phoenix, Arizona. (Frasher Photo Card F-7088.)

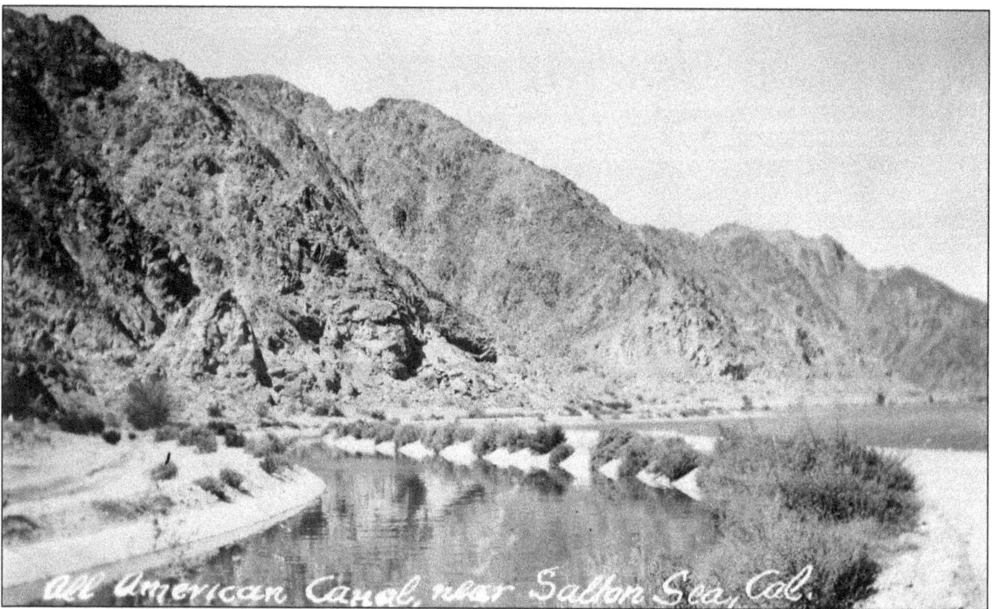

ALL AMERICAN CANAL, SALTON SEA, CAL. The All-American Canal provides drinking water for nine cities and irrigates over 500,000 acres. It is the largest irrigation canal in the world, carrying up to 26,155 cubic feet per second. Unused photo card. (740.6 m3).

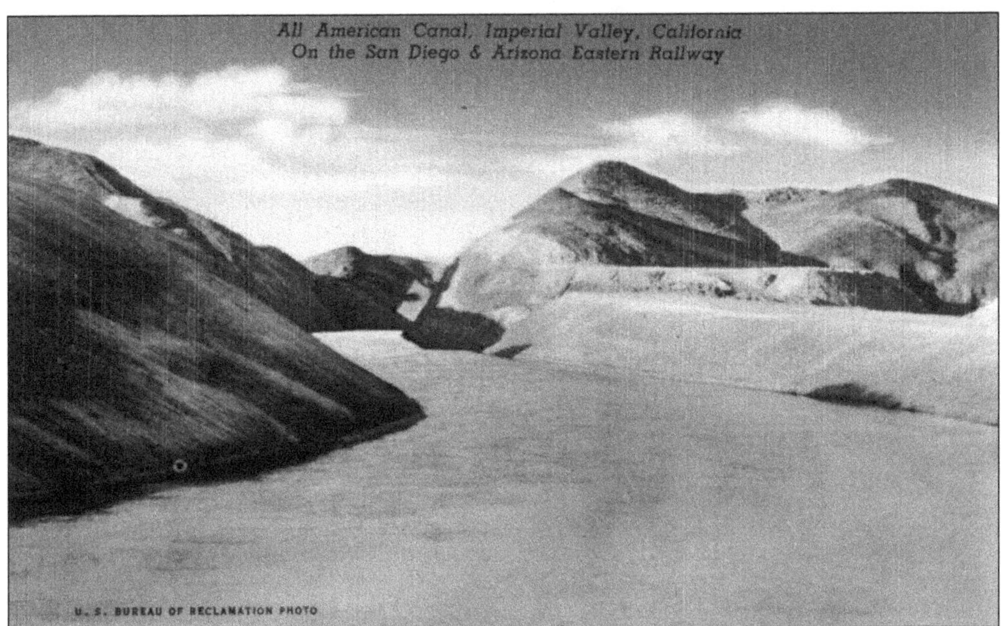

All American Canal, Imperial Valley, California. On the San Diego and Eastern Arizona Railway; U.S. Bureau of Reclamation Photograph. "The All American Canal is the largest and most outstanding irrigation enterprise in the Western Hemisphere. Water from Boulder Dam and the Colorado River passes through the main canal, 80 miles long, and branch canals, 130 miles, to irrigate over one million acres in the Imperial Valley." Unused photo card. (Genuine Curteich – Chicago, C.T. Art Colortone, Post Card Reg. US Pat. Off.)

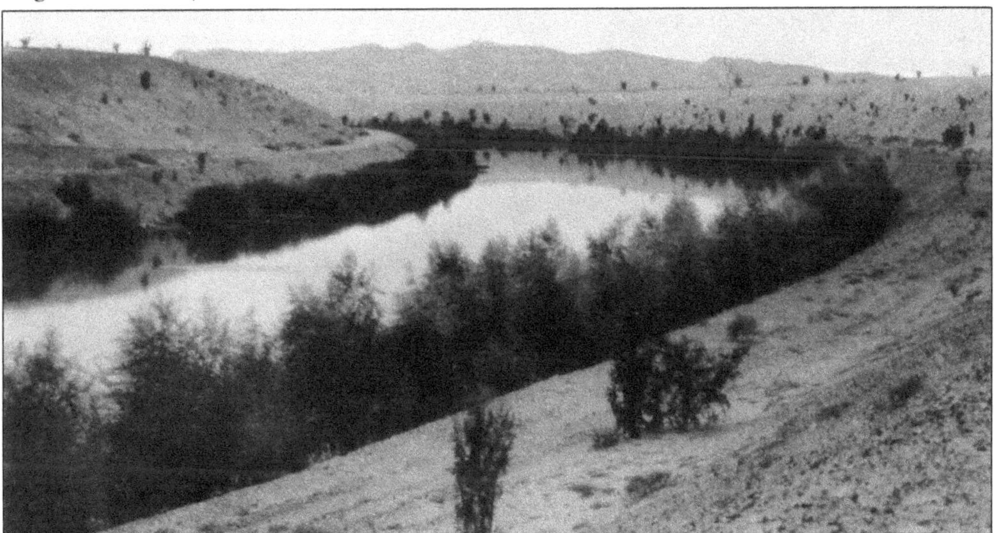

All-American Canal in the Southeastern Corner of California, Picks up Water at the Imperial Dam on the Colorado River and Delivers It to Imperial and Coachella Valley Ranchers. "Completion of the canal made possible the cultivation of 500,000 additional acres of land". With over 500 people drowning in the canal since 1997, it has been called the most dangerous body of water in the United States. (Union Oil Company's Natural Color Scenes of the West.)

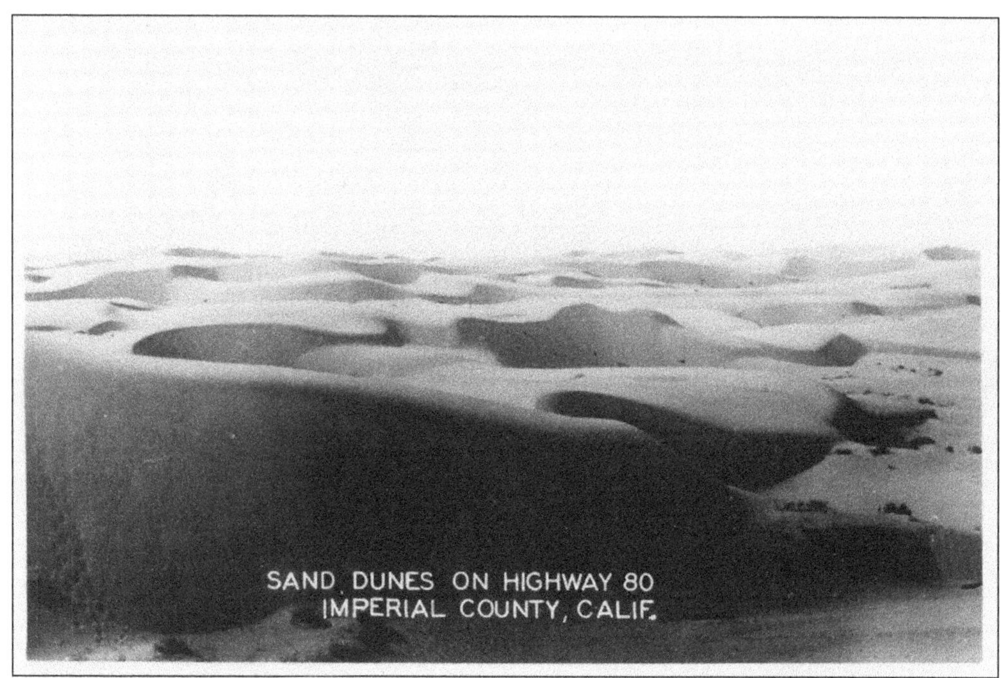

Sand Dunes on Highway 80, Imperial Valley, Calif. The Algodones Dunes, an 8-by-40 mile stretch of sand, is east of El Centro along Interstate 8. The dunes have no vegetation whatsoever. Unused photo card.

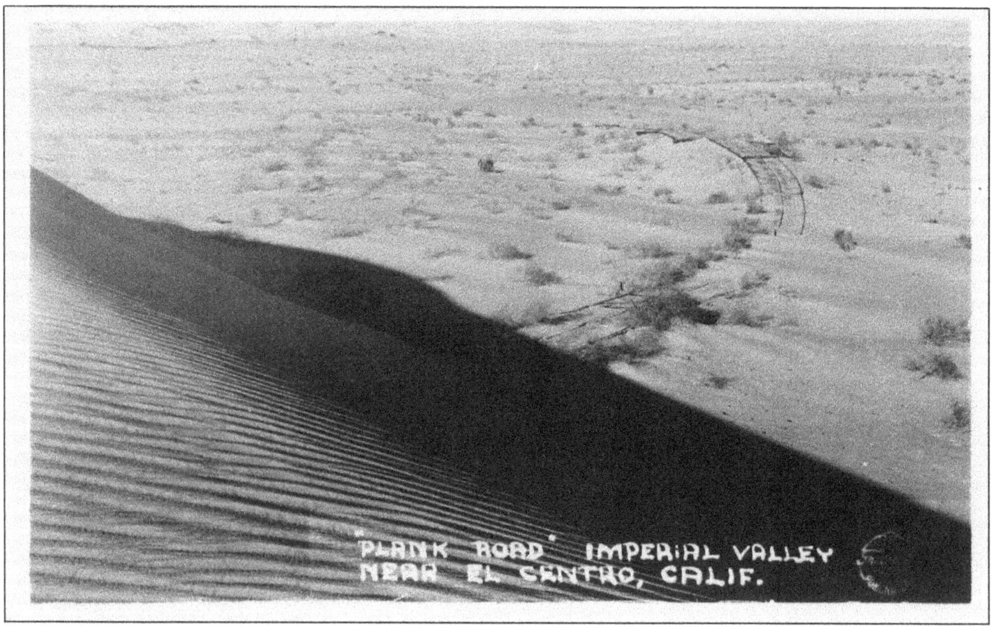

"Plank Road," Imperial Valley Near El Centro, Calif. The old Plank Road was built in 1914 as an east–west route over the Algodones Dunes. The plank road effectively connected the extreme lower section of Southern California to Arizona and provided the last link in a route between San Diego and Yuma. Unused photo card. (Frashers, Pomona, Calif.)

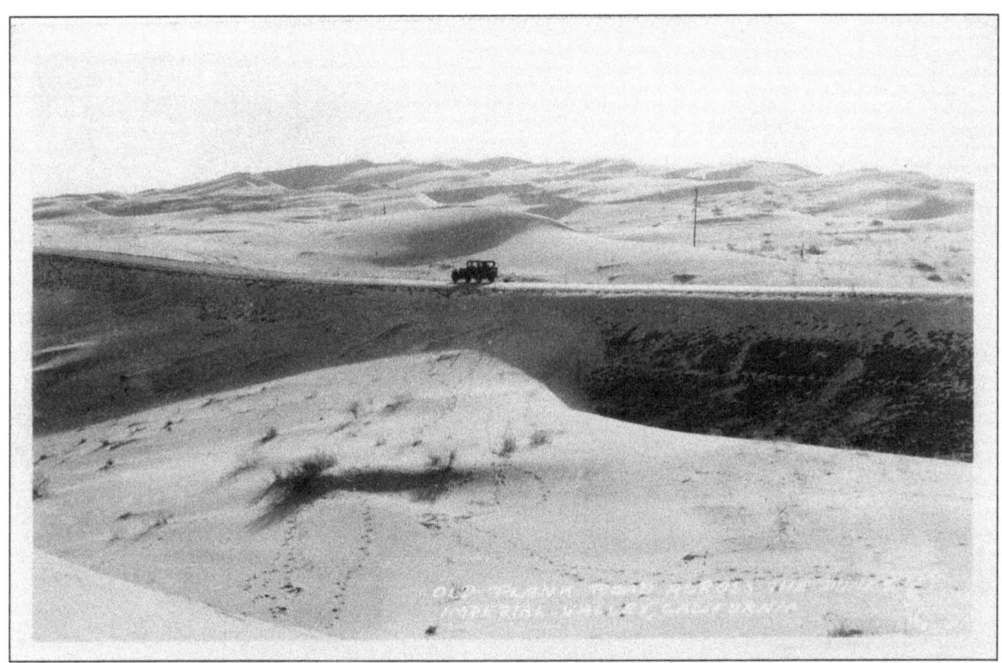

Old Plank Road Across the Dunes, Imperial Valley, California. A more sophisticated prefabricated plank road was commissioned in 1916. The sections were transported to the worksite by horse-drawn wagons and lowered in place using a crane. Unused photo card.

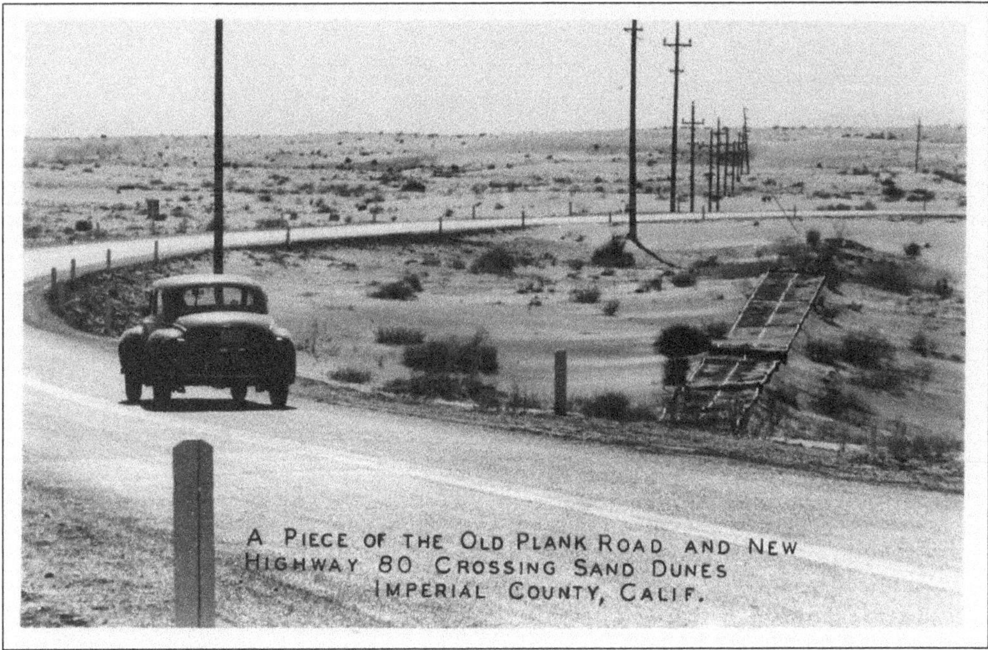

A Piece of the Old Plank Road and New Highway 80, Crossing Sand Dunes, Imperial Valley, Calif. Work crews struggled to keep the road open in the harsh desert environment. The road was only wide enough for one vehicle, and the ride was extremely rough. Unused photo card.

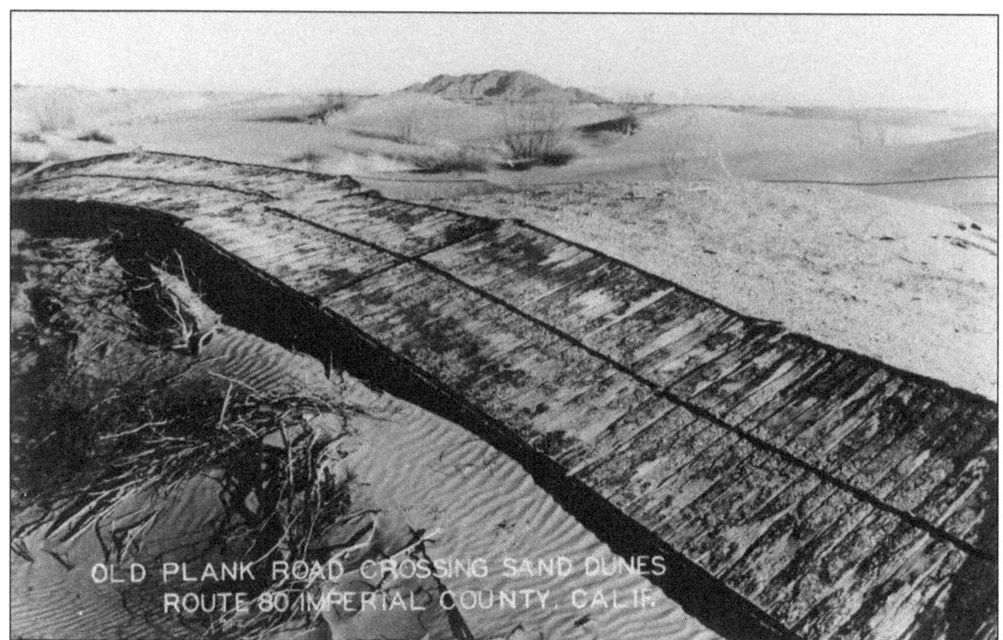

OLD PLANK ROAD CROSSING SAND DUNES ROUTE 80 IMPERIAL VALLEY, CALIF. A new asphalt and concrete road was constructed on top of a built-up sand embankment. It replaced the old plank road on August 12, 1926. The same highway later became Route 80 and more recently, Interstate 8. Unused photo card.

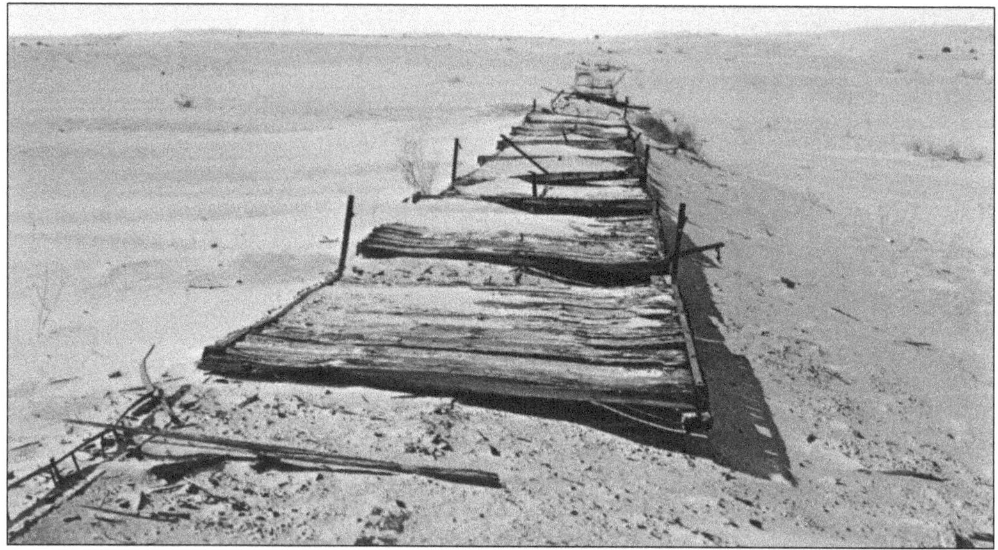

PLANK ROAD. "This road was built in 1914 and followed the contours of the shifting sand hills. It was over these hills that De Anza—the first white man to have crossed the Colorado Desert—made his way in 1774. This was the trail that the Butterfield Stage used along with explorers, trappers, traders, and others going to California. Because of the hostility of the Yuma Indians, some of the travelers bypassed Yuma. Today a modern highway crosses the desert . . . M.P." Only fragments of the plank road remain, but they are protected under the jurisdiction of the Bureau of Land Management. Unused photo card. (© & Published by Royal Pictures, Colton, California; Photo-color by Merle Porter.)

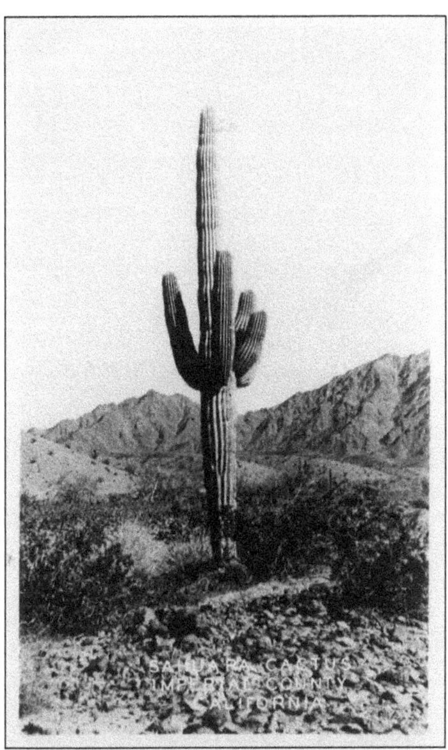

SAHUARA CACTUS, IMPERIAL COUNTY, CALIFORNIA. The Saguaro cactus grows only in the Sonoran Desert of southwestern Arizona and the Imperial Valley near the Colorado River. Mailed February 6, 1945, to Chicago, Illinois.

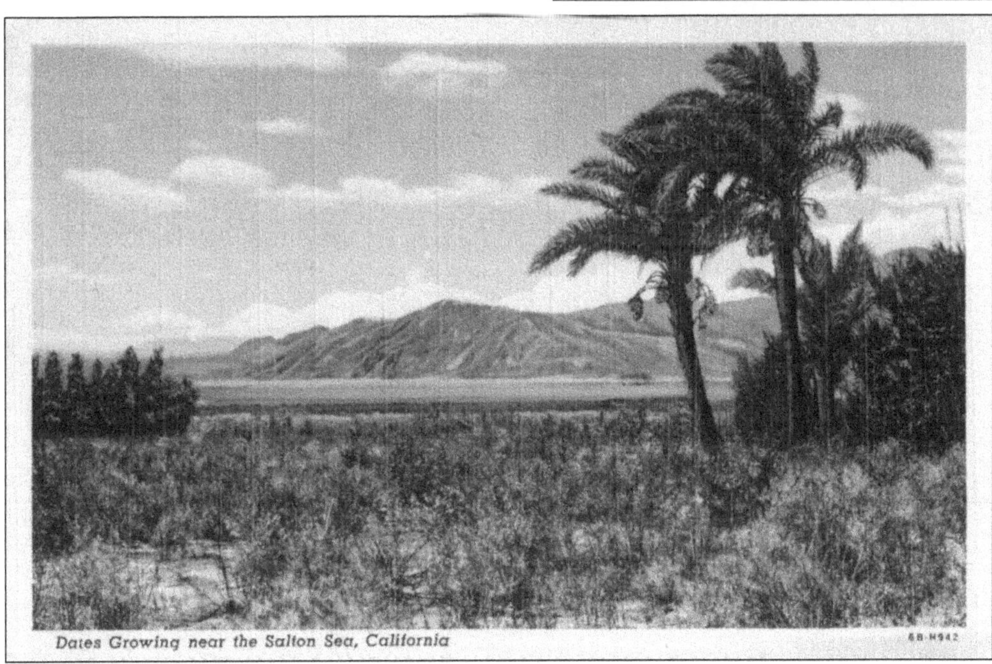

DATES GROWING NEAR THE SALTON SEA. In 1912, the American Date Company constructed the first date packing plant in the Coachella Valley. About 25,000 pounds of dates were produced in 1915 and 33 million pounds in 2005. There were 280 acres of dates under cultivation by 1920 and about 6,000 acres today. Mailed August 1958 to Terre Haute, Indiana. (Stephen H. Willard, Palm Springs, California.)

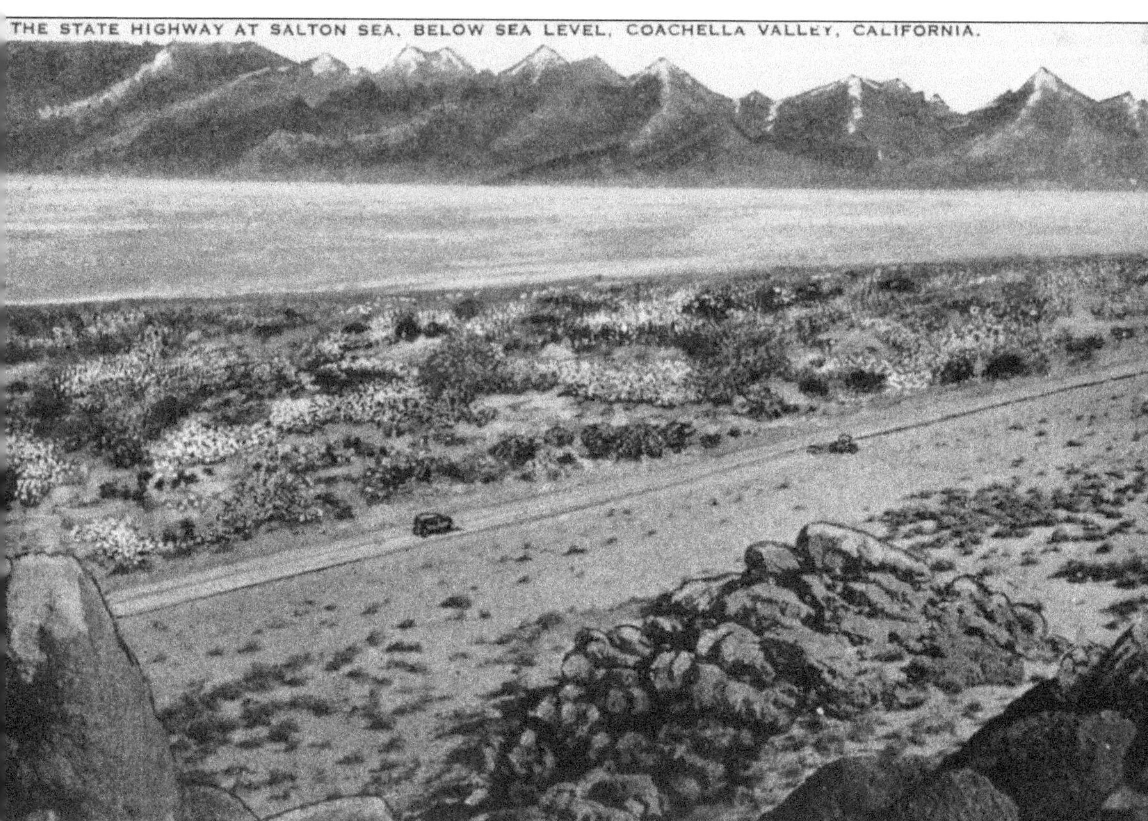

THE STATE HIGHWAY AT SALTON SEA, BELOW SEA LEVEL, COACHELLA VALLEY, CALIFORNIA. During the Salton Sea Boat Race of December 14, 1929, there were no graded roads down to the sea, so just getting to the water was an adventure. Mecca was the jumping off point, and Mecca farmers were called on with regularity to pull out stalled cars. Local residents also laid out the racing courses. State Highway 111 was first proposed in 1930. Unused. (Copyrighted by Desert Date Shop, Indio, California.)

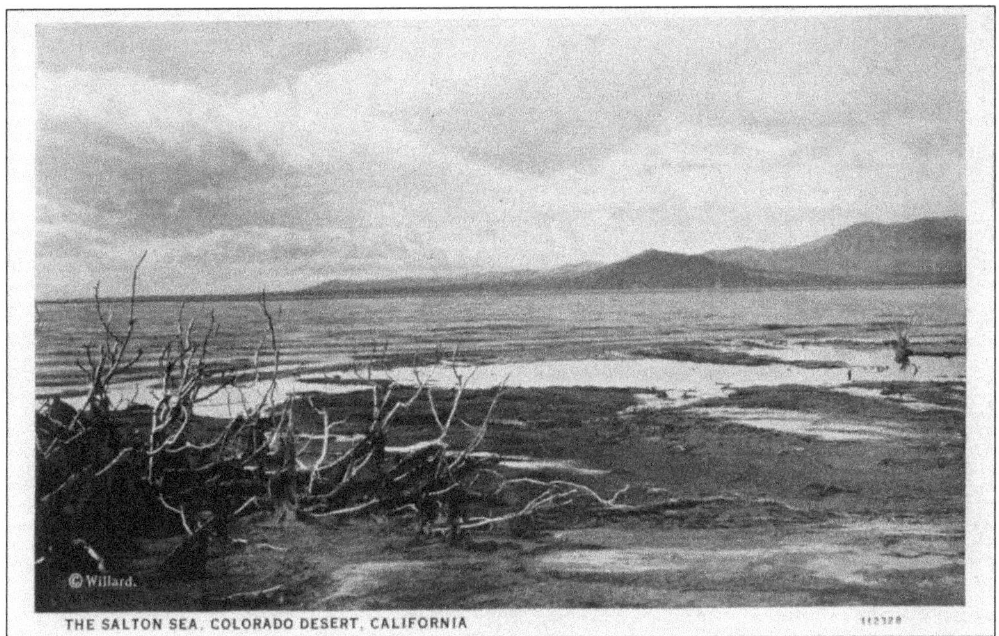

THE SALTON SEA, COLORADO DESERT, CALIFORNIA. This card was produced by Stephen Willard (1894–1965), who moved to Palm Springs, California, in 1920. He mastered a technique of transferring realistic tones to his photographs by tinting them with oils after meticulously developing the images. In 1947, he moved to the Owens Valley and made the eastern Sierra Nevada mountain range his subject matter. He died in 1965 at the age of 71. Unused. (© Willard – Published by Stephen H. Willard, Palm Springs, California.)

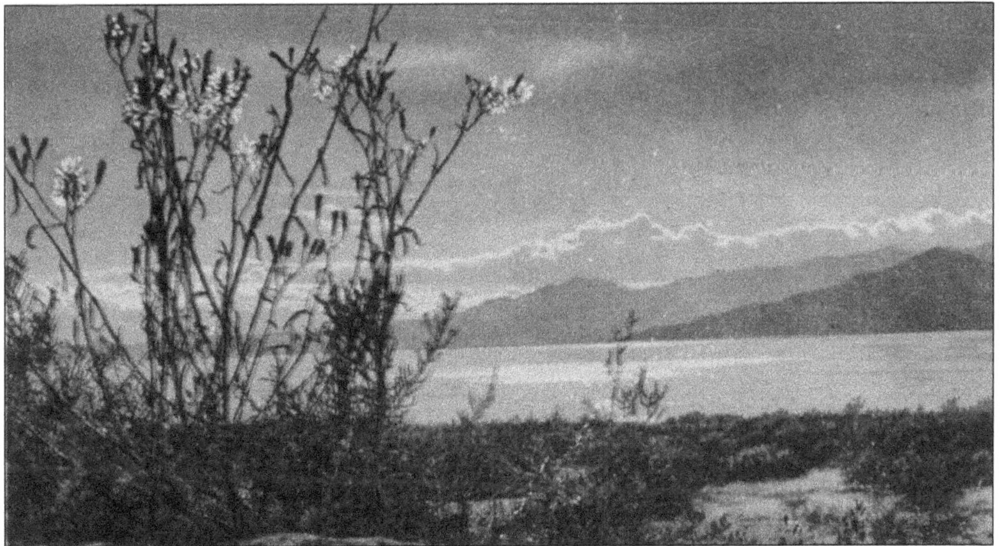

SALTON SEA, COACHELLA VALLEY, CALIFORNIA. The Sea History Museum is located in the renovated North Shore Beach and Yacht Club building. The structure was designed by noted architect Albert Frey and built by developers Ray Ryan and Trav Rogers in 1958. Although the yacht club was abandoned for decades, it was recently renovated with financial assistance from federal stimulus funding and help from the East Valley Historical Society. Mailed January 16, 1948, to Wethersfield, Connecticut. (Rubidoux Printing Co., Riverside, California.)

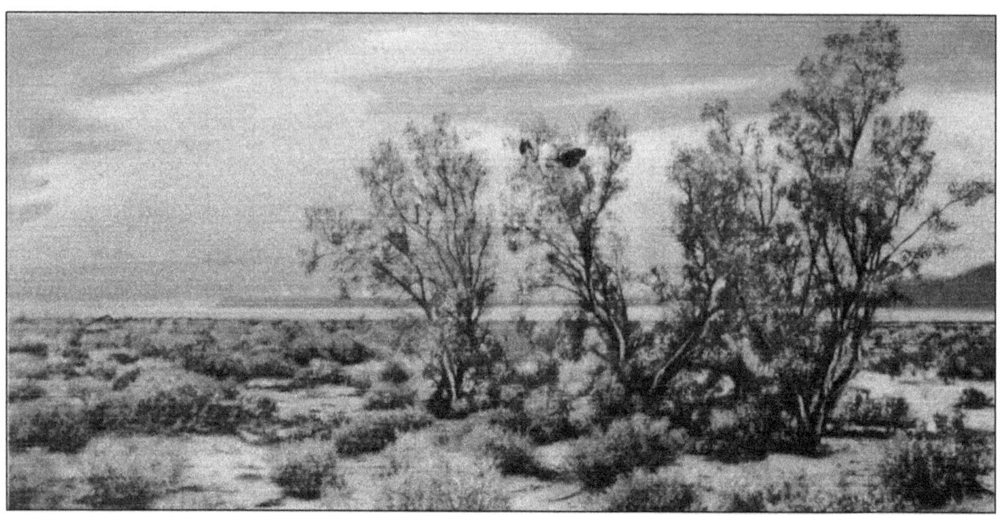

Smoke Trees on the Desert, California, Salton Sea, 260 Feet Below Sea Level in the Distance. The smoke tree, or *Psorothamnus spinosus*, is indigenous to the Sonoran Desert of southern Nevada, western Arizona, northwestern Mexico and southeastern California. It requires a relatively abundant supply of water. These trees are typically located along sandy or gravelly flats, arroyos, or washes. Creosote bushes are often found nearby, in elevations below sea level to 1,500 feet. Mailed August 11, 1943, to Johnson City, New York. (Webster Publishing & Novelty Co., Los Angeles, Calif.)

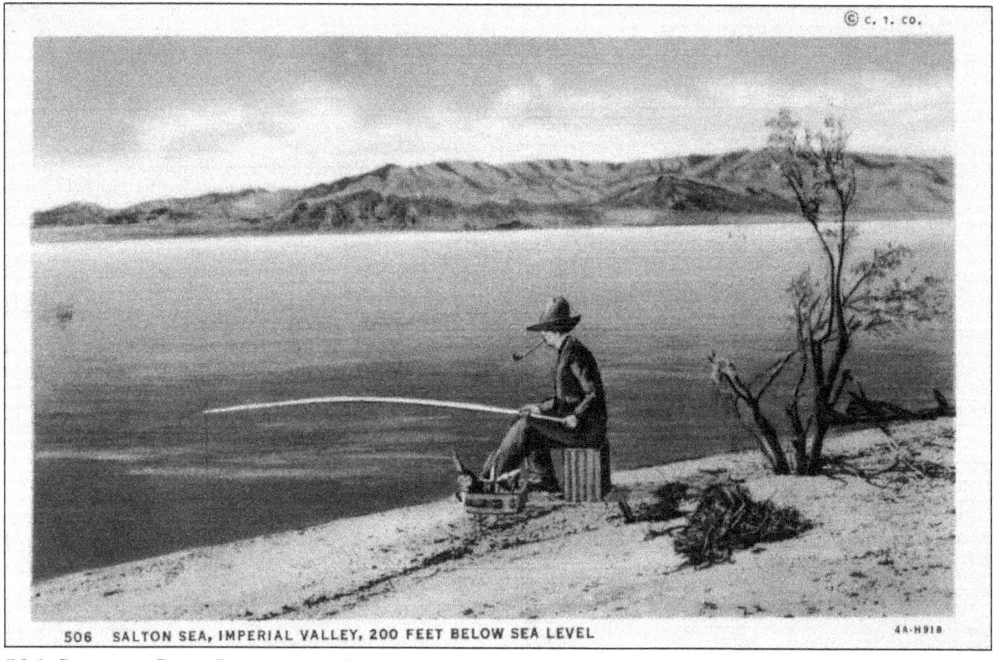

506 Salton Sea, Imperial Valley, 200 Feet Below Sea Level. From the 1920s to the 1940s, a commercial mullet fishery existed in the Salton Sea. During the 1950s, several species of saltwater game fish were introduced, including halibut, grunion, gulf croaker, sargo and corvina. Today, tilapia is the most abundant fish in the lake. Unused. (Harry Herz, 1565 Ebers St., San Diego, Calif.; "C.T. Colortone." Made only by Curt Teich & Co., Inc., Chicago, U.S.A.)

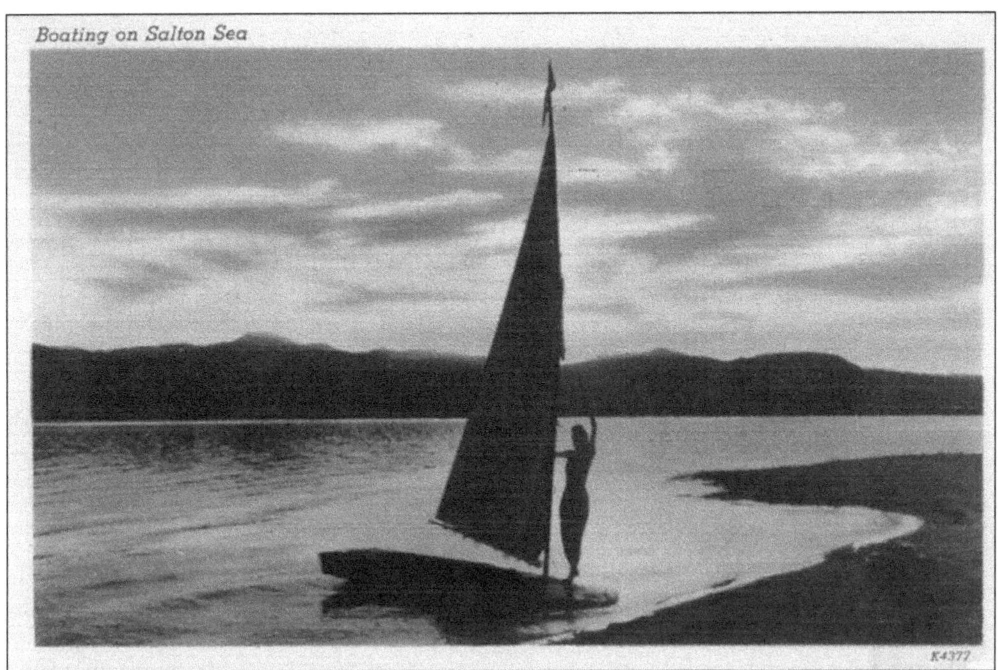

Boating on the Salton Sea / Salton Sea, near Indio, Calif. "252 feet below Sea Level. This body of water was formed in the early part of the century by an overflow of the Colorado River. You can Boat, Swim or Fish here." Mailed August 5, 1957 to Minneapolis, Minnesota. (A "Colourpicture" Publication, Boston 15, Mass. L.A. Office 2143 So. Alsace Ave. L.A.)

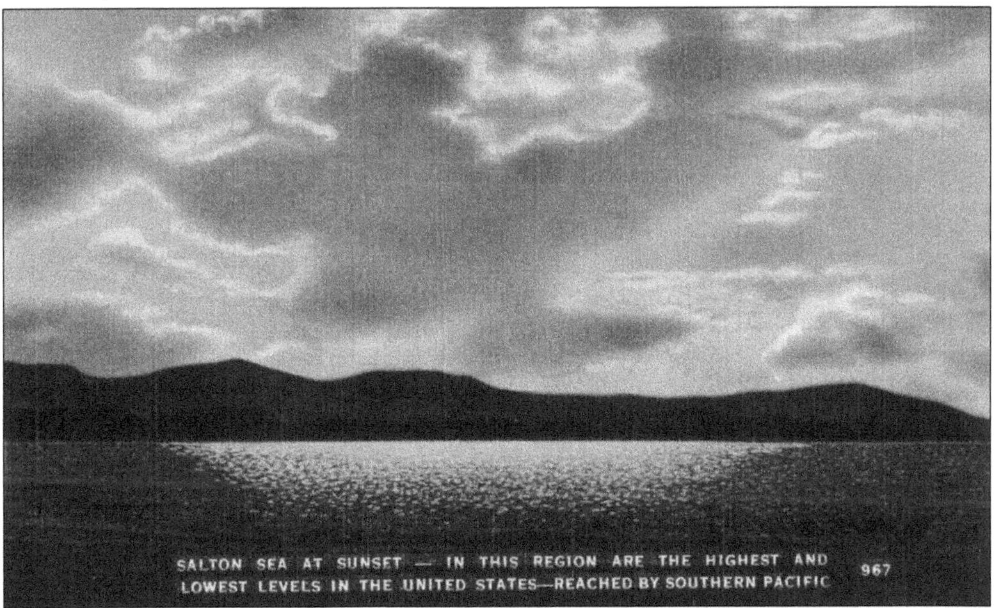

Salton Sea at Sunset—In This Region Are the Highest and Lowest Levels in the United States, Reached by the Southern Pacific 967; with Bag of Salt from Salton Sea, Calif. This postcard is interesting because it came attached with a small bag of "Salt from Salton Sea, Calif." Unused. (Deseret Book Company, Salt Lake City, Utah.)

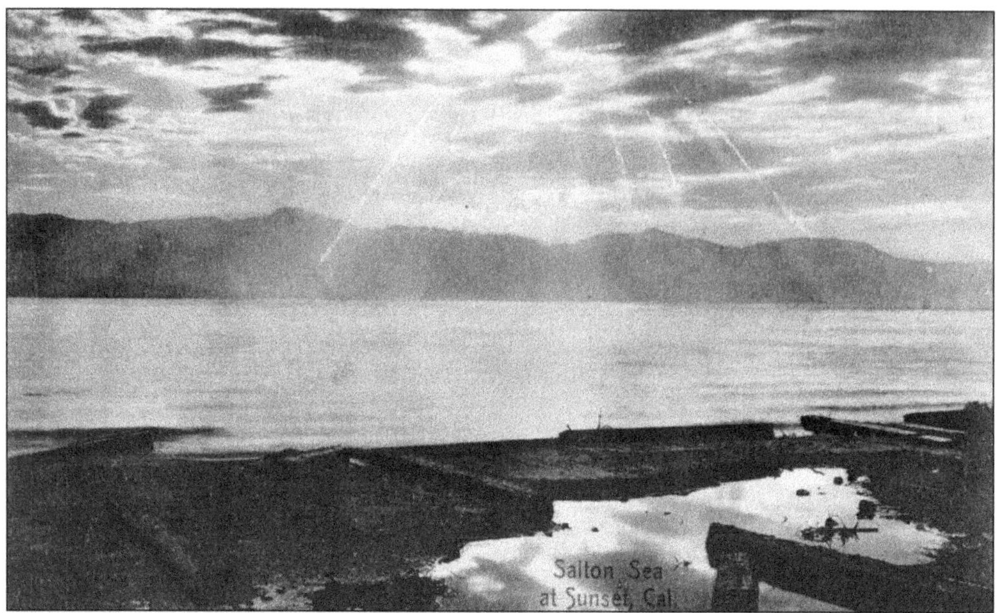

SALTON SEA, SALTON SEA AT SUNSET. Walter Lubkin was a photographer for the United States Reclamation Service. On glass negatives, he recorded some of the most compelling photographs of the American Southwest at the turn of the century. Lubkin took thousands of photographs documenting the reclamation service's irrigation projects in the West. The Lubkin Company produced photographs and postcards for the popular marketplace. Unused. (M. Rieder, Publ., Los Angeles, Cal., 24184; made in Germany; handcolored work; The Lubkin Co., Mesa, Arizona.)

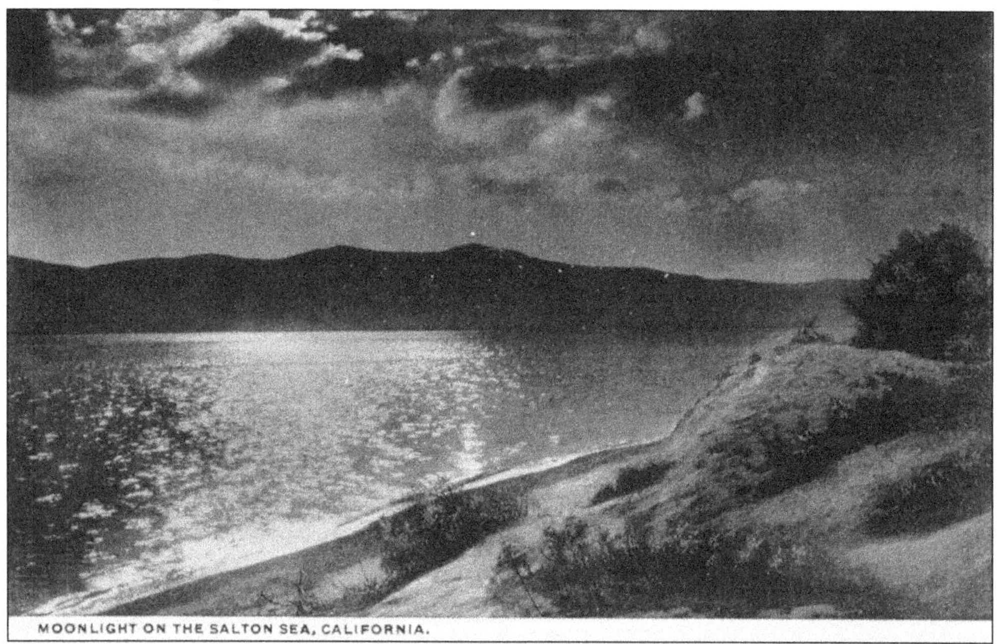

MOONLIGHT ON THE SALTON SEA, CALIFORNIA; UNUSED. The stark contrast of the desert landscape creates an incredible palette of colors with the water against the evening skies. (Published by NVC.)

Five

Glory Years of the Salton Sea

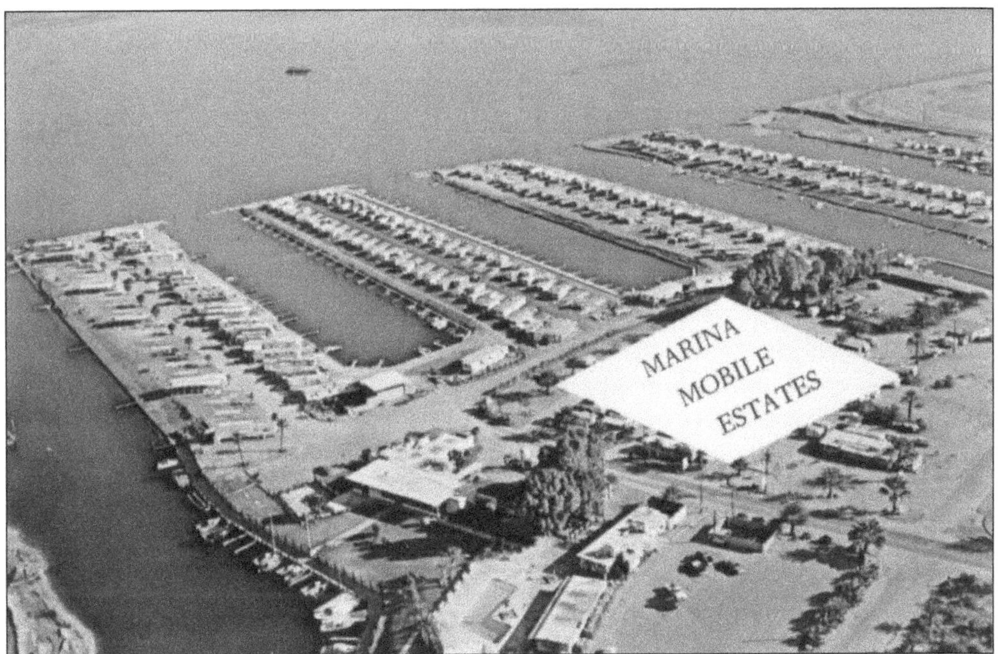

Marina Mobile Estates. "Rt. 2 – Box 444 – Thermal, Calif. / Desert Shore – Highway 86 – 25 Miles South of Indio / Recreation Center of the Salton Sea / The only park west of Florida where each mobile home has its own water frontage and dock space. / Ken & Judy Melson, Managers; Ph: EXpress 5-3511 and 5-3822 / Photo by Bert Lang." Unused photo card. (Pub. by Bert Lang, Sr., 2374 Chuckanut Lane, Bellingham, Wash.; made by Dexter Press, Inc. West Nyack, New York, 7731-C.)

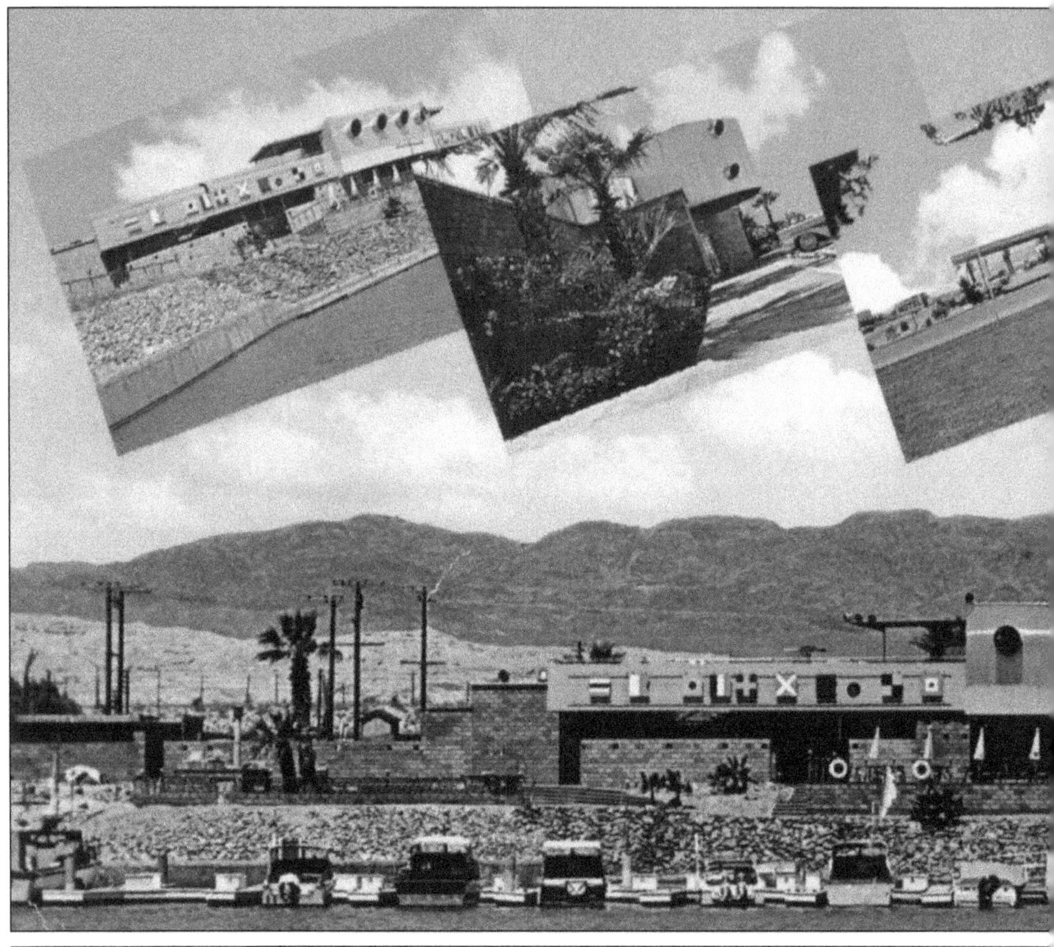

North Shore Beach

"The Glamour Capital of Salton Sea"

Co-Developers, Ray Ryan and Don Eastvold

POST

$2,000,000 ALREADY INVESTED IN . . .

NORTH SHORE YACHT CLUB, a Marine Clubhouse featuring excellent Restaurant, Cocktail Lounge and Entertainment.

NORTH SHORE LODGE MOTEL, a 50-unit air-conditioned motel overlooking the picturesque Salton Sea and the mysterious desert.

NORTH SHORE MARINA, a marina large enough to accommodate 400 boats and offering the finest of facilities including concrete launching ramp, hydraulic hoist, abundant boat slips with storage lockers, fresh water and electricity. Unexcelled docking and landing service. Water skiing supplies. Southern California's finest sport fishing year around. Riding stables near colorful bridle trails in the rugged Chocolate Mountains. Youth Village with playground equipment. Driving range and putting green. A paradise for flyers, North Shore's convenient landing strip is spacious enough to take care of any private or chartered plane with ample tie-down facilities and gas service. Conventions welcome up to 300 people.

Income, residential and business property available with fresh water and miles of paved roads. All of this in a complete . . .

ALL-YEAR MARINE COMMUNITY

LIVE — PROFIT — HAVE FUN!!

NORTH SHORE ESTATES on the SALTON SEA

LOS ANGELES, Pasadena, San Bernardino, Redlands, Beaumont, Pomona, Riverside, Perris, Palm Springs, Hemet, INDIO, Santa Ana, Long Beach, Newport, San Clemente, Ramona, Palm Desert, Anza, Aguanga, Temecula, Oceanside, PACIFIC OCEAN, Julian, Brawley, San Diego, El Centro, MEXICO, Mexicali

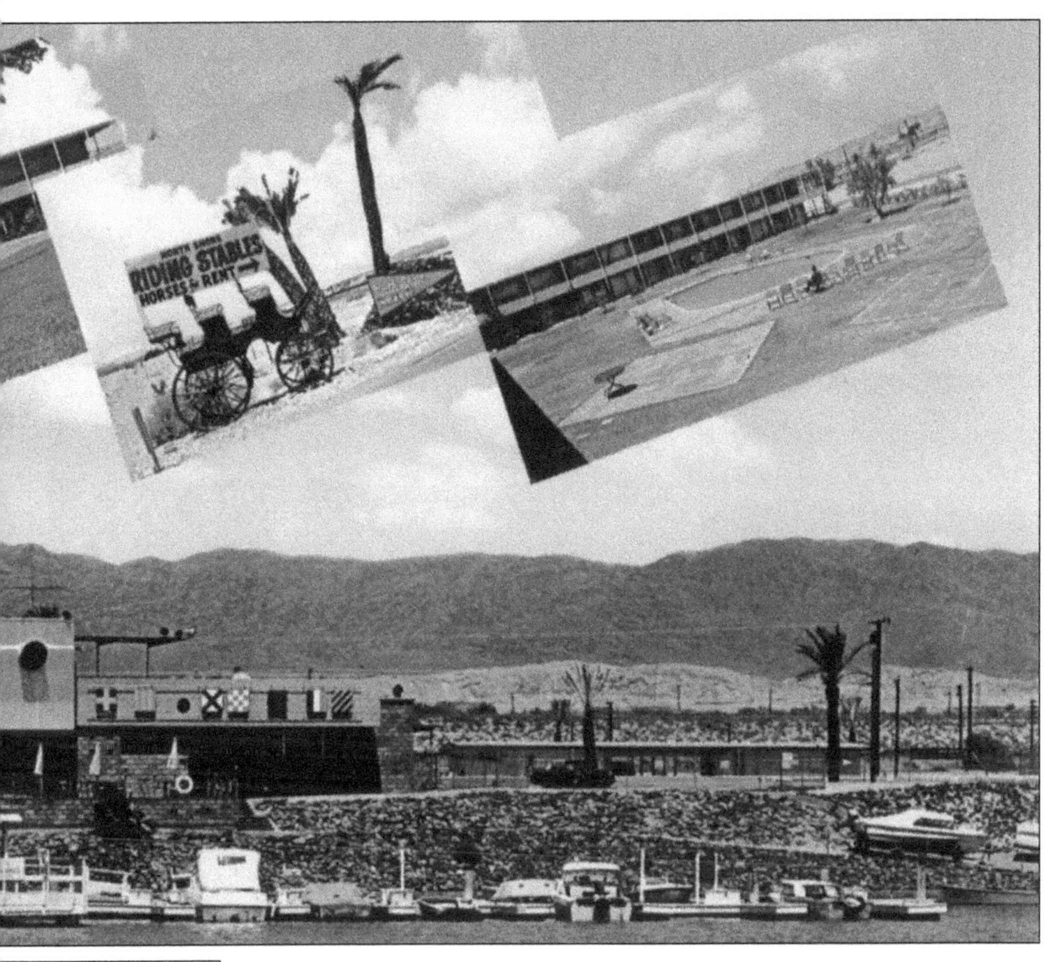

Mid-Century Design, New Age Glamour, and the Excitement of the Salton Sea. In 1958, millionaire oilman Ray Ryan and Trav Rogers bought the land that is now the town of North Shore. In 1960, they began construction on the North Shore Motel and North Shore Beach and Yacht Club. The resort opened in 1962 at a cost of $2 million. This paradise was promoted as one of the largest marinas in Southern California. The North Shore Beach and Yacht Club was Very Popular. The Beach Boys visited, and Jerry Lewis and the Marx Brothers had boats at the yacht club. In 1981, North Shore suffered from severe flooding that destroyed the jetty at the yacht club, making it impossible for boats to dock. The clubhouse was closed and never reopened.

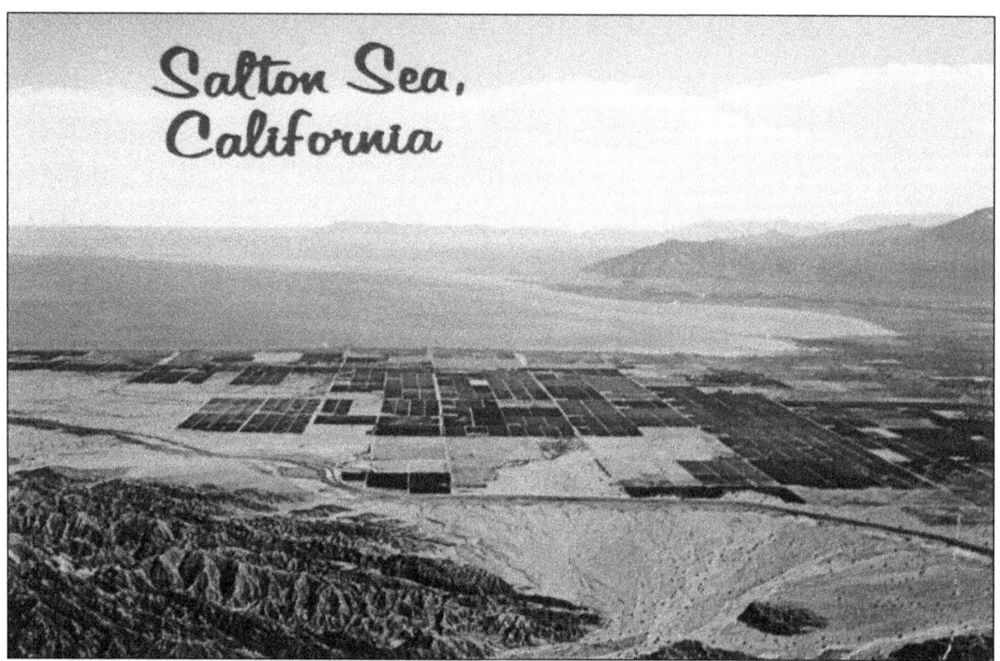

SALTON SEA, CALIFORNIA. "Just southeast of Indio, in the heart of the Coachella Valley, this 'Beach in the Desert' offers fishing, water skiing, camping, trailer facilities, and yacht clubs 54 miles from Palm Springs via Highway 111. Aerial photo by Bob Petley." Unused photo card. (Distributed by Petley Studios, 4051 E. Van Buren, Phoenix, Arizona.)

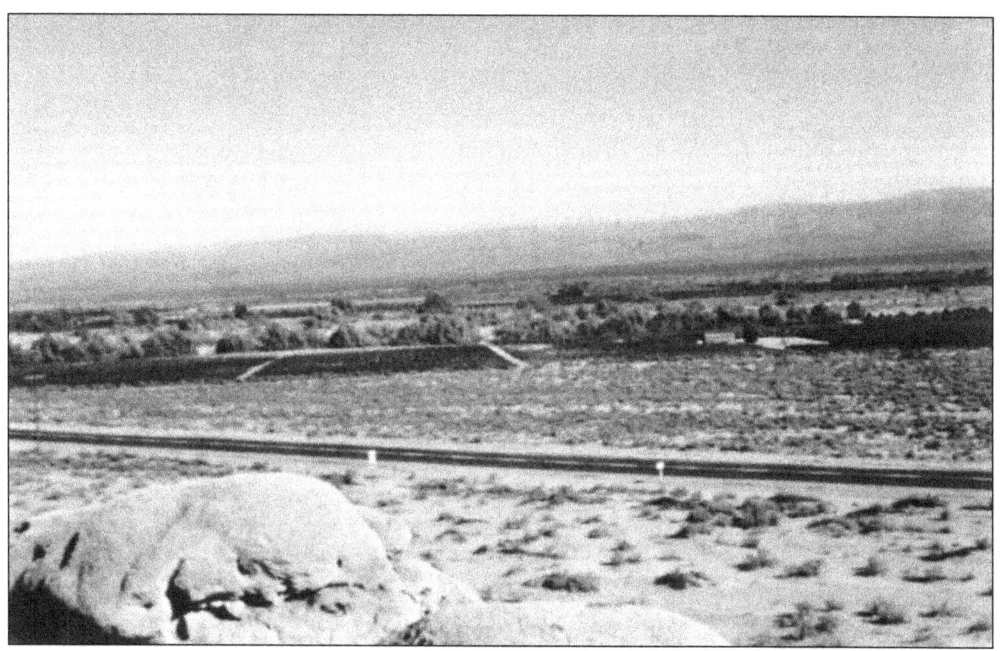

SALTON SEA, CALIFORNIA. "As viewed over the sand flats from the highway, 244 feet below sea level, this is the lowest point in the United States." Unused photo card. (Frye & Smith Ltd. San Diego California; 5344.)

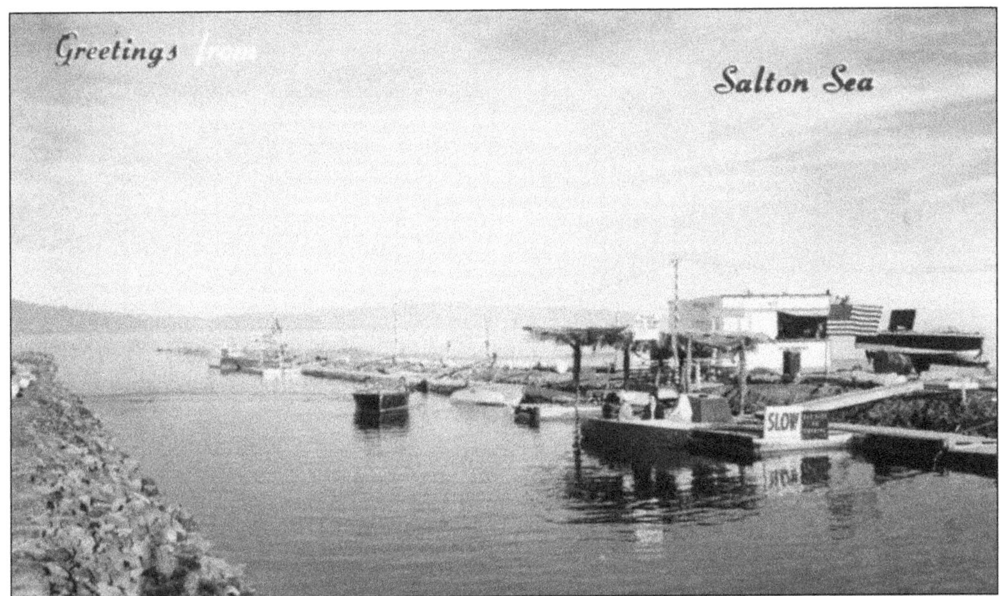

Greetings from Salton Sea; Salton Sea, California. This inland sea far below sea level was formed in 1907 when the Colorado River jumped its banks and threatened to wipe out the entire Imperial Valley. A heroic and million dollar battle eventually saved an inland empire, but the Salton Sea lived on. Color photo by David M. Mills. Unused photo card. (Copyright Ferris H. Scott, Santa Ana, Calif.; FS-135 and S4544-1; Western Resort Publications, 1320 N. Broadway, Santa Ana, Calif.)

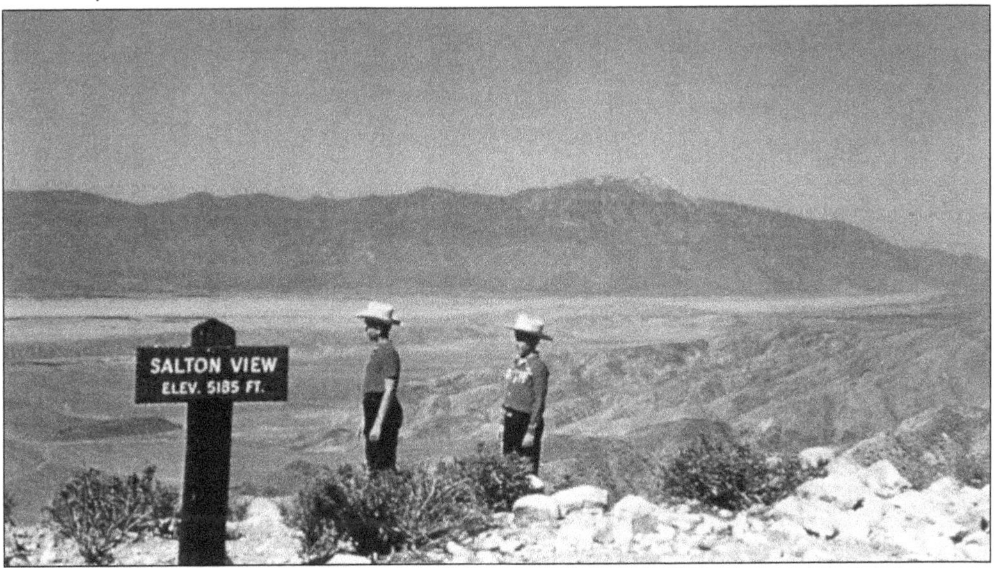

Salton View / Joshua Tree National Monument. "The outstanding scenic point in the Monument where from an elevation of 5,185 feet one obtains an unforgettable panorama of 'snow capped' San Jacinto (El. 10,837 feet), the 'date gardens' of Coachella Valley and the Salton Sea some thirty miles distance. On a clear day one can see Signal Mountain in old Mexico, over 95 miles away and the famous San Andreas fault extending almost north and south on the near side of Coachella Valley." Unused photo card. (Copyright Ferris H. Scott, Santa Ana, Calif. FS-380 & S-12645-1; Western Resort Publications, 1320 N. Broadway, Santa Ana, Calif.)

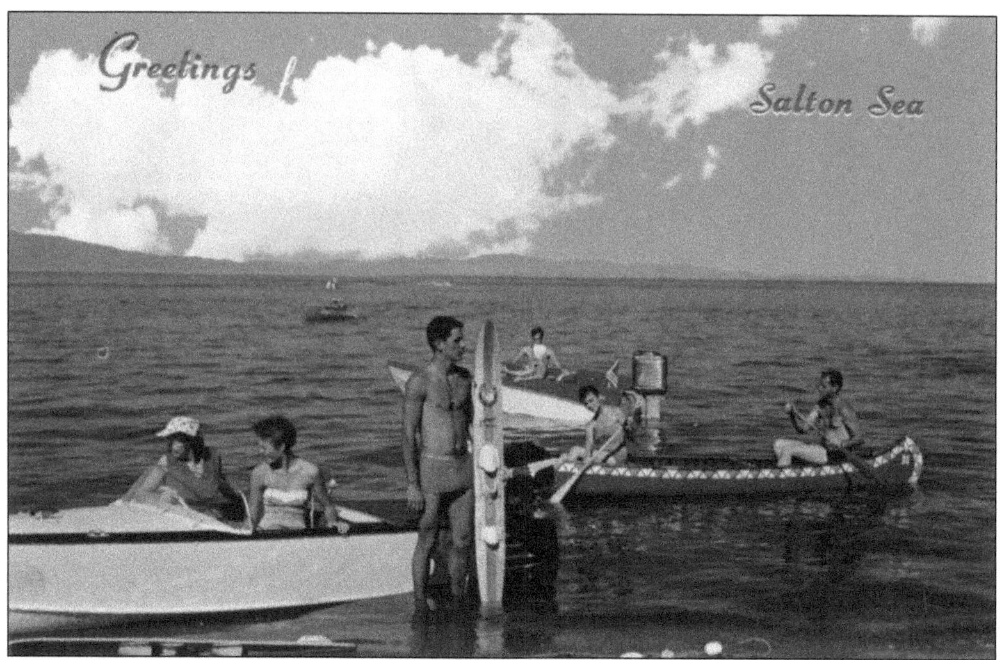

Greetings from Salton Sea. Jerry Lewis and the Marx Brothers are only a few of the many celebrities who, in its heyday, not only frequented the Salton Sea, but also kept their boats docked there. Color photo by David M. Mills. Unused photo card. (Copyright Ferris H. Scott, Santa Ana, Calif. FS-505 & S-18557L2; Western Resort Publications, 1320 N. Broadway, Santa Ana, Calif.)

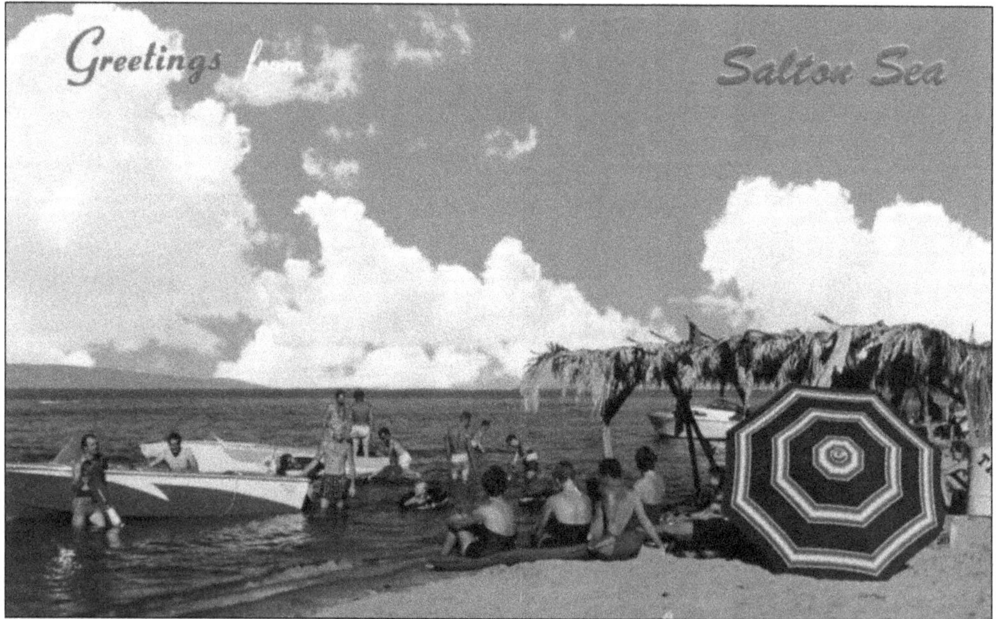

Greetings from Salton Sea. In the 1950s, the Salton Sea was to be Hollywood's more accessible Riviera and spring-breakers' hot spot for fun and sun. Color photo by David M. Mills. Unused photo card. (Copyright Ferris H. Scott, Santa Ana, Calif. FS-506 & S-18559L2; Western Resort Publications, 1320 N. Broadway, Santa Ana, Calif.)

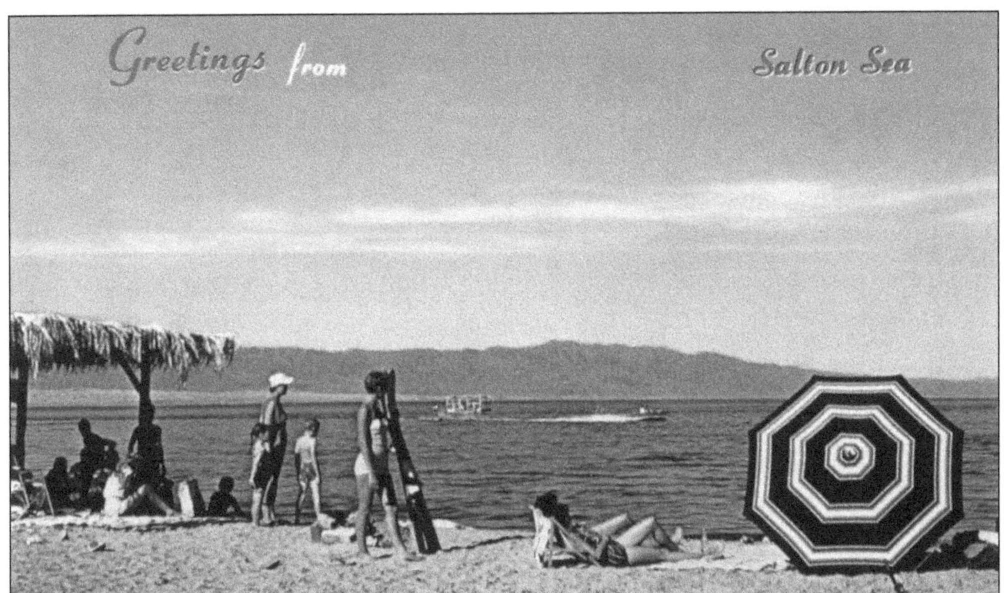

Greetings from Salton Sea. The Salton Sea became so immensely popular a vacation spot that during the mid-century it was a greater tourist draw than Yosemite National Park. Color photo by David M. Mills. Unused photo card. (Copyright Ferris H. Scott, Santa Ana, Calif. FS-507 & S-18560-2; Western Resort Publications, 1320 N. Broadway, Santa Ana, Calif.)

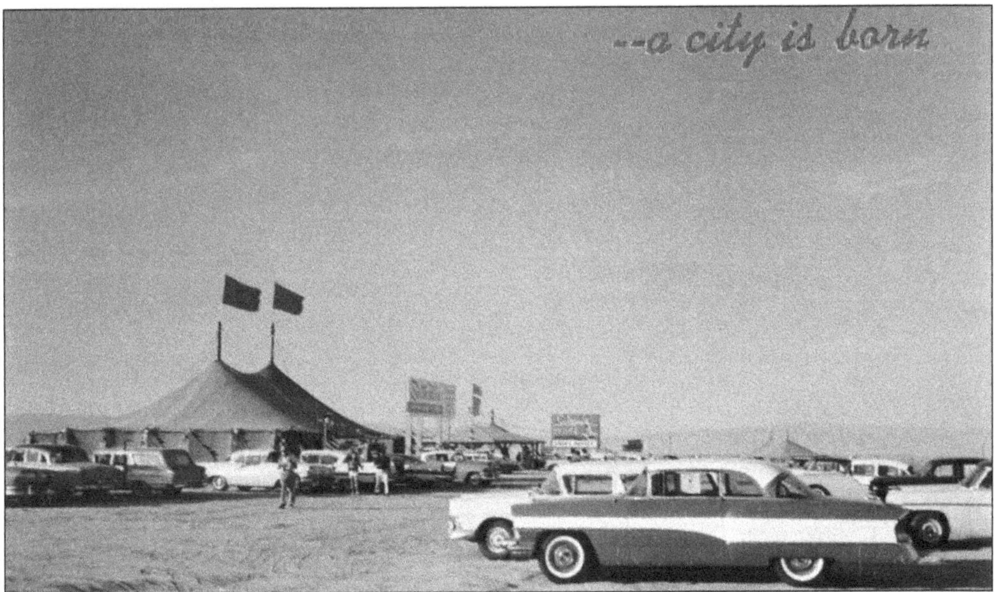

A City Is Born / Salton Sands, California. "This picture was taken in the spring of 1958 on the Salton Riviera's opening day—the day a city was born on the shores of the Salton Sea. A few months later these tents were replaced by permanent buildings and a beautiful modern city was on its way." During the 1950s, Salton City was built as a resort community along the Salton Sea. The town was developed primarily by M. Penn Phillips. He founded the M. Penn Phillips Company, as a subsidiary of Holly Development Corporation. This color photograph is by David M. Mills. Unused photo card. (Copyright Ferris H. Scott, Santa Ana, Calif. FS-508 & S18561; Western Resort Publications, 1320 N. Broadway, Santa Ana, Calif.)

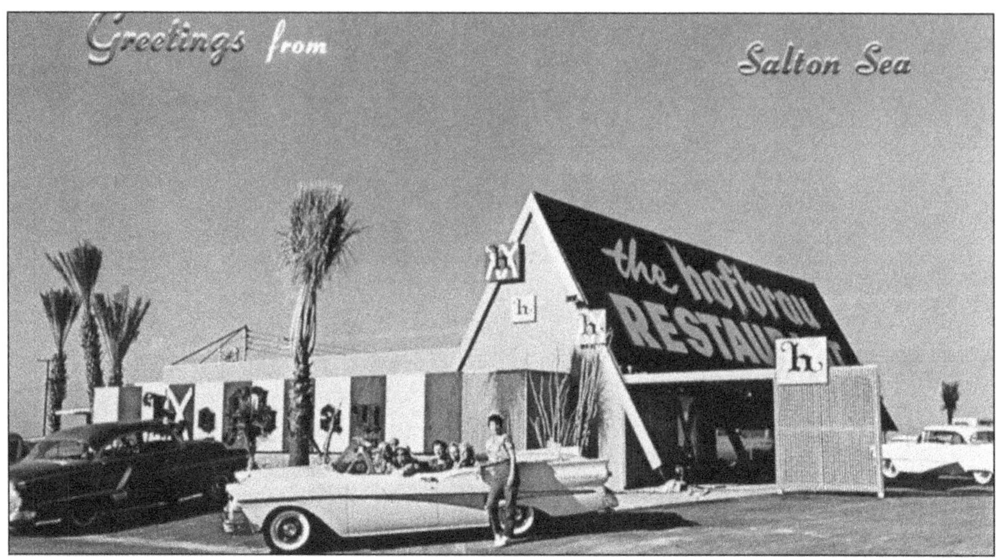

GREETINGS FROM SALTON SEA, THE HOFBRAU RESTAURANT, SALTON CITY, CALIFORNIA. "The most popular and picturesque restaurant on the shores of the Salton Sea, where the finest of foods and cocktails are served." Unused photo card. (Copyright Ferris H. Scott, Santa Ana, Calif. FS-597; Western Resort Publications, 1320 N. Broadway, Santa Ana, Calif.)

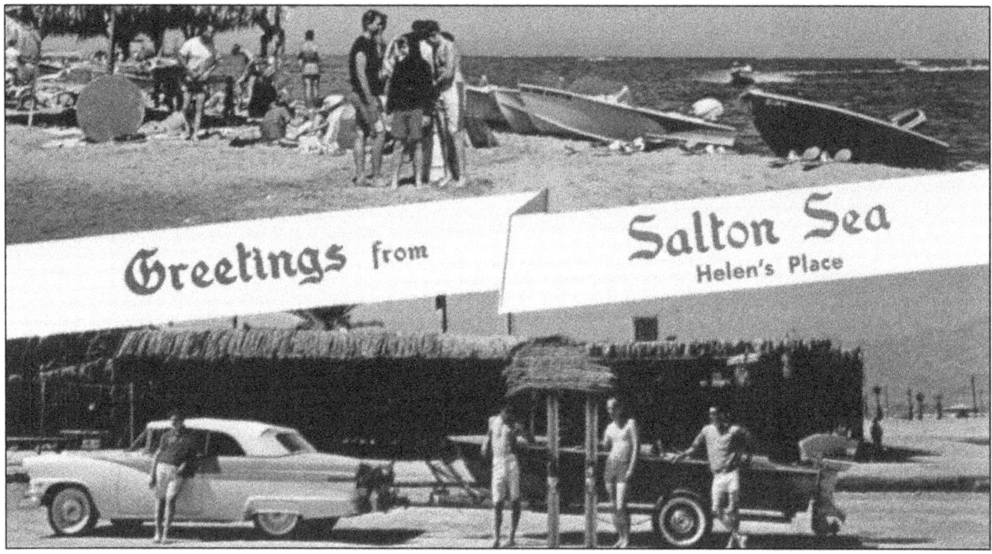

GREETINGS FROM SALTON SEA, HELEN'S PLACE. "This popular resort on the west shore of this desert sea provides all types of boating and swimming accommodations for the vacationing family. The Salton Sea boasts of the fastest water in the world because of its low elevation the greater water intensity provides a tremendous bite for the boat propellors [*sic*]." *Powerboat Magazine* in 2009 also credited the high salinity as a possible explanation. Others say the speed can be credited to lower barometric pressure and greater density. Helen Burns first came to the Salton Sea during the 1920s. During the 1950s, she developed her father's property from a small snack shop and souvenir stand into a restaurant, nightclub, and marina. Like many Salton Sea resorts, Helen's Beach House flooded several times and burned to the ground on June 28, 1979. Unused photo card. (Copyright Ferris H. Scott, Santa Ana, Calif. FS-635 & S129540L2; Western Resort Publications, 1320 N. Broadway, Santa Ana, Calif.)

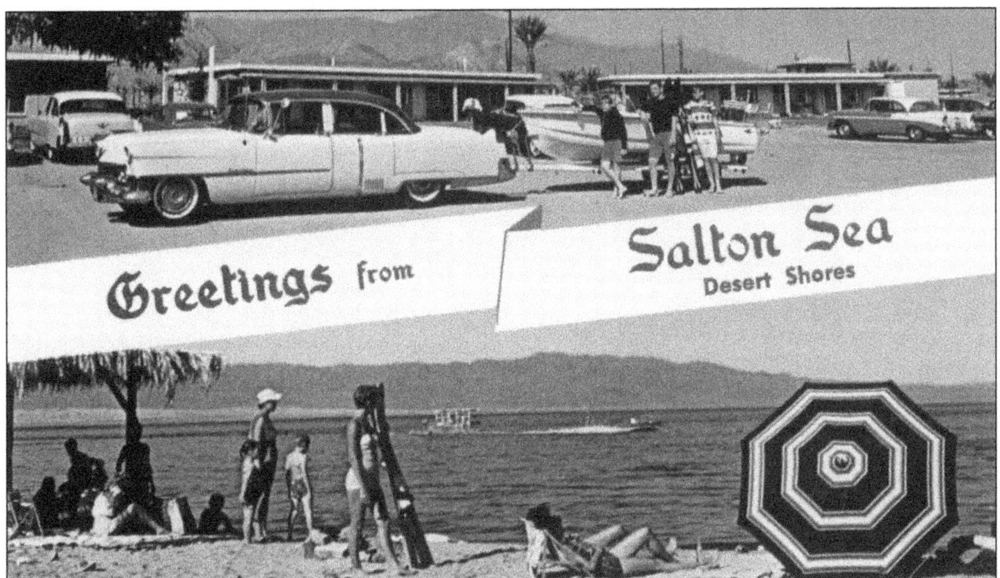

GREETINGS FROM SALTON SEA, DESERT SHORES. "This popular resort on the west shore of this sea in the desert provides all types of accommodations for the vacationing public. The boating facilities are the best and a modern motel, trailer part and cafe will add to your vacationing pleasure here on the shores of the world's fastest body of water." Unused photo card. (Copyright Ferris H. Scott, Santa Ana, Calif. FS-636 & S129539L2; Western Resort Publications, 1320 N. Broadway, Santa Ana, Calif.)

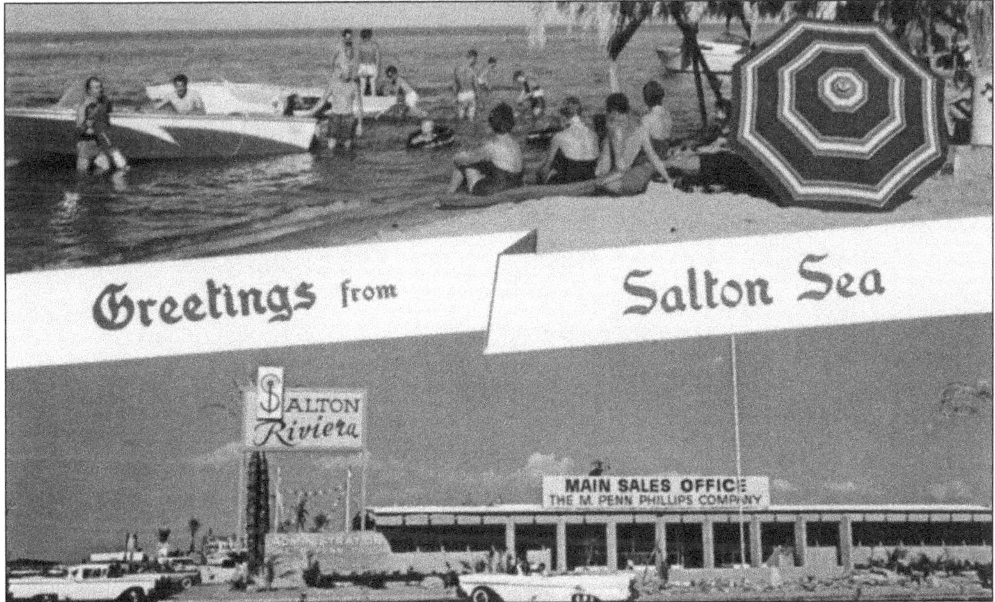

GREETINGS FROM SALTON SEA. "This famous all-year resort Community on the west shore of the Salton Sea is one of the fastest growing areas in the U.S.A. and represents investments that will exceed $20,000,000. Some 19,600 acres have been acquired and a master plan of development will transform it into America's No. 1 resort area on the shores of this fabulous inland sea." Unused photo card. (Copyright Ferris H. Scott, Santa Ana, Calif. FS-637 & S129541L2; Western Resort Publications, 1320 N. Broadway, Santa Ana, Calif.)

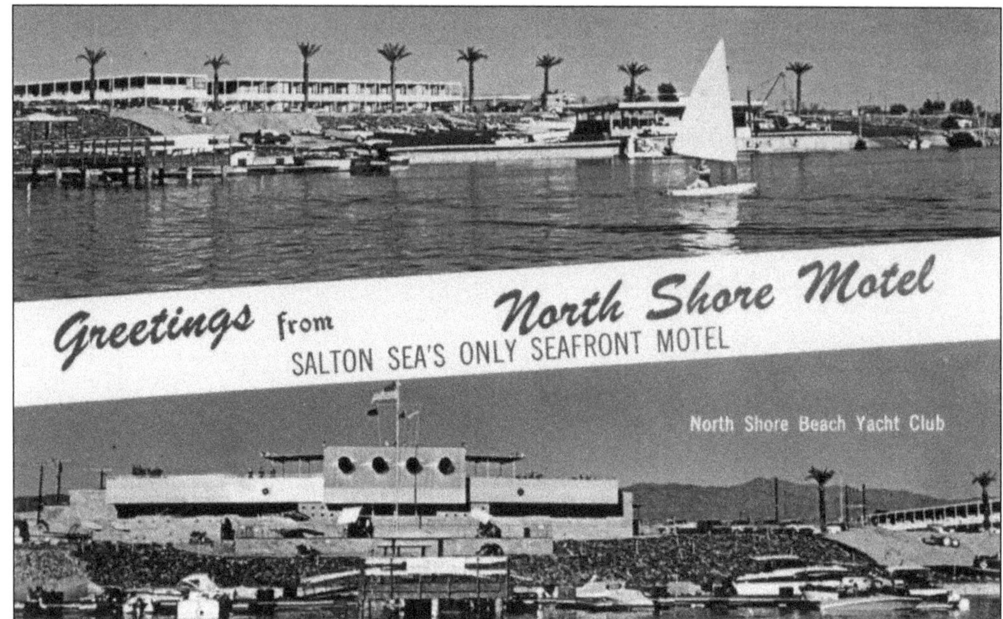

Greetings from North Shore Motel, Salton Sea's Only Seafront Motel / North Shore Beach Yacht Club / North Shore Motel. "Reached via Highway 111, this beautiful 48-unit seafront motel adjoins famed North Shore Beach Yacht Club. Bright gem of North Shore Beach, water sports capital of the Salton Sea, the resort by-the-sea affords incredibly breath-taking seascapes and mountain vistas. North Shore Motel overlooks the yacht club's magnificent clubhouse, 400-boat marina and busy boating, water skiing and fishing activity." Unused photo card. (Copyright Ferris H. Scott, Santa Ana, Calif. FS-694 & S2806L2; Western Resort Publications, 1320 N. Broadway, Santa Ana, Calif.)

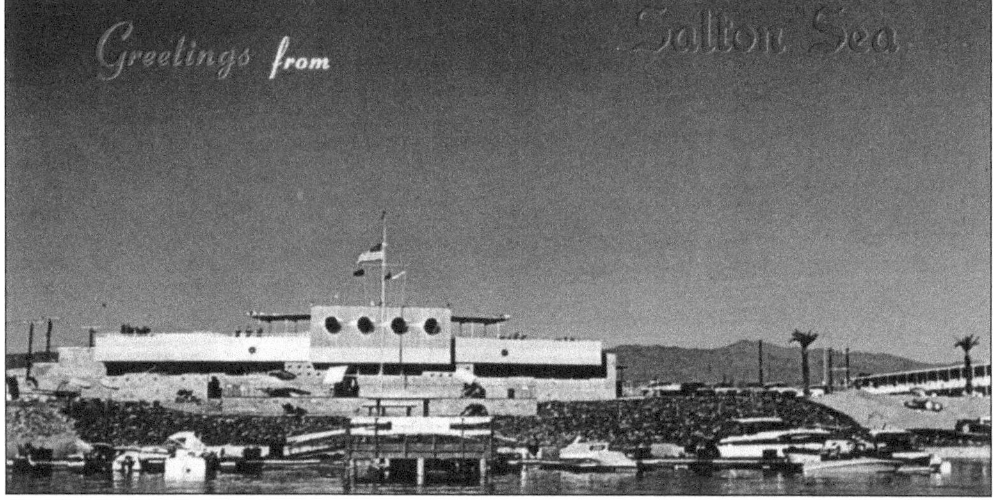

Greetings from Salton Sea / North Shore Beach and Yacht Club. "This picturesque yacht club is known as the glamour capital of the Salton Sea. Over $2,000,000 in improvements have made this facility with its 400 boat marina, one of the most beautiful and well equipped yacht clubs in the west." Unused photo card. (Copyright Ferris H. Scott, Santa Ana, Calif. FS-695 & S-32804-1; Western Resort Publications, 1320 N. Broadway, Santa Ana, Calif.)

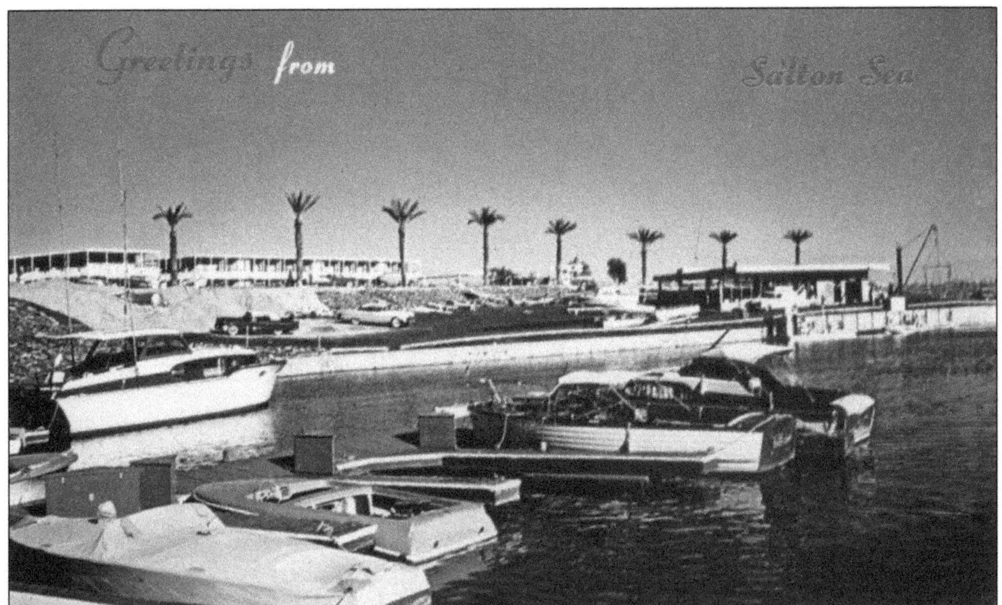

Greetings from Salton Sea / North Shore Motel. "This beautiful 48 unit seafront motel adjoins the famed North Shore Beach Yacht Club and affords incredibly breath-taking seascapes and mountain vistas. This motel overlooks the Yacht Club's magnificent clubhouse and 400 boat marina." Unused photo card. (Copyright Ferris H. Scott, Santa Ana, Calif. FS-696 & S-32805-1; Western Resort Publications, 1320 N. Broadway, Santa Ana, Calif.)

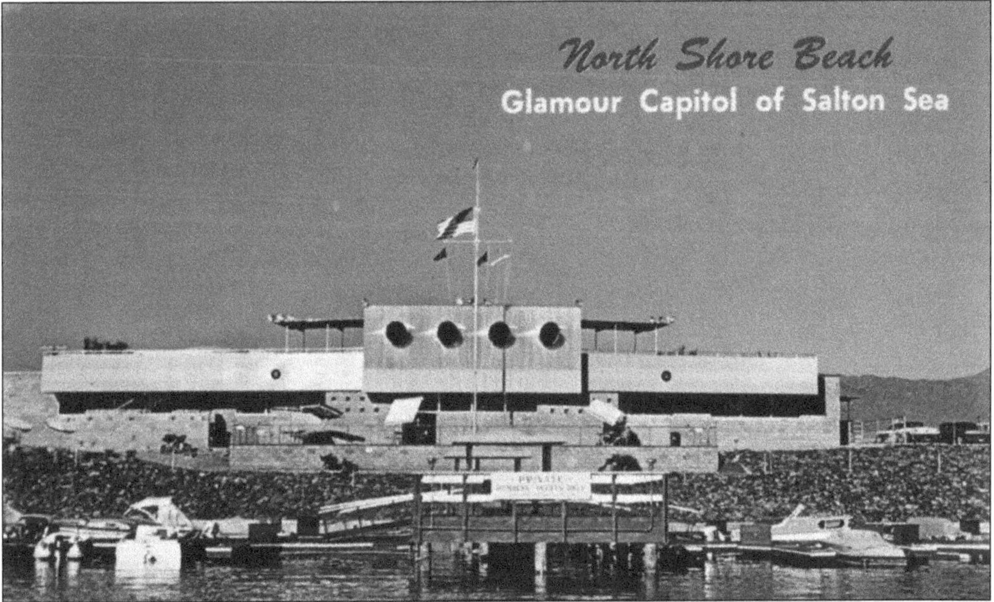

North Shore Beach, Glamour Capitol of Salton Sea / North Shore Beach and Yacht Club. "This magnificent club house overlooking the Salton Sea is one of the best equipped facilities of its kind on the West Coast. Over $2,000,000 has been invested to care for every need of the water sports enthusiast." Unused photo card. (Copyright Ferris H. Scott, Santa Ana, Calif. FS-697 & S-32801; Western Resort Publications, 1320 N. Broadway, Santa Ana, Calif.)

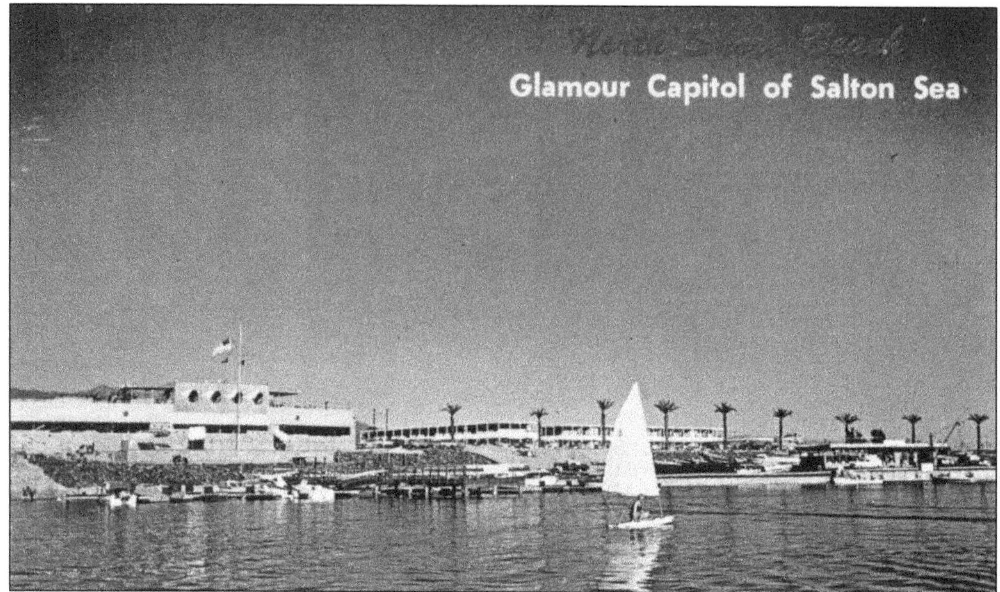

North Shore Beach, Glamour Capitol of Salton Sea / North Shore Beach and Yacht Club. "A picturesque panorama of the complete facilities of this $2,000,000 investment on the shore of the Salton Sea. A magnificent club house, a 48 unit motel and a 400 boat marina await the pleasure of the water sports enthusiast." Mailed on January 2, 1978 Minneapolis, Minnesota. (Copyright Ferris H. Scott, Santa Ana, Calif. FS-698 & S432802; Western Resort Publications, 1320 N. Broadway, Santa Ana, Calif.)

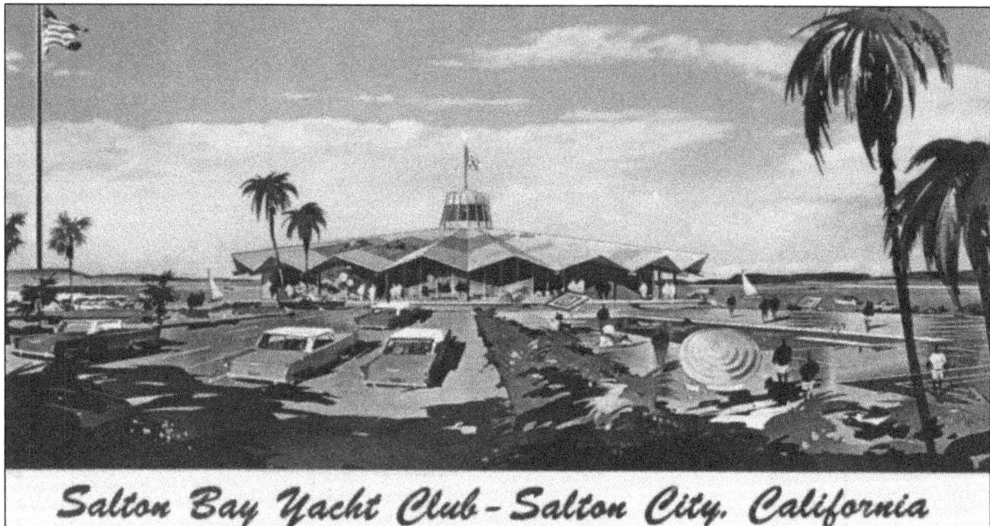

Salton Bay Yacht Club – Salton City, California, South of Palm Springs, between Indio and El Centro via Highway 99 / Salton Bay Yacht Club. "This picturesque Yacht Club is considered to be one of the most luxurious Yacht Clubs in the Western United States. This unique facility is situated in the heart of the Inland Desert Empire on the shores of the fabulous Salton Sea." Unused photo card. (Copyright Ferris H. Scott, Santa Ana, Calif. / FS 725 / S-34233-1; Western Resort Publications, 1320 N. Broadway, Santa Ana, Calif.)

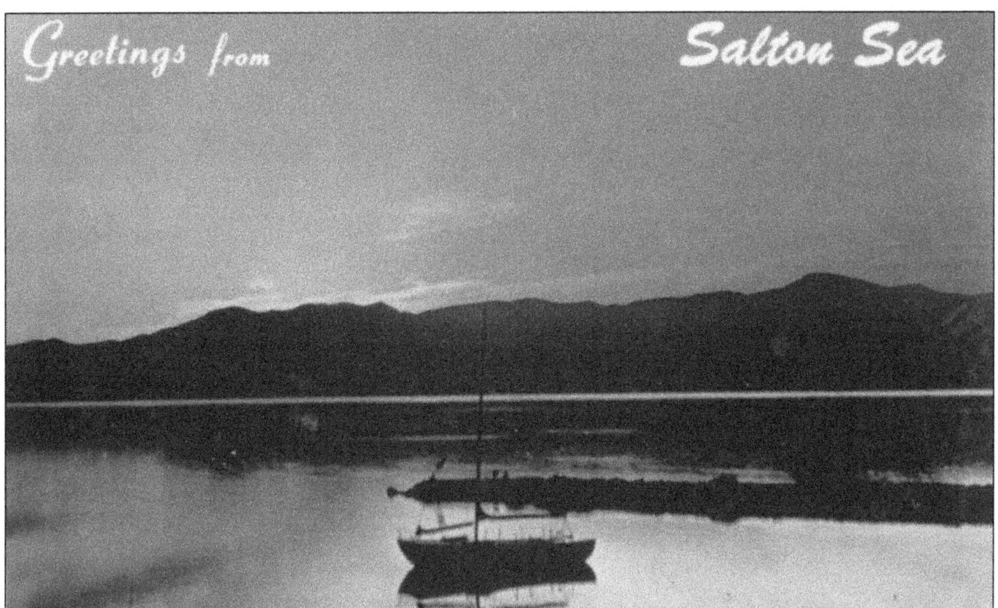

Greetings from Salton Sea. "A colorful sunset over the Salton Sea is a sight long to be remembered. This inland sea far below sea level was formed in 1907 when the Colorado River jumped its banks but today it is one of the great recreational areas in the West, a real haven for the water sports enthusiast." Unused photo card. (Copyright Ferris H. Scott, Santa Ana, Calif. FS-737 & S-4046L2-1; Western Resort Publications, 1320 N. Broadway, Santa Ana, Calif.)

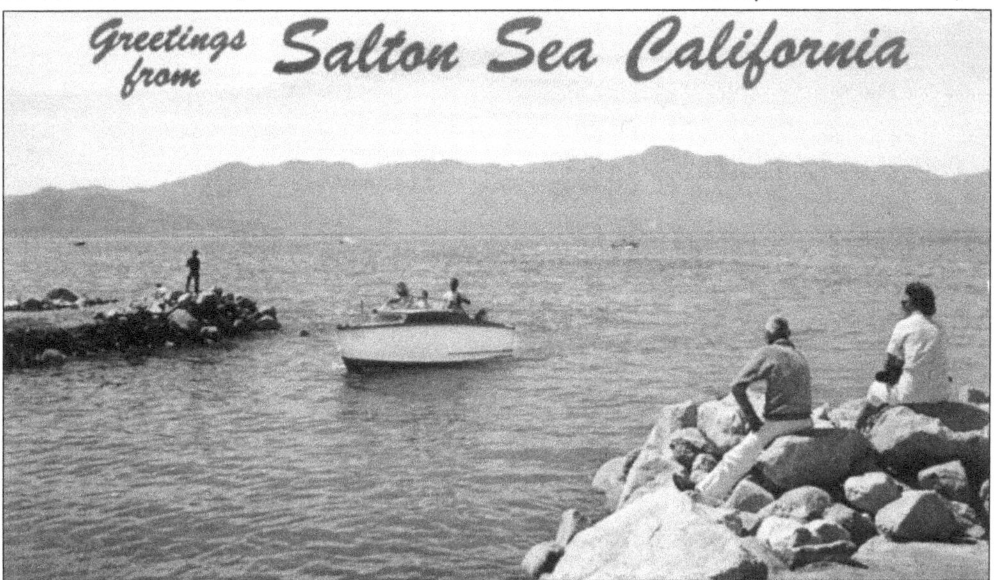

Greetings from Salton Sea / Scene at Salton Sea State Park, California. "Salton Sea is California's newest inland playground. Over 30 miles long, 14 miles wide, and 236 feet below sea level. It is the world's fastest speedboat course. Popular for sailing, water-skiing, swimming, fishing, and hunting." Salton Sea State Park was dedicated on February 12, 1955. During its heyday, it was the second most popular state park in California. More than 400,000 boats crowded its waters each year. Unused photo card. (Desert-Seens, P.O. Box 134, Palm Springs, Calif. / G-224.)

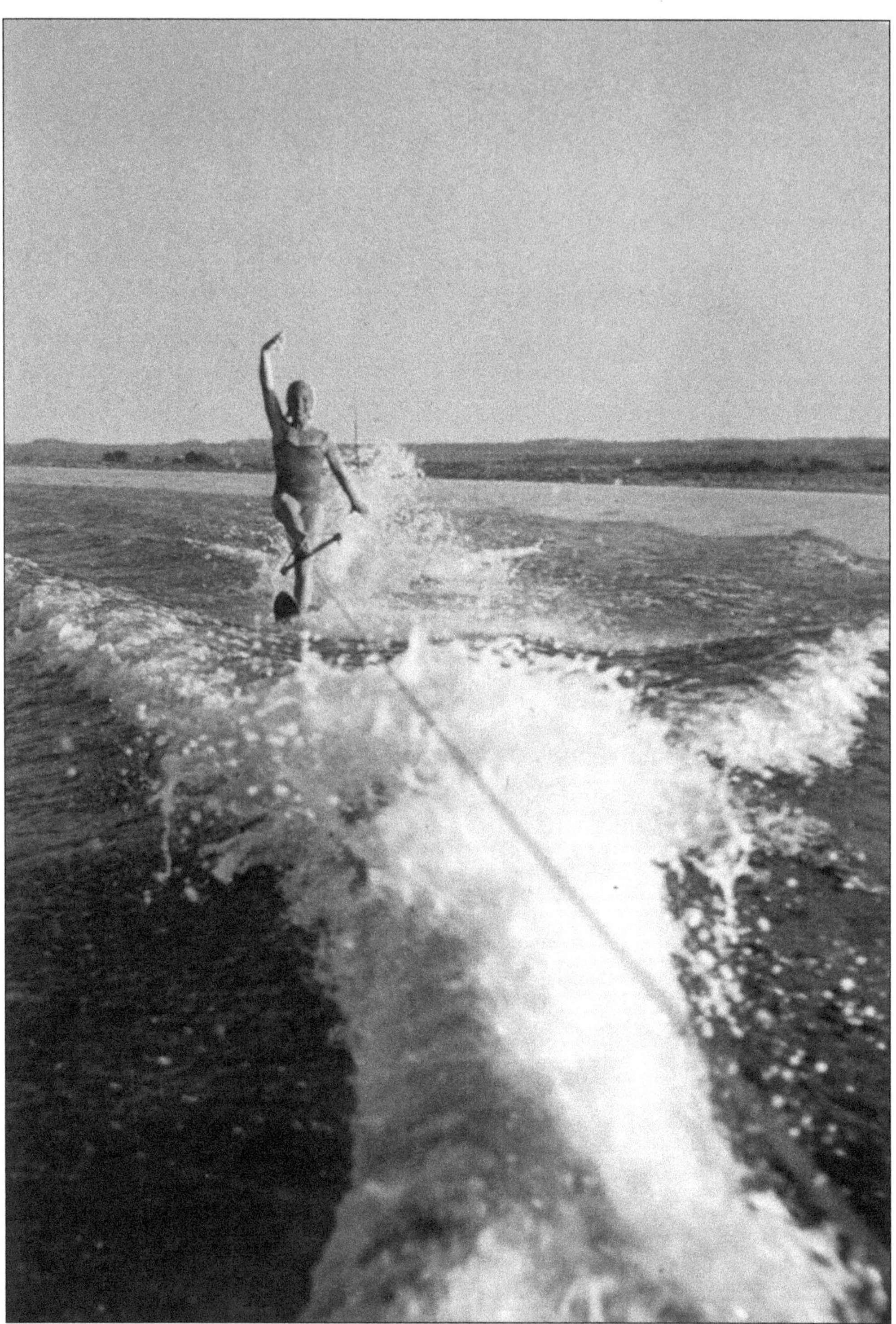

UNTITLED. "The most popular sport at the Salton Sea is water skiing. Anyone from 4 to 84 can learn and take full advantage of this warm, calm, inland sea." (Another Chris Card; Plastichrome by Colourpicture Publishers, Inc. Boston 13, Mass., U.S.A. 27947 / P27949.)

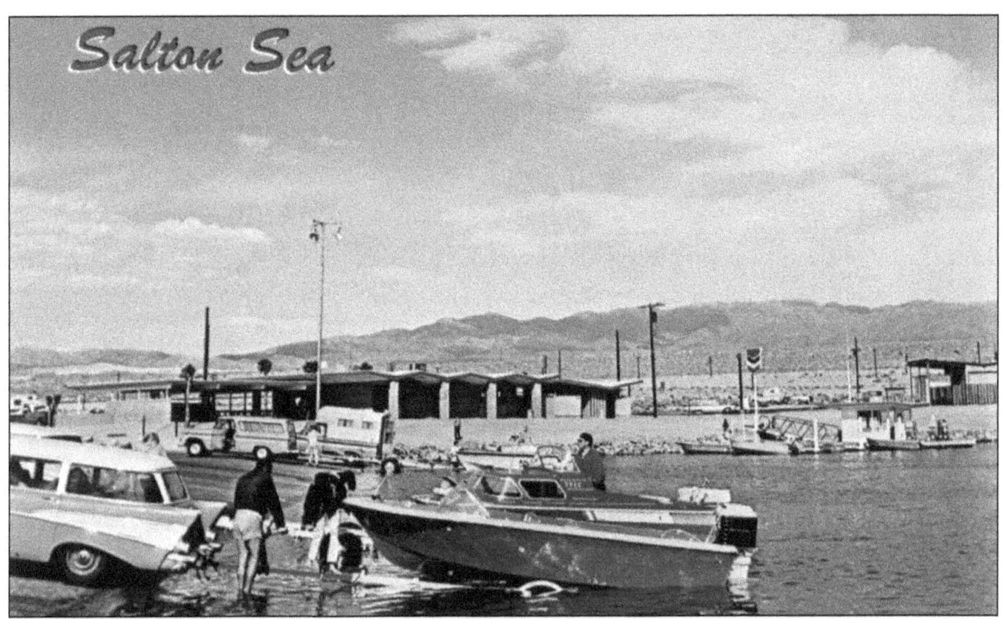

SALTON SEA / SALTON SEA STATE PARK, NORTH SHORE, CALIFORNIA. "On the boat ramp of this popular 2 million dollar facility on the North Shore of this great inland sea some 34 miles long, 11½ miles wide, an average center depth of 40 feet and 232 feet below sea level. The new modern restaurant and snack bar in the background." Unused photo card. (Copyright Ferris H. Scott, Santa Ana, Calif. FS-1038 & S-62048; Western Resort Publications, 1320 N. Broadway, Santa Ana, Calif.)

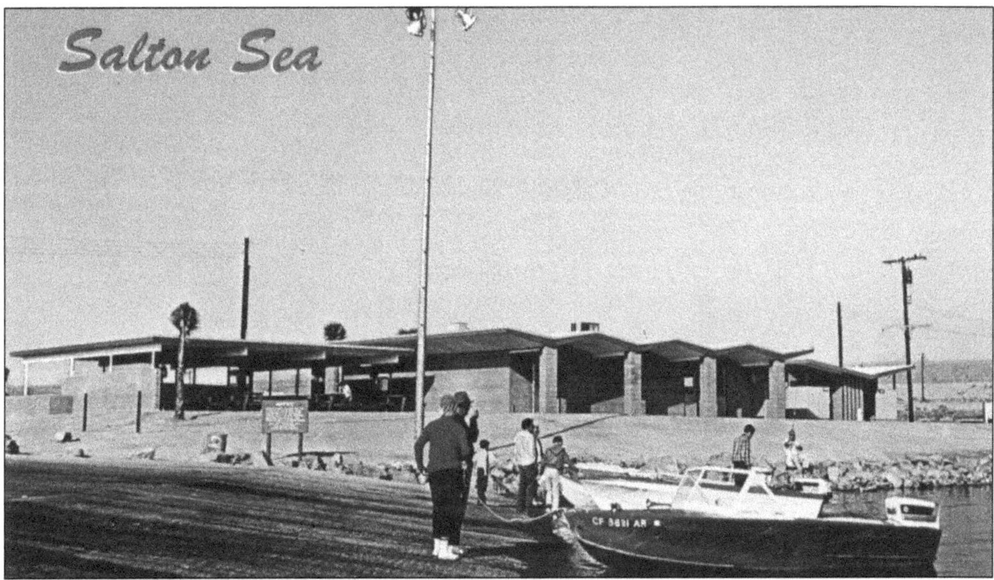

SALTON SEA / SALTON SEA STATE PARK, NORTH SHORE, CALIFORNIA. "The well designed boat ramp of this popular 2 million dollar facility on the North Short of this great inland sea some 232 feet below sea level. The new modern restaurant and snack bar in the background. The seas' length is 34 miles, width 11½ miles and has an average center depth of 40 feet." Unused photo card. (Copyright Ferris H. Scott, Santa Ana, Calif. FS-1039 & S-62049; Western Resort Publications, 1320 N. Broadway, Santa Ana, Calif.)

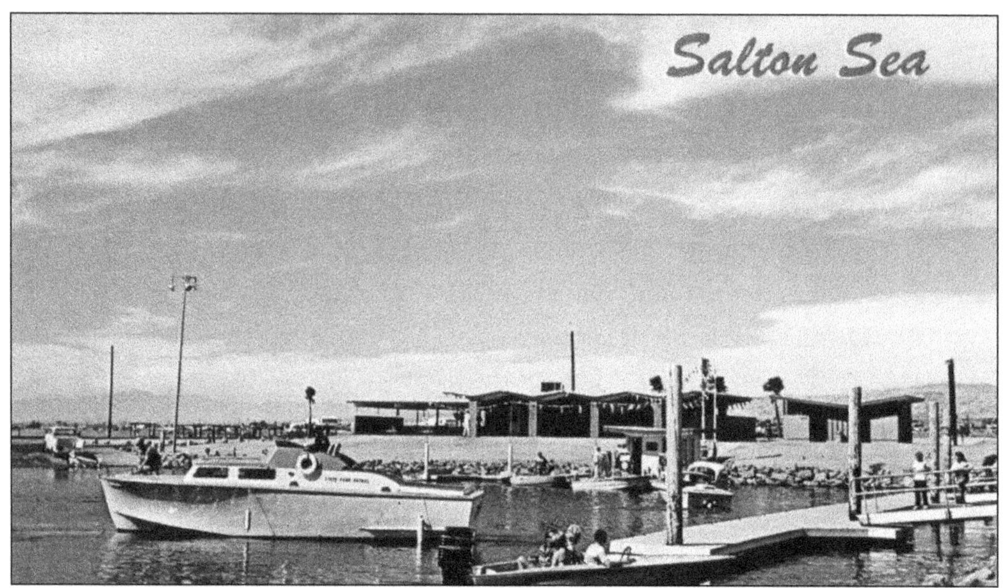

Salton Sea / Salton Sea State Park. "The 31 foot state patrol boat in the foreground and the new restaurant and snack bar beyond. This State Park facility represents a 2 million dollar investment and has developed into a most important California recreation area. This inland sea is 232 feet below sea level, 34 miles long, 11½ miles wide, while the average center depth is 40 feet." Unused photo card. (Copyright Ferris H. Scott, Santa Ana, Calif. FS-1040 & S-62050; Western Resort Publications, 1320 N. Broadway, Santa Ana, Calif.)

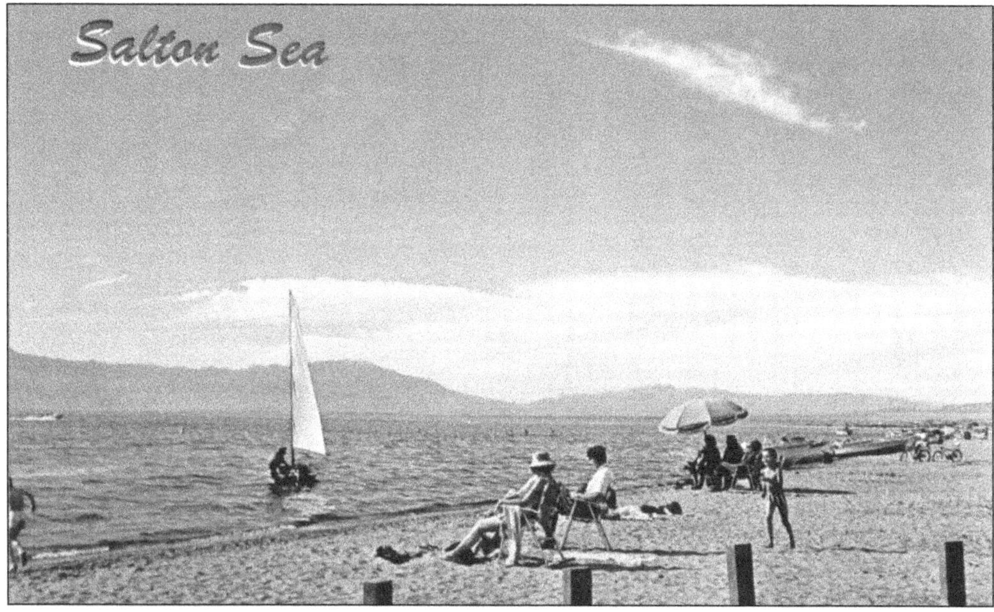

Salton Sea / Salton Sea State Park. "Relaxing on the shores of this inland sea, some 34 miles long, 11½ miles wide and 232 feet below sea level. Close to 2 million dollars has been spent to make this State Park one of the finest recreational areas in the west." Today, the Salton Sea State Park features five campground sites, a boat launch facility, and a recently renovated visitor center. Unused photo card. (Copyright Ferris H. Scott, Santa Ana, Calif. FS-1041 & S-62051; Western Resort Publications, 1320 N. Broadway, Santa Ana, Calif.)

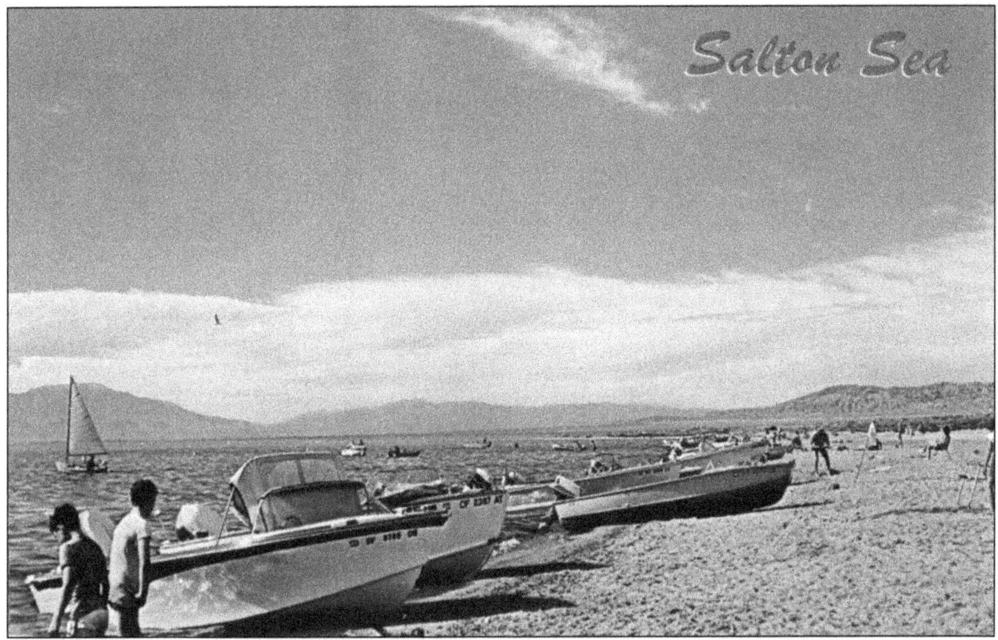

Salton Sea / 232 Feet below Sea Level – 34 Miles Long – 11½ Miles Wide – Average Center Depth 40 Feet. "This popular area is fast becoming the water skiing and boating capital of the west. The low elevation and greater water intensity makes for the fastest water in the world as well as one of California's most popular year around recreational areas." Unused photo card. (Copyright Ferris H. Scott, Santa Ana, Calif. FS-1042 & S-62052; Western Resort Publications, 1320 N. Broadway, Santa Ana, Calif.)

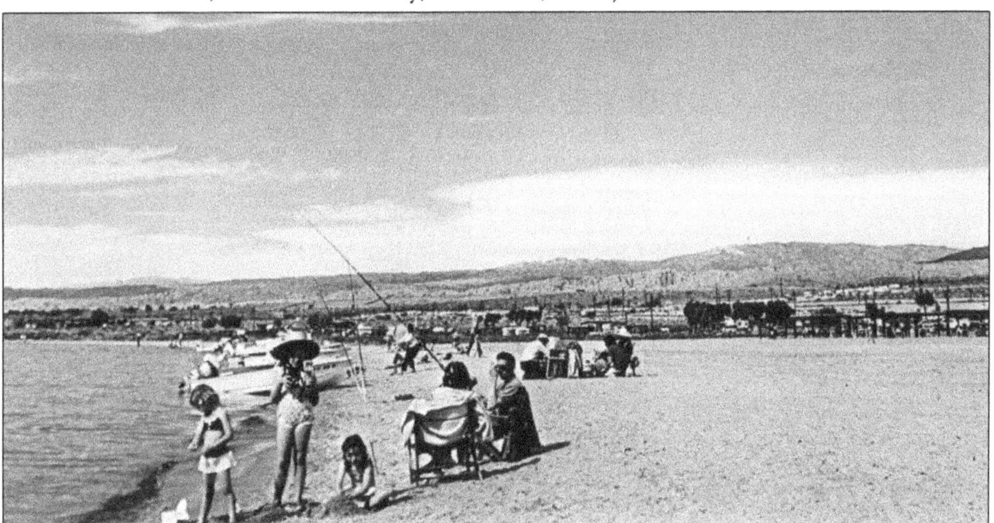

Salton Sea / Salton Sea State Park. "Relaxing on the shores of this great inland sea where close to 2 million dollars has been spent to make this State Park one of the finest recreational areas in the West. This sea was formed in 10907 when the Colorado River jumped its banks and threatened to wipe out the entire Imperial Valley. 232 feet below sea level – 34 miles long – 11½ miles wide / Average center depth 40 feet." Unused photo card. (Copyright Ferris H. Scott, Santa Ana, Calif. FS-1043 & S-62053; Western Resort Publications, 1320 N. Broadway, Santa Ana, Calif.)

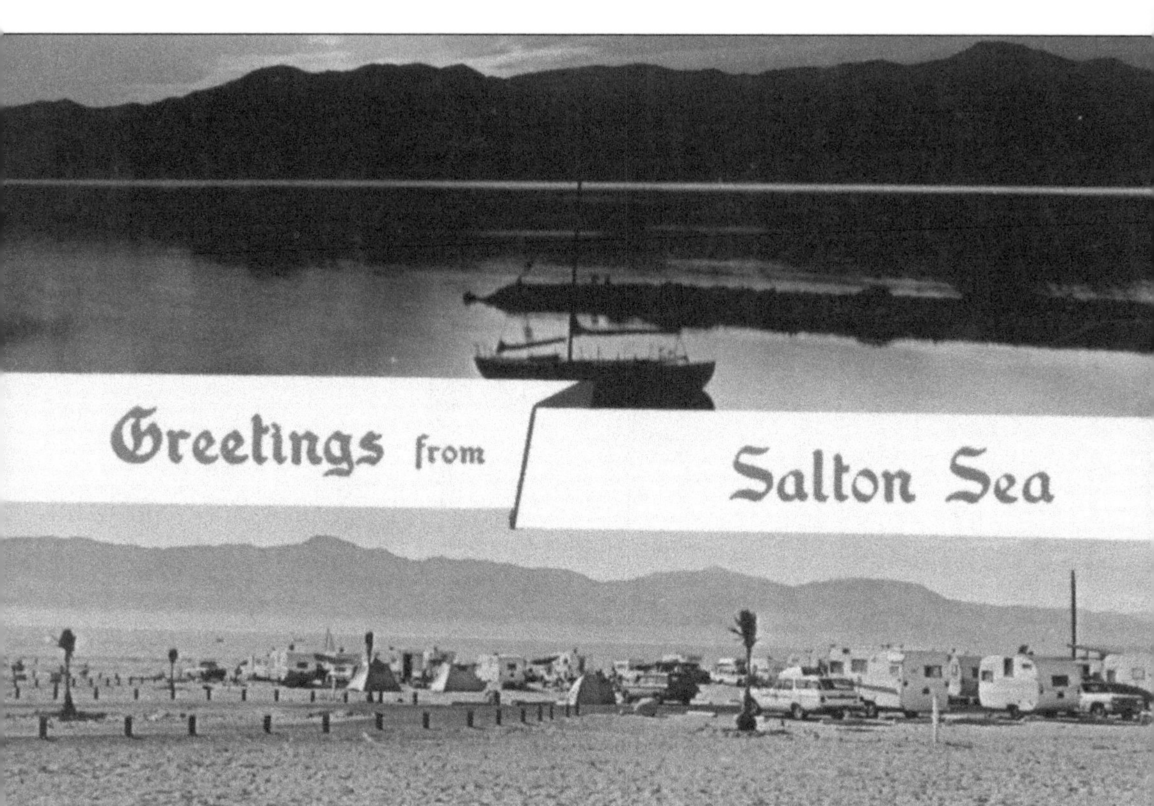

Greetings from Salton Sea / Salton Sea State Park, Salton Sea State Park, North Shore, California. "(Top) A colorful sunset on this most picturesque of inland seas, some 232 feet below sea level, 34 miles long and 11½ miles across. (Below) Trailers line the shore of this State Park where some 2 million dollars has been spent to make this facility one of the finest of its kind in the West." Color photographs by Jerry Chaney. Unused photo card. (Copyright Ferris H. Scott, Santa Ana, Calif. FS-1044 & S620540L2; Western Resort Publications, 1320 N. Broadway, Santa Ana, Calif.)

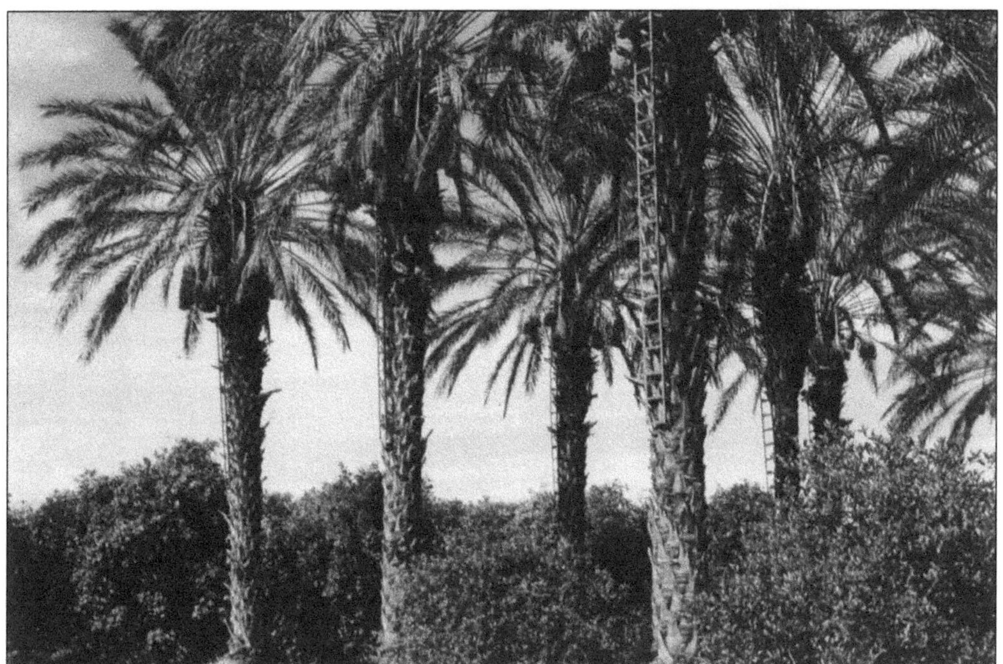

DATELAND – SOUTHERN CALIFORNIA. "Enormous date palms Backed by Citrus groves flourish in the so-called desert region north of the Salton Sea." Unused photo card. (Published and distributed by Columbia Wholesale Supply, 11401 Chandler, North Hollywood, Calif. / H-148 &19627.)

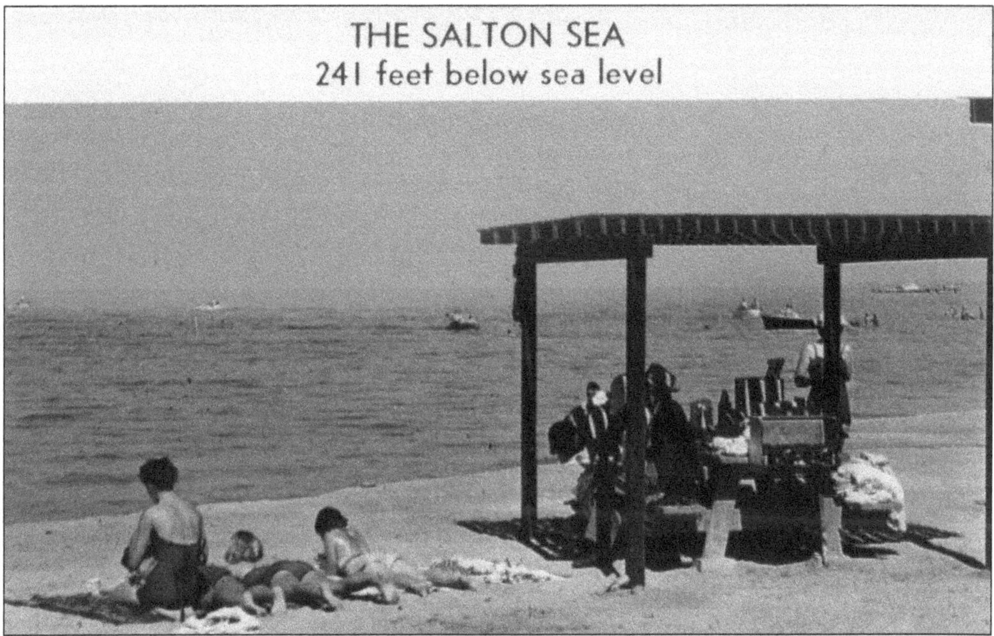

THE SALTON SEA, 241 FEET BELOW SEA LEVEL. "The Great Salton Sea, a few miles southeast of Indio, California. An interesting and popular area." Unused photo card. (Published and distributed by Columbia Wholesale Supply, 7609 Santa Monica Blvd., Hollywood 46, Calif. / H-2329 / 22884.)

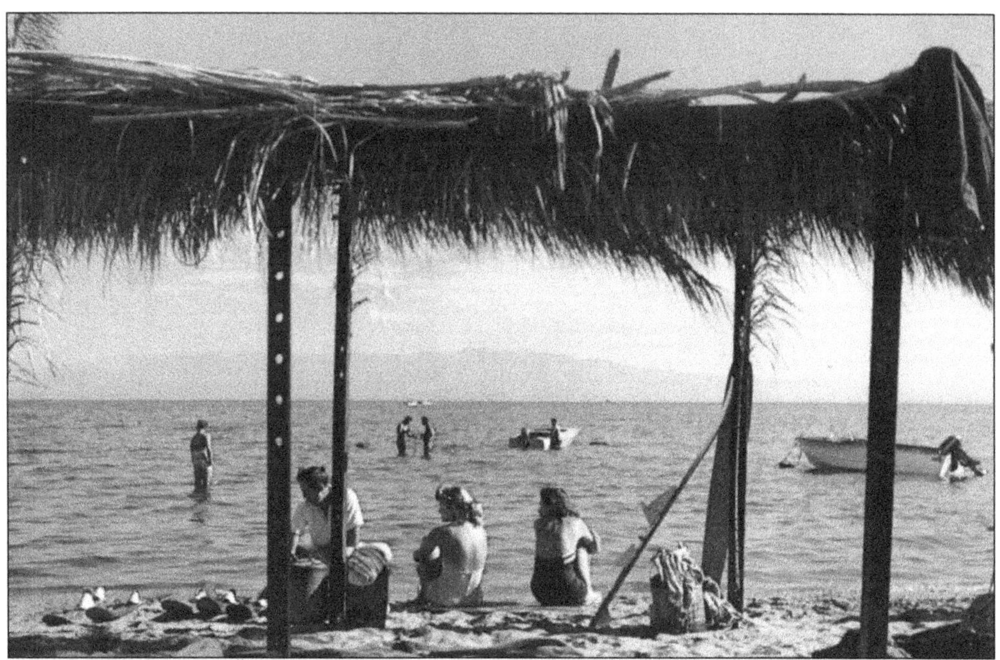

"WATER FUN" AT SALTON SEA. The Salton Sea has been known for powerboat races since around 1929. During the Salton Sea Regatta of 1951, a total of 21 world records were broken. The American Power Boat Association's three-day Kilo races resumed at the Salton Sea in 2008. Several other races have also returned to the "fastest water" in the world. Color photography by Carlos Elmer; unused photo card dated March 26, 1961. (Published and distributed by Columbia Wholesale Supply, 7609 Santa Monica Blvd., Hollywood 46, Calif. / H-1572 / 34188.)

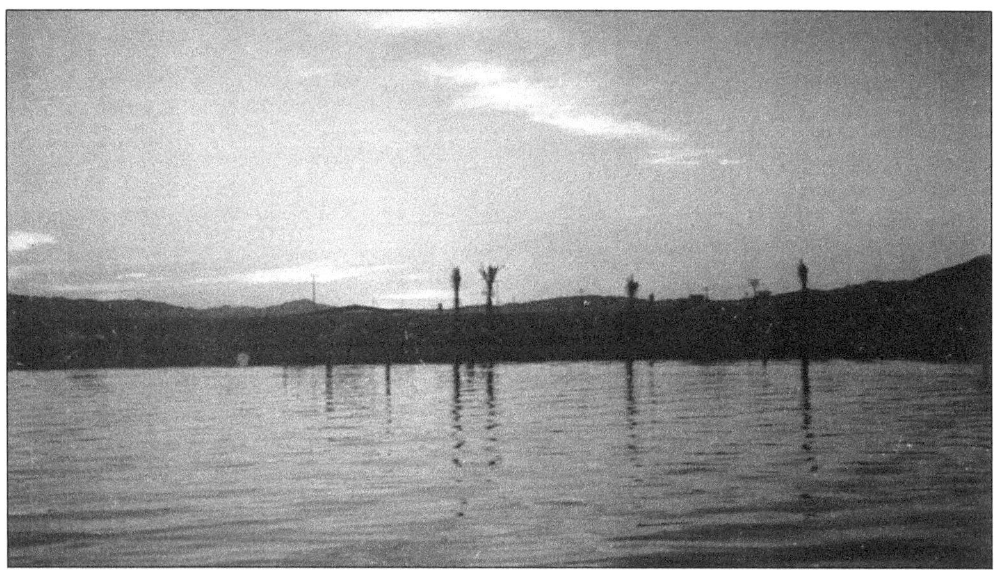

SALTON SEA, CALIFORNIA. "235 feet below sea level. Sunsets on the fabulous Salton Sea prove a never ending wonder to the thousands of daily visitors." Color photo by Bill Stover; unused photo card. (Published and distributed by Columbia Wholesale Supply, 11401 Chandler, North Hollywood, Calif. / H-2213 & 53484.)

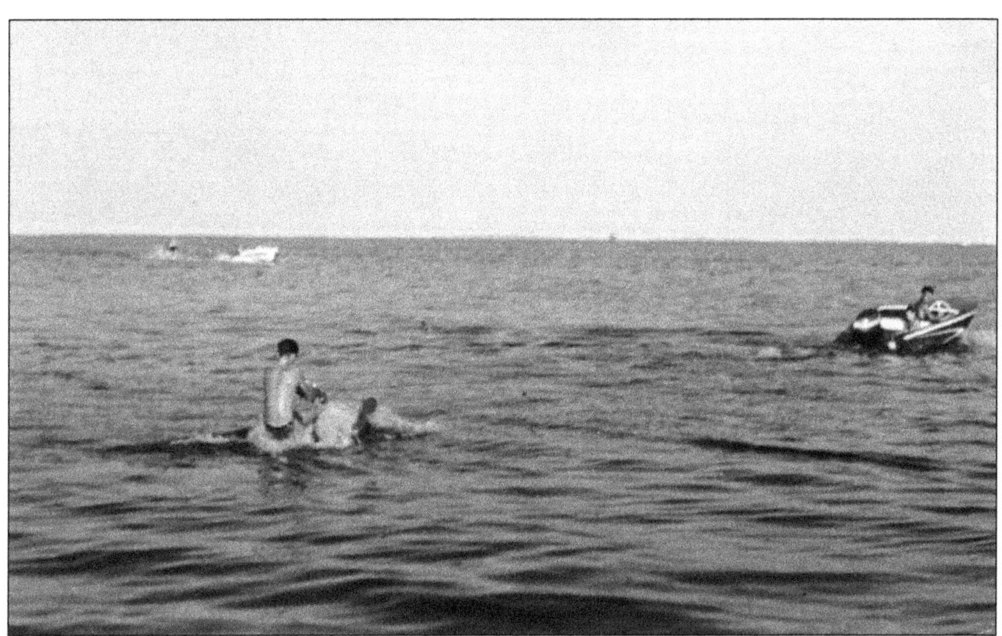

SALTON SEA, CALIFORNIA. " 'Just getting up' for an almost endless ride on the fastest water in the world. Because it is 235 ft. below sea level, it permits new world speed records for boats. Salton Sea is rapidly becoming the ski capitol of Southern California." Color photo by Bill Stover; mailed on January 30, 1964 to Calumet City, Illinois. (Published and distributed by Columbia Wholesale Supply, 11401 Chandler, North Hollywood, Calif. / 53487.)

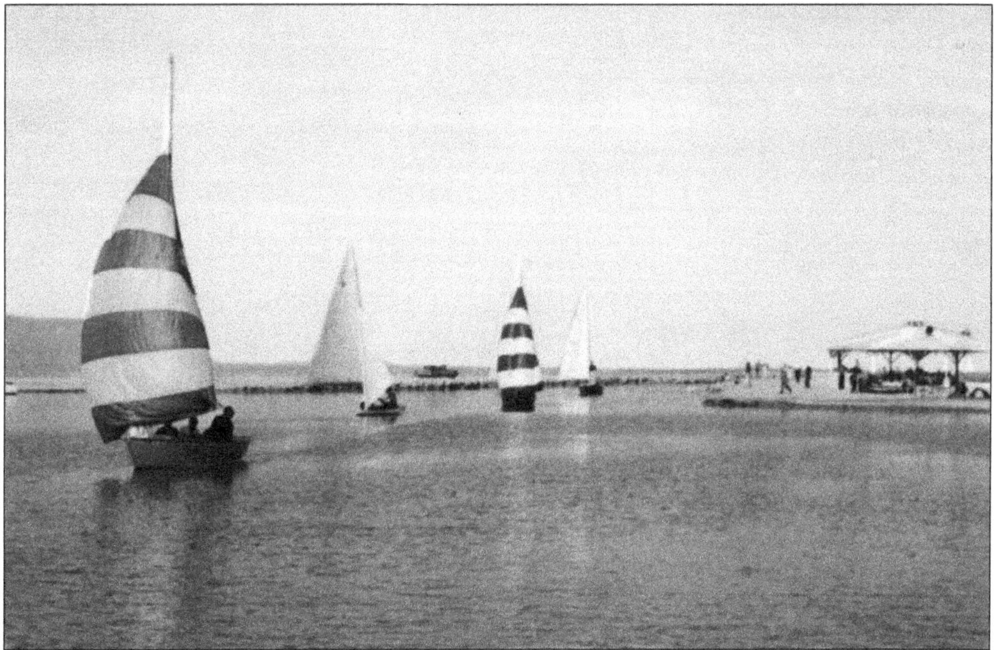

SALTON SEA, CALIFORNIA. "235 feet below sea level. Sailboats, a familiar sight on Salton Sea, offer a graceful, relaxing scene for the visitors." Color photo by Bill Stover; unused photo card. (Published and distributed by Columbia Wholesale Supply, 11401 Chandler, North Hollywood, Calif. / H-2210/ 53488.)

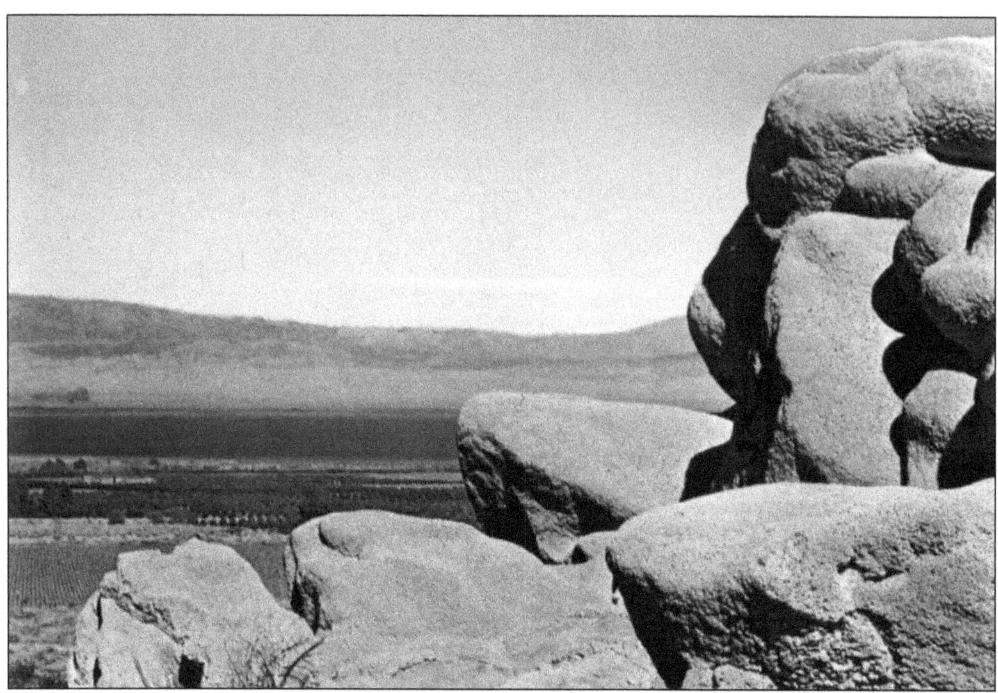

Travertine Rock. "Off Highway 99 near the Salton Sea – At one time this whole area was part of the Gulf of California. Coral was built on the rocks which are now exposed." Color photo by Louis & Virginia Kay. (Published and distributed by Columbia Wholesale Supply, 11401 Chandler, North Hollywood, Calif. / H-2153 & 58030.)

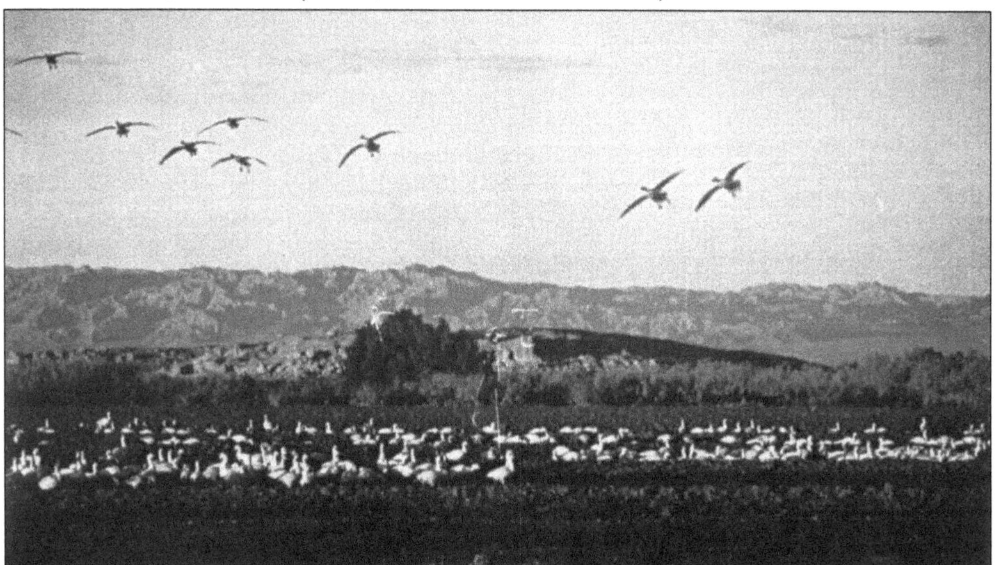

Snow Geese Landing on Wildlife Refuge Feeding Grounds Located on the South End of the Salton Sea. The Sonny Bono Salton Sea National Wildlife Refuge has 826 acres of manageable wetland units and provides habitat for over 375 species of birds. It is the winter home for up to 30,000 geese and 60,000 ducks. Color photo by Louis & Virginia Kay; unused photo card. (Published and distributed by Columbia Wholesale Supply, 11401 Chandler, North Hollywood, Calif. / H-3057 & 58048.)

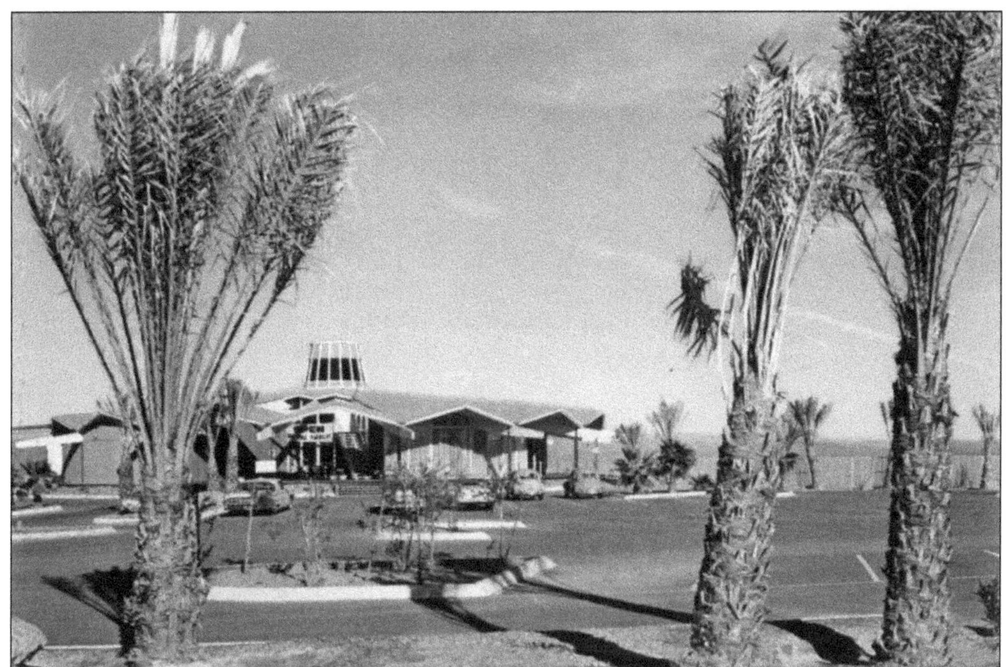

Beautiful Yacht Club Situated on the West Side of the Salton Sea. Color photo by Louis & Virginia Kay; mailed July 10, 1964 to Canisteo, New York. (Published and distributed by Columbia Wholesale Supply, 11401 Chandler, North Hollywood, Calif. / H-3059 / 58049.)

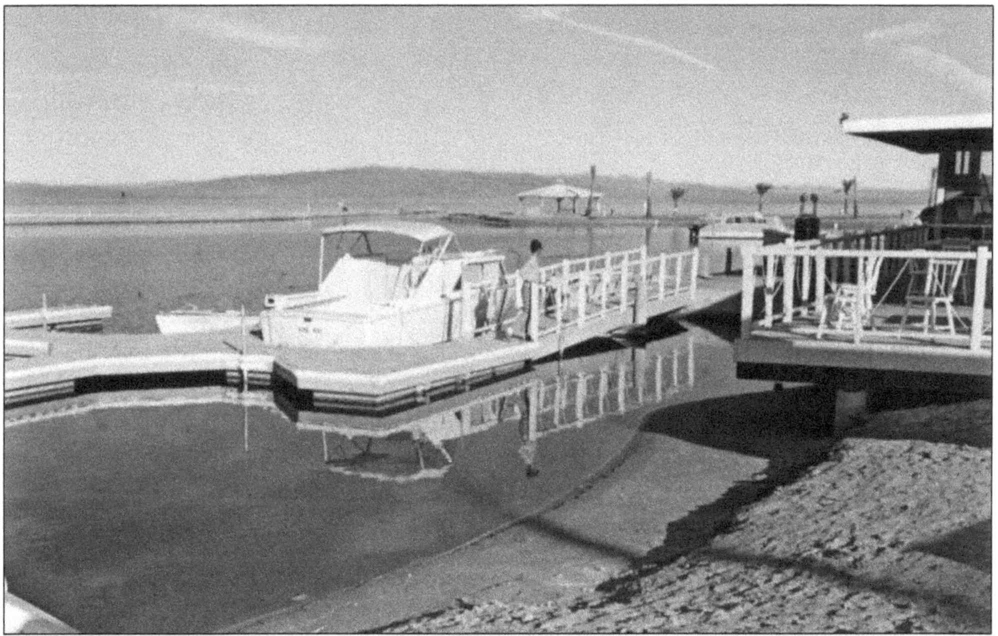

Popular Yacht Harbor on the West Side of the Salton Sea. "Facilities are available for launching boats." Color photo by Louis & Virginia Kay; unused photo card. (Published and distributed by Columbia Wholesale Supply, 11401 Chandler, North Hollywood, Calif. / H-3058 & 58050.)

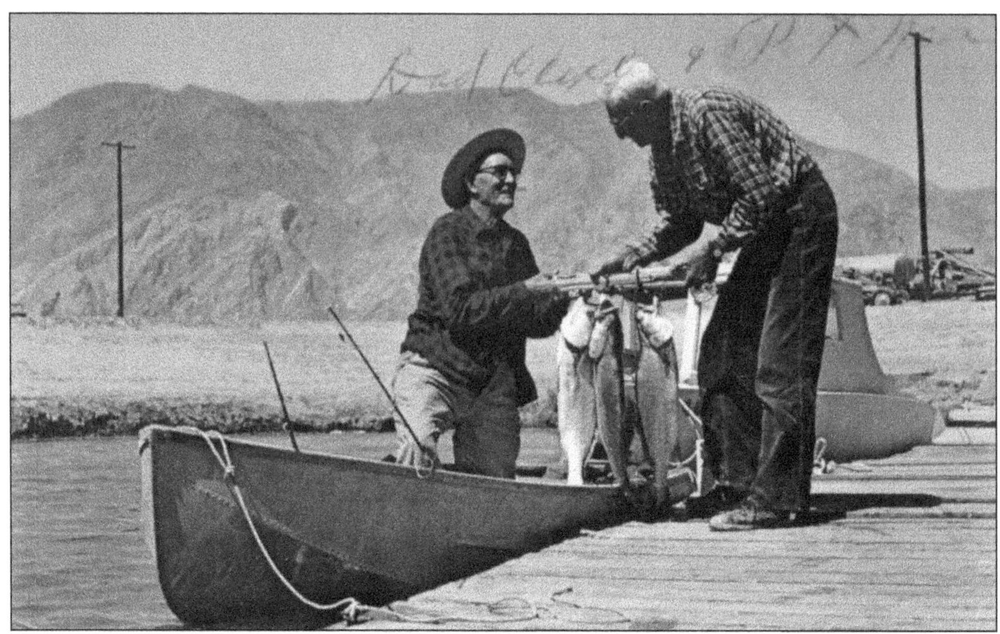

SALTON SEA, CALIFORNIA. Sonny Bono Salton Sea Refuge maintains and improves habitat for wintering waterfowl and shorebird habitat. The refuge provides habitat for over 375 bird species, including up to 30,000 snow, Ross's, and Canada geese, and 60,000 ducks daily from November through February. Endangered species observed on the refuge include the southern bald eagle, peregrine falcon, California brown pelican, Yuma clapper rail, and desert pupfish. Salton Sea, California; unused photo card. (Published and distributed by Columbia Wholesale Supply, 11401 Chandler, North Hollywood, Calif. / H-3308 / 64566.)

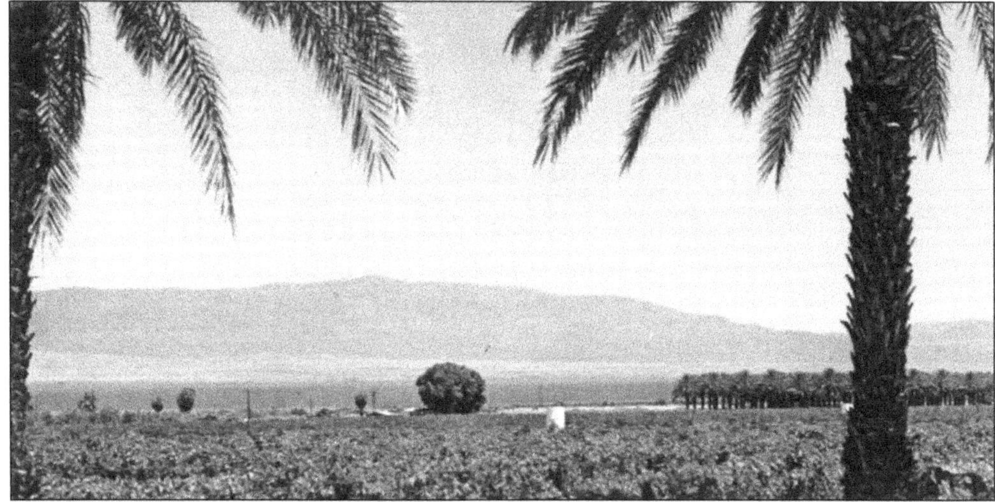

SALTON SEA, CALIFORNIA. Salton Sea State Recreation Area lies along the northeast edge of the lake. The park includes 14miles of trails, campsites and shoreline. This agency reports more than 200,000 visitors each year. However, tourists should be advised that there is a noticeable lack of quality motels, restaurants or comfort facilities around much of the lake. However, the Salton Sea is only a 45 minute drive from Palm Springs and other Coachella Valley destination locations. Salton Sea, California; Unused photo card. (Published and distributed by Columbia Wholesale Supply, 11401 Chandler, North Hollywood, Calif. / H-3309 & 64567.)

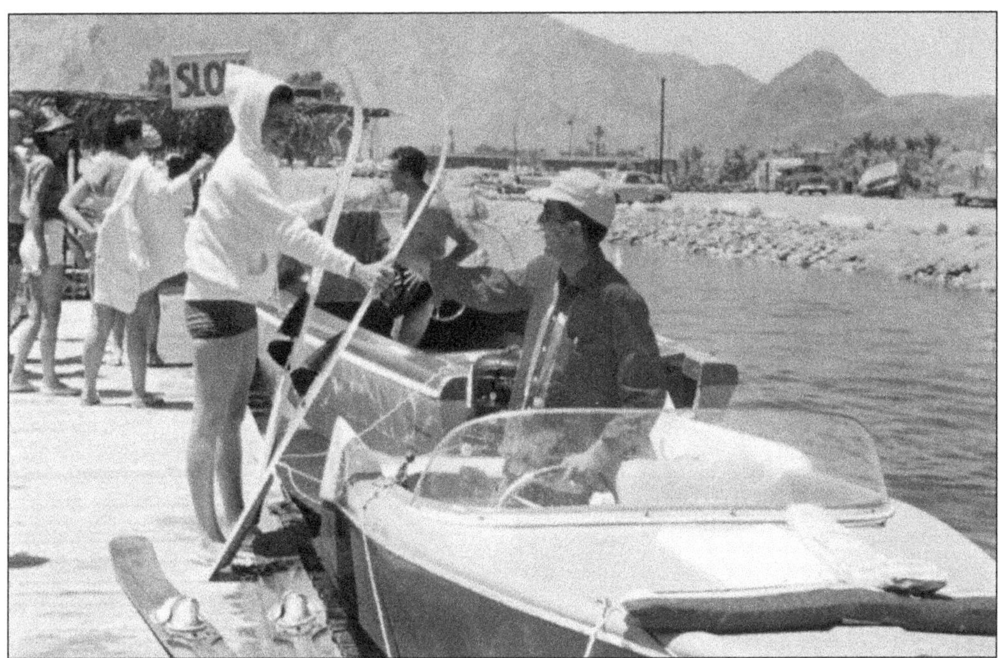

UNTITLED. "The colorful boats and costumes of motor boating and skiing enthusiasts add to the beauty of the desert, sea, and mountains in the Salton Sea area." Unused photo card. (Another Chris Card; Plastichrome by Colourpicture Publishers, Inc. Boston 13, Mass., U.S.A.)

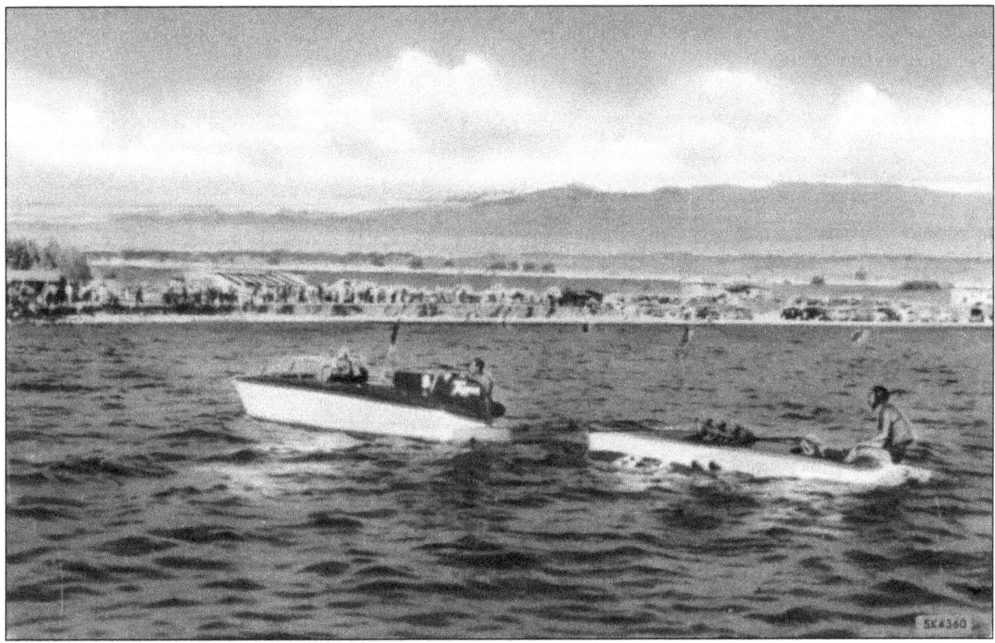

BELOW SEA-LEVEL SALTON SEA, NEAR INDIO, CALIF. "Boating, Swimming and Fishing are enjoyed here. This large body of water was formed the early part of this century by an overflow of the Colorado River." Unused photo card. (A "ShiniColor" by Colourpicture," Boston 15, Mass. U.S.A. 2143 So. Alsace Ave., L.A.)

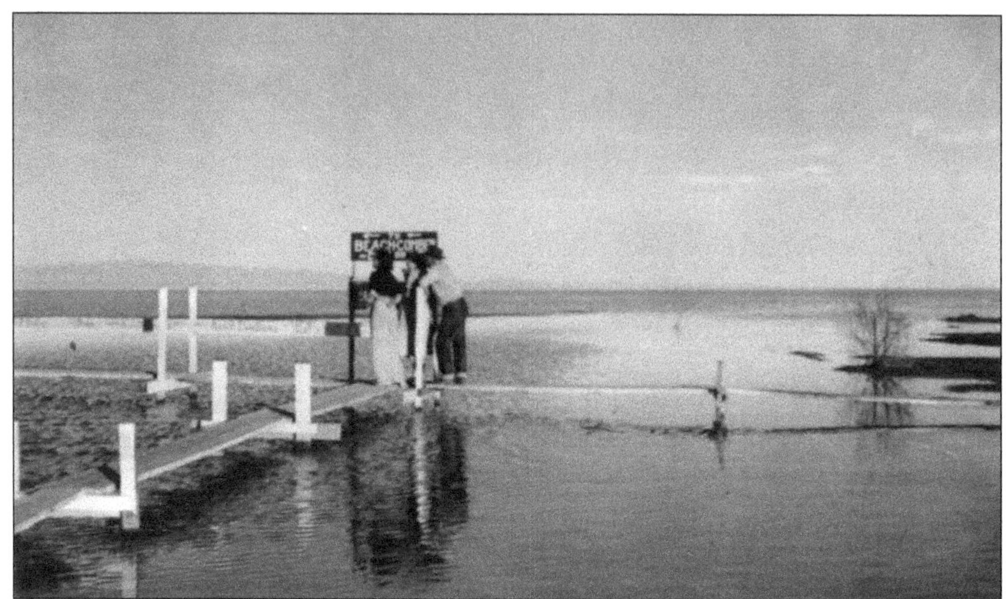

SALTON SEA BEACH ON SALTON SEA. "Elevation 238 below sea-level. First notations of the Salton Sea were made in 1853. The Salton Sea as we know it now was formed in 1905, 1906, and 1907 by overflow of flood waters of the Colorado River. It is about 32 miles long and 13¼ miles wide. Evaporation from the surface is about 7 feet yearly." Unused photo card. (Pub. & Dist. by Larry Holland, El Centro, Cal. / P2897; "Plastichrome" by Colourpicture, Boston 15, Mass., U.S.A.)

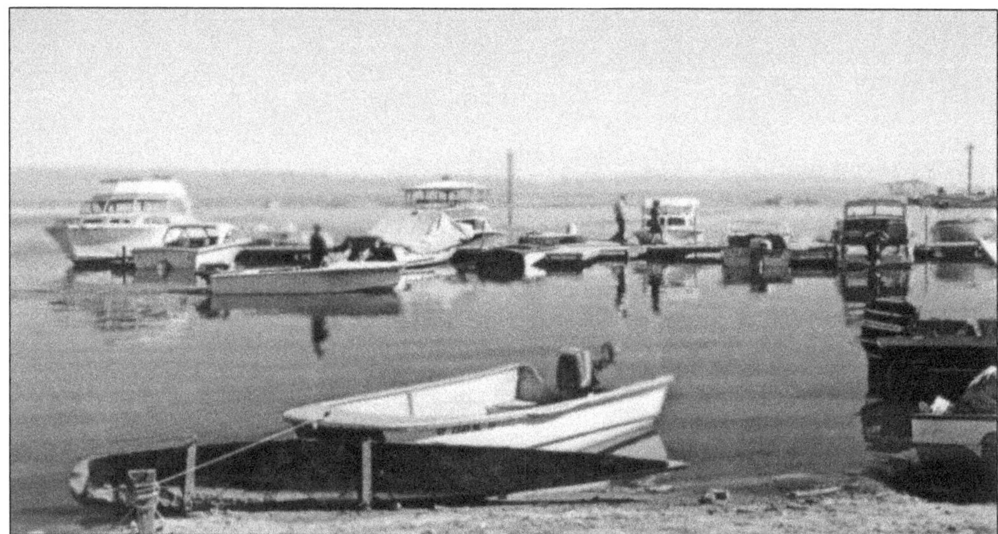

SALTON SEA. "This inland sea was formed in 1905 when the Colorado River overflowed into the sandy depression that was once a remnant of prehistoric Lake Cahuilla. The old lake dried up leaving behind enormous beds of fossil shark's teeth, oyster and conch shells. The sea is located in lower Coachella Valley. A printer's error in setting conchilla (Sp. small sea shell) gave the valley its unusual name. Today this 40 mile long body of water is known for its fishing and water sports. There are a number of resorts around the sea . . . M.P." Photo-color by Merle Porter; unused photo card. (© & Published by Royal Pictures, Colton, California C-189 & 5-76334.)

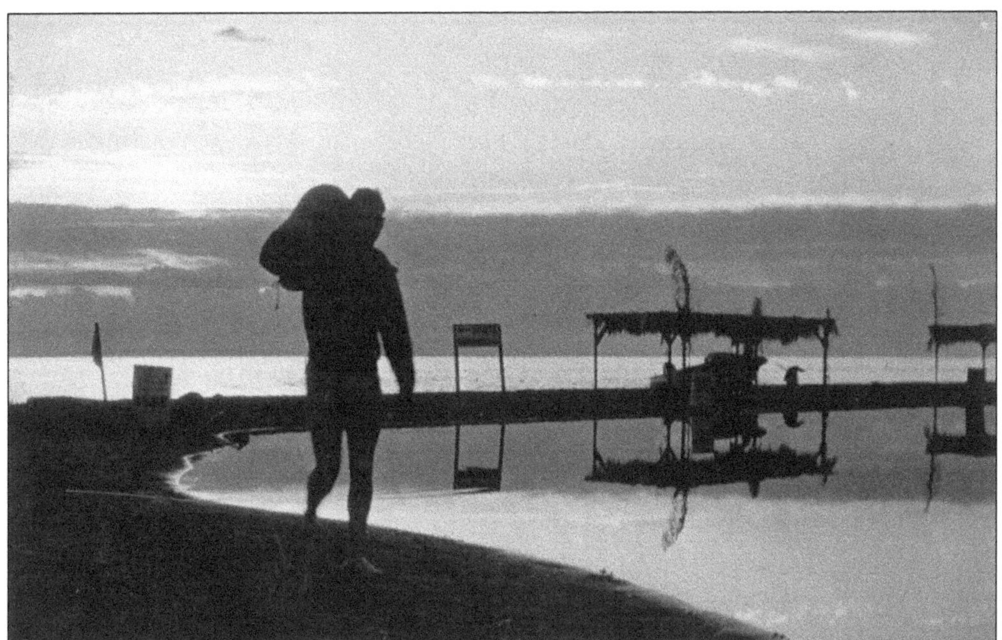

UNTITLED. "Nowhere are the sunrises and sunsets as beautiful as at Salton Sea. The combination of sea-mountains-desert and South Sea Island atmosphere make the sunrises and sunsets at the Salton Sea incomparable." Unused photo card. (Another Chris Card; Plastichrome by Colourpicture Publishers, Inc. Boston 13, Mass., U.S.A. 27947 / P27950.)

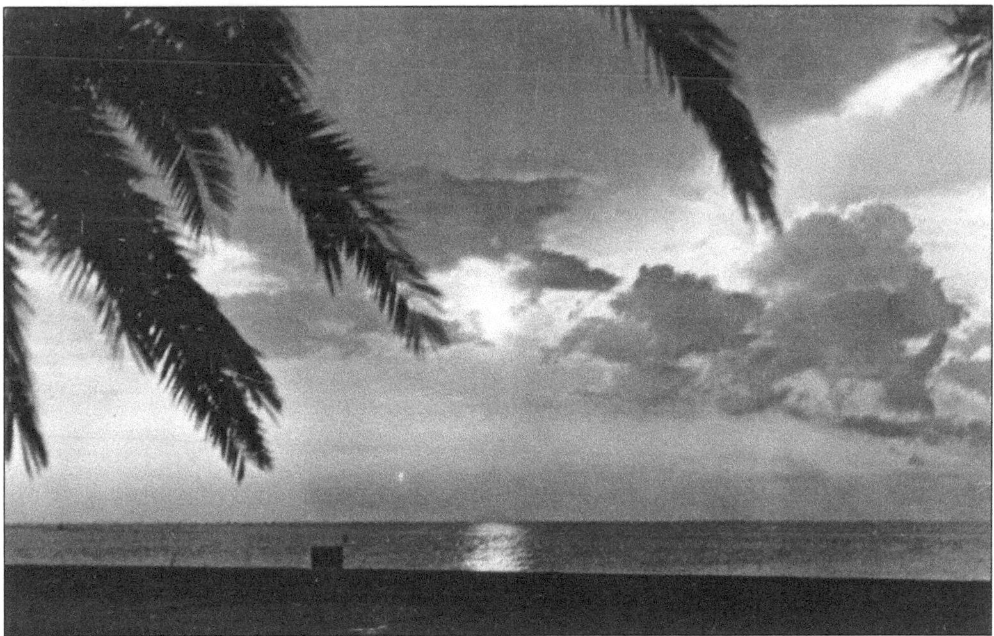

SALTON SEA, CALIFORNIA AND A STORMY SUNSET. "This inland sea, far below sea level, was formed in 1907 when the Colorado River jumped its banks and threatened to wipe out the entire Imperial Valley, A heroic and million dollar battle eventually saved an inland empire but the sea lived on." Unused photo card dated March 26, 1961. (Pub. by Western Resort Publications, Santa Ana, Calif., / P732.)

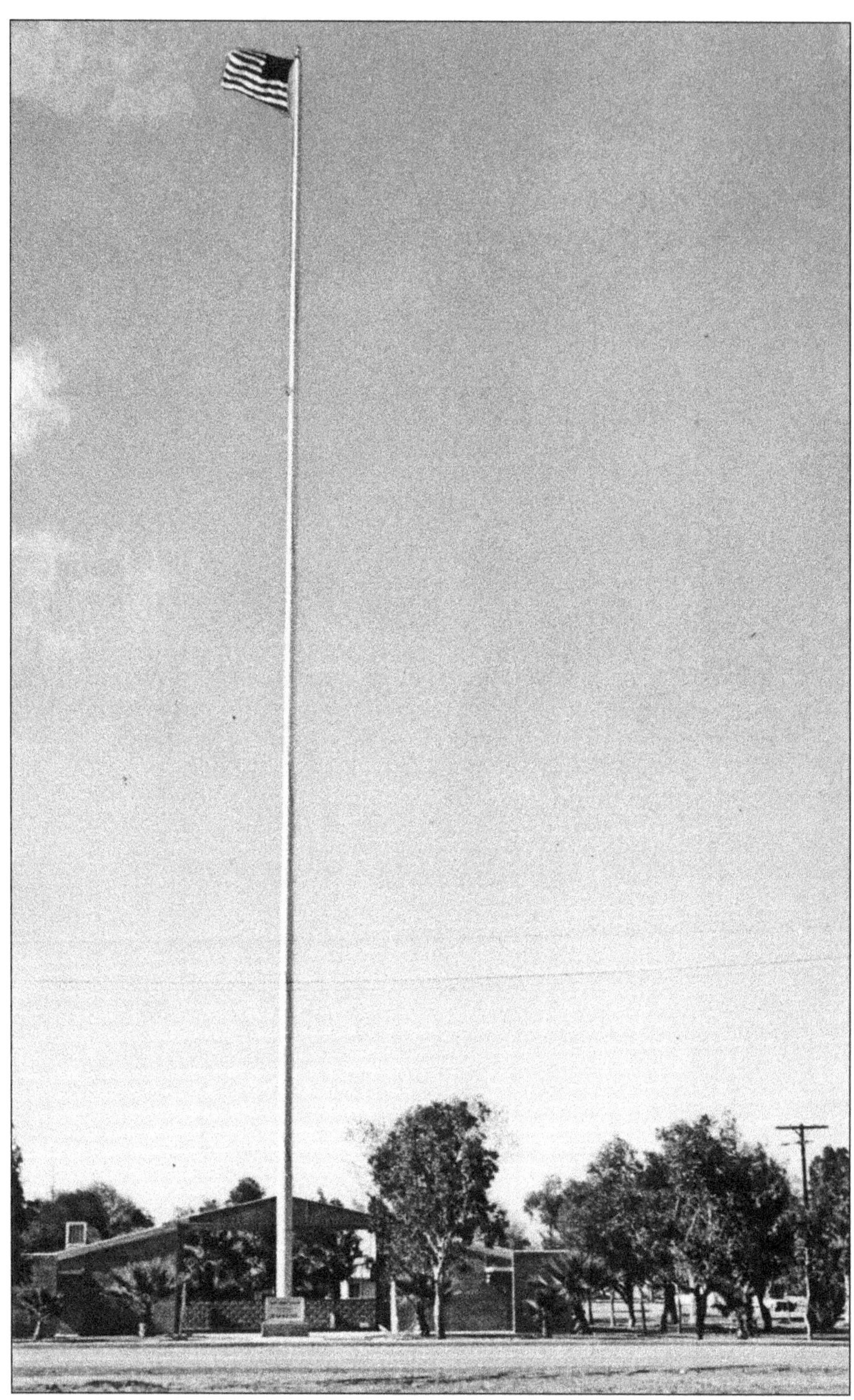

CALIPATRIA, CALIFORNIA. "The 'lowest down' city in the western hemisphere, 184 feet below sea level. World's tallest flagpole, the top of which is at sea level." Unused photo card; photo by Walter S. Hubbard. (Published and distributed by Columbia Wholesale Supply, 11401 Chandler, North Hollywood 46, Calif. / H-3681 / 90035.)

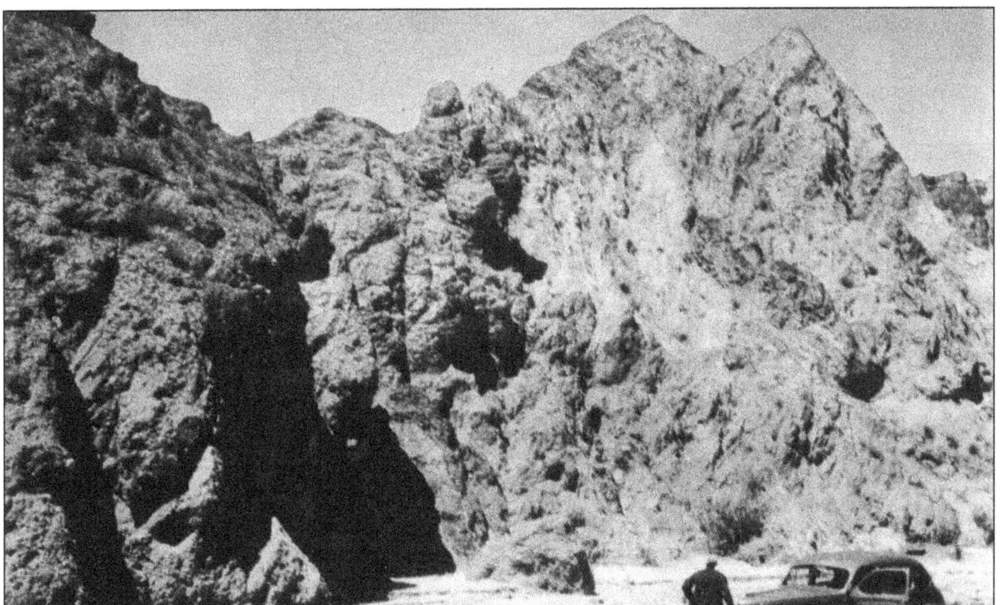

PAINTED CANYON. "Painted Canyon, near Mecca, California is an outstanding example of vivid desert coloring and strange formations resulting from ancient volcanic action. Salton Sea and Joshua Tree Monument are nearby features of the great American Desert." Unused photo card. (Union Oil Company's Natural Color Scenes of the West.)

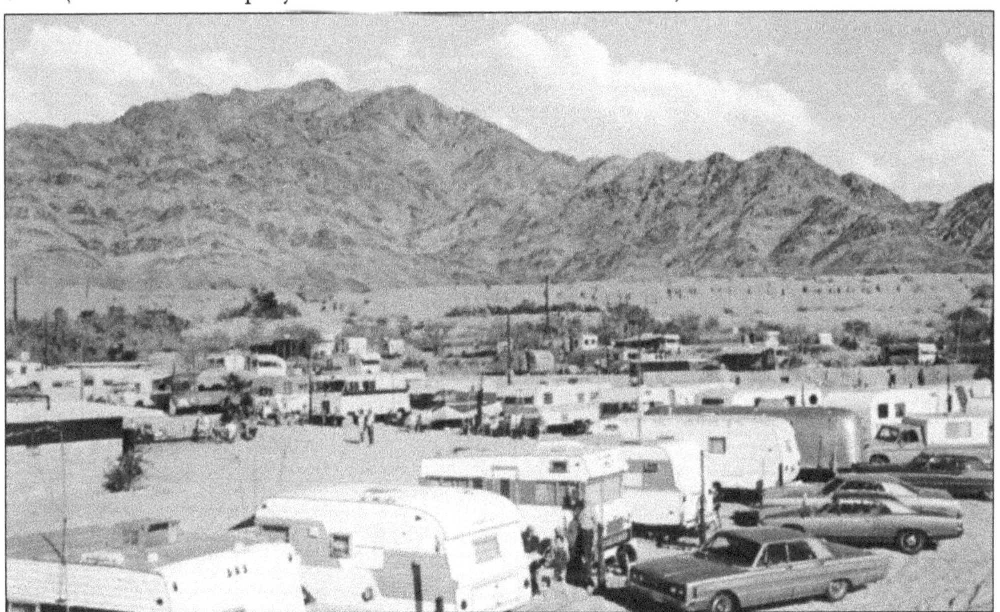

BASHFORD'S HOT MINERAL SPA. "Salton Sea – Highway 111, Star Rt., Box 26, Niland, Calif. 92257. Individual Mineral Baths – Swimming Pool – Hydro Therapy Pool, Hot water spilling from the lap of Chocolate Mts. for bathers in Imperial sunlight or desert night. Midway Salton Sea and fresh water canal. Winter place for trailer or camper our 'Hot Mineral Well.' " The city of Niland was named by the Imperial Farm Lands Association after "Nile Land" and referred to the fertility of the area. Unused photo card. (Pub. by California Color Photos, 595 Buckingham Way, San Francisco, 94102.)

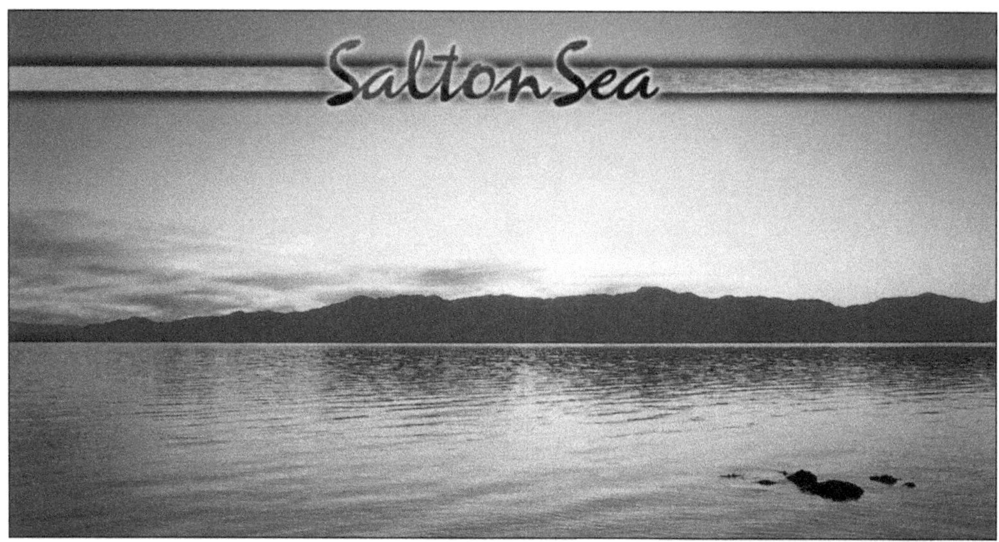

SALTON SEA. "A new day begins at the Salton Sea located at the southern end of the Coachella Valley near the desert resort cities of Palm Springs and Palm Desert. This large inland sea was formed when the Colorado River overflowed its banks in the early 1900s." Photo © Al Scott. (© Western Resort Publications & Novelty, PO, Box 4465 Palm Springs, CA 92263. Printed in U.S.A. / AS-403 / K26830.)

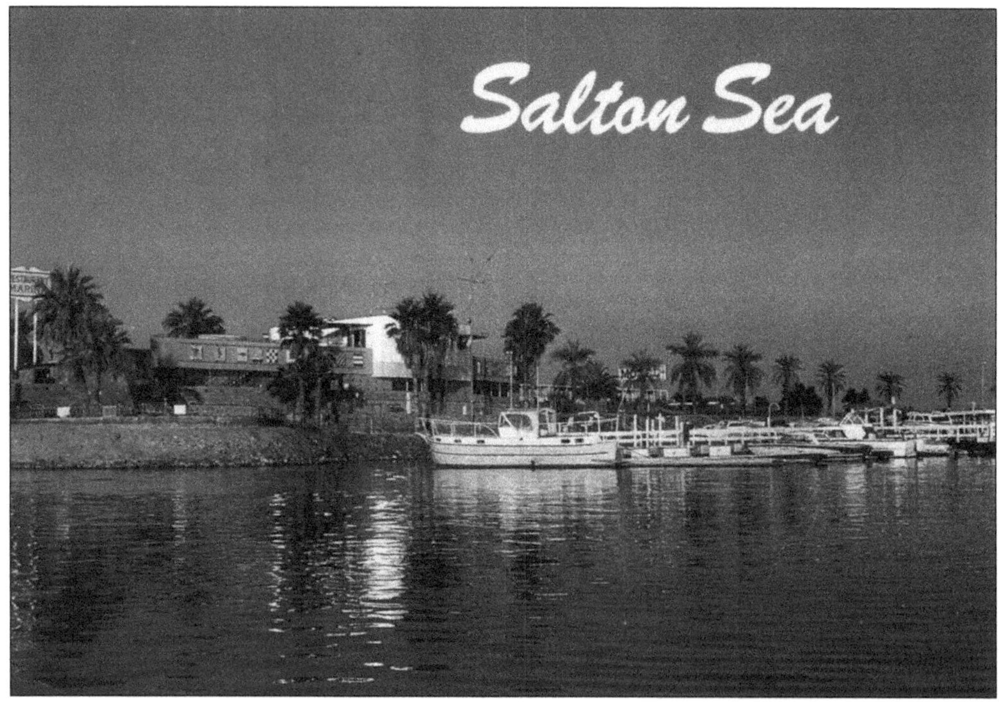

SALTON SEA. "North Shore, Salton Sea, California. Motel, Marina Campground, Landing Strip. Located on the Northeast corner of the Salton Sea 22 miles Southeast of Indio on Highway 111. Only 2 hours and 30 minutes from Los Angeles." Unused photo card. (Published by Petley Studios, 4051 E. Van Buren, Phoenix, AZ 85008 / B13431.)

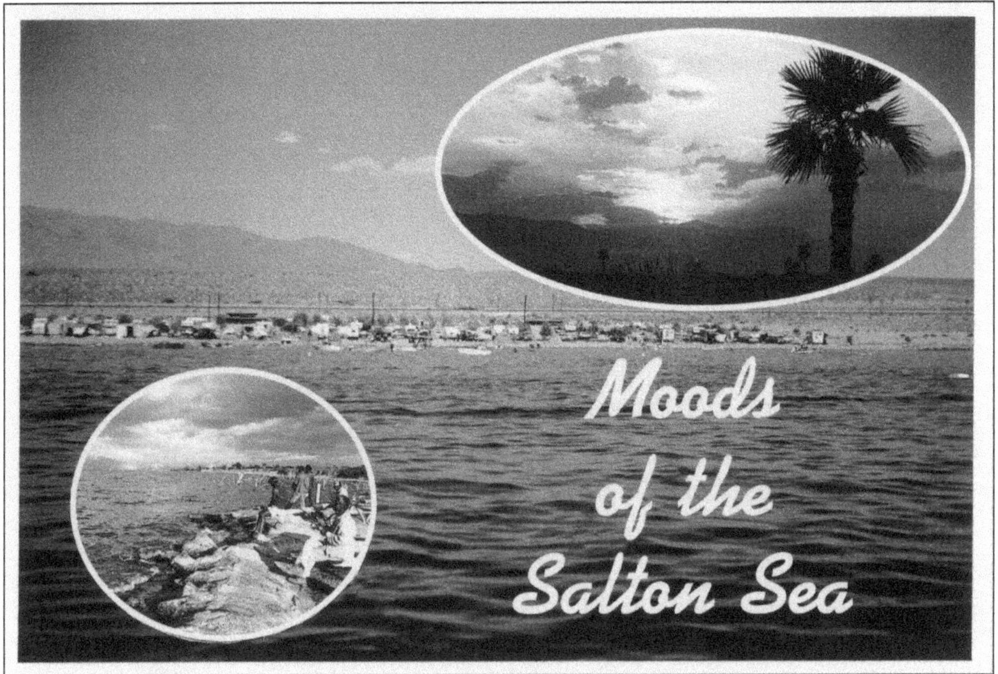

Moods of the Salton Sea. "Year long recreation can be found at the Salton Sea Recreation Area, one hour drive south of Palm Springs, California." Unused photo card. (© Woody Barnes, P.O. Box 1570 Julian, CA 92036.)

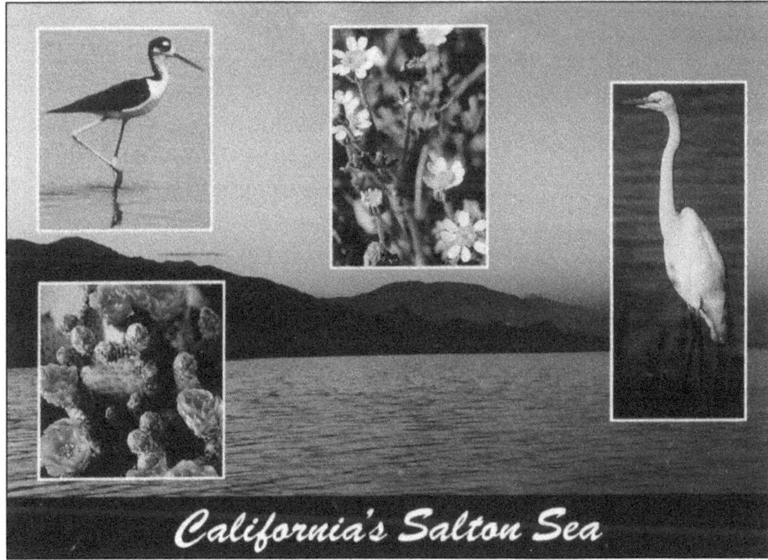

California's Salton Sea. "As the shades of night gently enfold this desert sea, and stars hang low in the heavens, there are lingering memories of the haunting bird calls, of colorful blossoms on rare desert plants. Its beauty, whispering breezes, and the wonders of Nature surrounding the Salton Sea will always remain with you. Upper left: Black Neck Stilt, Center: Rock Daisies, Right: Great Egret, Lower Left: Beavertail Cactus. Photographs courtesy of State Park Rangers, Salton Sea, and Sue Myers. Unused photo card. (Amescolor II, Palm Springs, CA (760) 327-5334.)

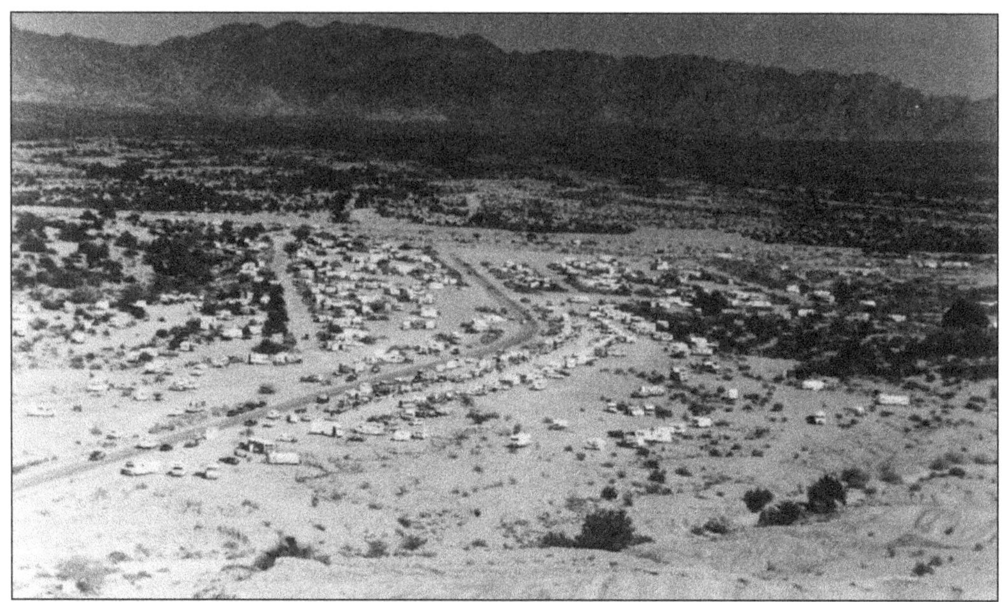

Slab City – Niland, California. "Thousands of Snowbirds flock to 'Slab City' near Niland, California, each winter form all U.S. states and Canada. The concrete foundations – 'Slabs' – are relics of an abandoned Navy Base used during World War II." Slab City is a free RV oasis located in the desert near Niland, California. The area is an abandoned World War II base formerly known as Camp Dunlap. The only remains of the camp are concrete slabs of the buildings, guardhouse and a couple of old bunkers. The enclave is an encampment of former hippies and snowbirds, as well as abandoned buses, trailers and vehicles. There is an eclectic array of solar panels, junk art and a real American subculture. Unused photo card. (44821-E.)

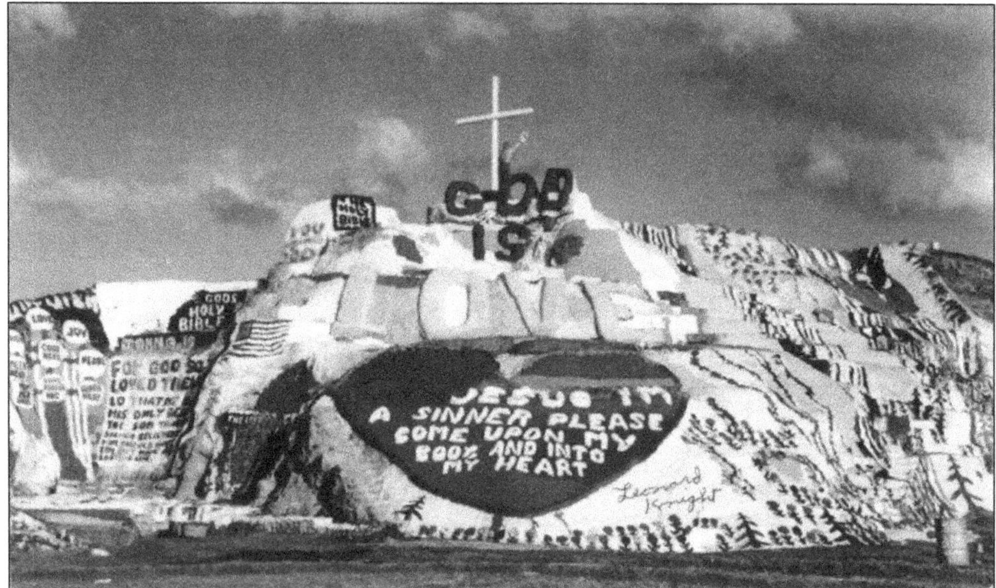

Slab City – Niland, California. Leonard Knight came to the Niland area in 1983. He only planned to stay a few days. However, he decided to stay. With only a 100,000 gallons of paint later, he created Salvation Mountain with the focal cross and reminder that "God Is Love."

Resources

archiver.rootsweb.ancestry.com/th/read/CADATA/2006-02/1139893508
geology.about.com/od/geology_ca/ig/saltonseepfield/
icfb.net/countyag.html
Laflin, P. *The Salton Sea: California's overlooked treasure.* The Periscope, Coachella Valley Historical Society, Indio, CA: 1995.
ngm.nationalgeographic.com/ngm/0502/feature5/index.html
nilandchamber.org/_tomato_festival.htm
saltonsea.sdsu.edu/
saltonseadoc.com/saltonSeaStatePark.html
www.allbusiness.com/specialty-businesses/1083233-1.html
www.americansouthwest.net/california/algodones_dunes/
www.desertusa.com/Cities/ca/imperial-valley-irrigation.html
www.desertusa.com/july96/du_saguaro.html
www.hbw.addr.com/index.htm
www.sandiegohistory.org/journal/71spring/highway.htm
www.sandiegohistory.org/journal/76winter/imperial.htm

www.ingramcontent.com/pod-product-compliance
Lightning Source LLC
LaVergne TN
LVHW060626110826
845147LV00015B/945
* 9 7 8 0 7 3 8 5 7 4 5 5 4 *